THE HOUSING STATUS
OF BLACK AMERICANS

THE HOUSING STATUS
OF BLACK AMERICANS

Wilhelmina A. Leigh
James B. Stewart

Transaction Publishers
New Brunswick (U.S.A.) and London (U.K.)

Library of Congress Catalog Number: 91-33116
ISBN: 1-56000-579-3
Printed in the United States of America

Library of Congress Cataloging-in-Publication Data
The Housing status of Black Americans/[compiled by] Wilhelmina A. Leigh, James B. Stewart.
    p.   cm.
    Articles from a special issue of the Review of Black political economy.
    Includes bibliographical references.
    ISBN 1-56000-579-3
    1. Afro-Americans—Housing—United States.   I. Leigh, Wilhelmina.
II. Stewart, James B. (James Benjamin), 1947–
HD7288.72.U5H67   1992
363.5'9996073—dc20   91-33116
                                                                              CIP

Acknowledgment of Financial Support by the
Federal National Mortgage Association (FNMA)

Financial support for the publication of the special issue of *The Review of Black Political Economy* on which this book is based was generously provided by Fannie Mae. The views reflected in these articles, however, should be attributed only to their authors. They do not necessarily reflect positions of Fannie Mae or its officers.

CONTENTS

I. OVERVIEW

II. GENERAL HOUSING CONDITIONS AND SPECIAL POPULATIONS

III. CASE STUDIES

IV. POSTSCRIPT   241

I

Overview

1

CIVIL RIGHTS LEGISLATION AND THE HOUSING STATUS OF BLACK AMERICANS: AN OVERVIEW

Wilhelmina A. Leigh

This article explores the relationship between civil rights legislation and the housing status of black Americans. An economic and judicial history of the pursuit of fair housing (or equal opportunity in access to housing) is provided for two major periods—from the late 1800s to the 1950s, and from the years of the civil rights movement to the present. An exploration of the housing status of black Americans throughout these periods follows, in which measures such as crowdedness and tenure—attributable partly to inequality in access to housing—are examined, and comparisons of black and whites are made.

Equal opportunity in access to housing, or fair housing, as used in this article means the ability of households of any racial or ethnic group to seek out and acquire housing they can afford in any market area. That is, fair housing exists if all households of all racial groups have access to all neighborhoods, with income as the only limiting factor. Although the concept of equal opportunity in access to housing certainly encompasses residence in racially integrated neighborhoods—that is, neighborhoods that both blacks and whites can move into and that both groups are continuing to move into—its use here is broader than integration alone. Equal opportunity in access to housing also could include residence in racially segregated neighborhoods (that is, neighborhoods in which only one racial group lives), if the decisions to so reside are not coerced.

This article first presents an economic and judicial history of the pursuit of fair housing by black Americans, from the late 1800s up to and including the decentralization of industry that began in the 1950s. Since the 1800s, major changes in the U.S. economic system have been accompanied by locational shifts in the population. Although black Americans, as all other Americans, have sought to take advantage of these economic changes by relocating, the lack of equality of opportunity in access to housing—often enforced by actions of the legislative or the judicial branch of government—has limited their ability to do so.

A legislative and judicial history of fair housing from the years of the civil rights movement up to the present is provided. A focal point of this history is the passage of the Civil Rights Act of 1968 (P.L. 90–284) on April 11, 1968.[1] Also noted are some of the major court decisions rendered in tests of the Act as they have contributed to the fair housing "landscape" since the passage of the 1968 Act.

Finally, the article explores the housing status of black Americans. Certain condition measures such as crowdedness and tenure that can be attributed in part to inequality in access to housing are examined. Comparisons of blacks with whites/all races are made. The final section synthesizes these discussions and draws conclusions.

ECONOMIC AND JUDICIAL HISTORY OF EQUAL OPPORTUNITY IN ACCESS TO HOUSING (LATE 1800s TO EARLY 1950s)

The period from the post-Civil War era up to the passage of the 1968 Fair Housing Act provides several examples of measures enacted to limit equality of access to housing for blacks. First, during the Reconstruction period, when the South in particular and the nation overall, were adjusting to the dismantling of the slave system and were establishing a new economic order, the doctrine of "separate but equal" was promulgated, with its associated constraints on access to housing by blacks. Second, while the northern states were industrializing, their localities used racially restrictive covenants and racial zoning to limit the access to housing of blacks seeking employment opportunities in the North. Third, the decentralization of industry that began in the middle of the twentieth century was accompanied by federal government housing policies that limited the ability of black Americans to suburbanize along with the industries that might employ them. (See Exhibit 1 for a summary of these trends.)

Developments during these three economic periods are discussed in detail in the following sections.

The Post-Civil War Era

After the Civil War, in addition to the fourteenth and fifteenth amendments, the Civil Rights Acts of 1866 and 1875 were passed to accord

EXHIBIT 1
Economic History of Fair Housing

Period	Approximation to Fair Housing	Contemporary Political Economy
After the Civil War	· Civil Rights Act of 1866 established same rights to purchase, sell, and hold property for black Americans as for white Americans.	· After the end of the economic system that depended on slavery, the nation began to industrialize; population began leaving the agricultural South.
	· Plessy versus Ferguson (1896) established doctrine of separate but equal.	· Legislative branch of federal government tried in vain to establish equality in housing and all other aspects of life for former slaves.
Industrialization	· Racially integrated neighborhoods dominated northern cities until World War II.	· Adam Smith's laissez faire doctrine guided industrialization that used recent European immigrants in low-wage jobs.
	· Southern cities passed municipal racial zoning ordinances to define blocks of residence for blacks and whites.	· Short-lived residential integration was squelched by use of racial zoning and racially restrictive covenants.
	· When the Supreme Court found residential zoning ordinances illegal, racially restrictive covenants often were added to deeds to maintain segregated residential areas.	· Judicial branch of federal government was major actor in behalf of rights of blacks.
Decentralization of Industry	· Federal assistance for ownership through the FHA furthered patterns of segregated living, after World War II.	· Executive branch was beginning to develop postures favoring fair housing.
	· President Truman established a President's Committee on Civil Rights.	· Judicial branch was major actor on behalf of rights of blacks.

EXHIBIT 1 (continued)

Period	Approximation to Fair Housing	Contemporary Political Economy
	· Supreme Court decided in Shelley versus Kraemer that racially restrictive covenants were unenforceable in state courts although they remained valid in private transactions.	
Civil Rights Movement (1954–1968)	· Two federal laws passed—Civil Rights Act of 1964 and Fair Housing Act of 1968.	· War fueled the economy and generated inflation.
	· Executive Order 11063 (1962) was issued to outlaw racial discrimination in certain types of federally assisted housing.	· Efforts were made to provide employment opportunities, perhaps as an antidote to rioting.
	· Supreme Court reaffirmed the Civil Rights Act of 1866 that precludes discrimination by race in the sale or rental of real property.	· The legislative, executive, and judicial branches of the federal government all made efforts to enhance fair housing access for blacks.

rights to blacks. Among other provisions, the Civil Rights Act of 1866 guarantees to all U.S. citizens in every state and territory the same right as is enjoyed by the white citizens thereof to inherit, purchase, lease, sell, hold, and convey real and personal property. Although the fourteenth amendment was intended to give the backing of the Constitution to the rights afforded to blacks under the Civil Rights Act of 1866, the amendment does not limit discrimination by private individuals. In fact, in the Civil Rights Cases (109 U.S. 3) of 1883, Justice Bradley presented the racial philosophy of the Supreme Court at that time: (1) Discrimination by a state violates the fourteenth amendment; and (2) private racial discrimination does not confer an inferior status on black Americans.[2] The Civil Rights Act of 1875 (18 STAT 335), popularly known as the Ku Klux Klan Act, was invalidated by the Supreme Court decisions in the Civil Rights Cases of 1883.

Over a decade later, in *Plessy v. Ferguson* (163 U.S. 537) in 1896, the Supreme Court established the doctrine of "separate but equal" to govern race relations in the nation. In this case, the Supreme Court upheld the right of a state to pass a statute providing separate railway cars for blacks and whites.[3] This doctrine also was used to justify such actions as the exclusion of blacks from residential neighborhoods occupied by whites.

Industrialization

At the turn of the century, a propertied class of blacks that was able to afford decent housing in racially integrated neighborhoods had begun to develop in northern and western cities. In places such as Chicago, Columbus, Minneapolis, New York City, Pittsburgh, Portland, San Francisco, and San Diego, blacks resided in limited racial concentrations and in integrated living patterns.[4]

However, in the early years of the twentieth century, especially in the urbanizing North, European immigrants provided cheap plentiful labor, almost to the exclusion of blacks in some industries. Competition for low-wage industry jobs in the North between European immigrants and blacks who had migrated there from the South sparked race riots during the early part of the twentieth century. One result of these riots was that blacks began to seek the protection that segregated neighborhoods could provide.[5]

The potential for residential integration for the growing propertied class of northern blacks was thwarted by the local use of racial zoning. In 1910, Baltimore passed a municipal residential segregation ordinance that effectively designated white and black residential blocks. Over a dozen southern cities, including Atlanta, Birmingham, Louisville, New Orleans, and Richmond, enacted similar ordinances.[6] In the 1917 decision in *Buchanan v. Warley* (245 U.S. 60), the Supreme Court found the exclusion of "Negroes" from certain residential areas to be a denial of the equal protection clause of the fourteenth amendment.[7]

Although many localities continued to zone racially after the 1917 decision, in some municipalities a racially restrictive covenant began to be used for similar effect instead. These covenants were private contracts or agreements that the property would not be sold, leased, or rented to "Negroes," Jews, Orientals, or whatever group local prejudice found to be undesirable. In 1926, in *Corrigan v. Buckley* (271 U.S. 323), the Supreme Court upheld private restrictive covenants on properties. The Court continued to uphold the sanctity of these covenants as a product of the free market, protected under freedom of contract and freedom to determine the disposal of one's property.[8] By the 1930s, several other factors could be noted that fostered racial residential segregation— decline in the number of domestic servants, exclusion of blacks from newly developed residential areas in the cities, general policies and practices of the real estate industry to foster racial segregation, and growth of the black population.[9]

Decentralization of Industry

After World War II, when U.S. servicemen returned to civilian life and began to follow their industry jobs to the suburbs, blacks were left behind, in large measure, due to the manner in which federal government housing programs were operated. From 1935 to 1950, most of the eleven million homes built and marketed with federal guarantees or insurance were in suburban areas that excluded blacks.[10] The loan guarantee program of the Veterans Administration (VA) and the mortgage insurance program of the Federal Housing Administration (FHA) helped few blacks move to the suburbs.[11] The military had excluded blacks for so long that few blacks were eligible for VA loans after World War II. The FHA provided mortgage loan insurance in a manner that kept suburban subdivisions racially distinct and established patterns of residential segregation that the civil rights movement and subsequent legislation still are struggling to eliminate.

The policies governing the federal programs providing mortgage guarantees and insurance were at variance with contemporaneous statements of federal civil rights policies. For instance, in 1946, President Harry Truman had established a President's Committee on Civil Rights. One of the four rights deemed important by this committee was the right to equality of opportunity, including access to services in the fields of education, housing, health, recreation, and transportation, whether free or at a price, and with complete disregard for race, color, creed, and national origin. The President's Committee on Civil Rights also recommended the enactment of state laws banning restrictive covenants and a renewed court attack on restrictive covenants.[12]

As if in response to the committee's recommendations, on May 3, 1948, the Supreme Court decided, in Shelley v. Kraemer (334 U.S. 1), that restrictive covenants were unenforceable by state courts. The Supreme Court reasoned that when restrictive covenants are enforced they deny to excluded groups equal protection of the law as guaranteed by the fourteenth amendment. Even though racially restrictive covenants were invalidated in 1948, thereafter, many owners holding deeds bearing these covenants alleged that they felt a moral obligation to uphold them in private transactions.[13]

In December 1949, the FHA and the VA reversed their policies that had promoted racial segregation in housing. After February 15, 1950, the FHA and the VA no longer provided mortgage insurance for properties with racially restrictive covenants on their deeds. In 1951, the FHA began selling all repossessed FHA-insured housing on a nonsegregated basis. Although FHA and VA policies changed, little additional housing was made available to blacks. As of 1959, less than 2 percent of the new homes provided through FHA mortgage insurance since the end of World War II had been made available to minorities.[14]

LEGISLATIVE/JUDICIAL HISTORY (CIVIL RIGHTS MOVEMENT TO PRESENT)

The Civil Rights Movement

As already noted, in the early 1950s, before the civil rights movement had begun, the large majority of black Americans continued to experience unequal access to housing opportunities. The last piece of enforceable federal civil rights legislation had been passed in 1866. Although racially restrictive covenants had been outlawed in 1948, the ''separate but equal'' doctrine continued to govern race relations throughout the land with respect to education, public facilities, transportation, and accommodations. Increasingly, blacks were living largely in segregated neighborhoods in urban areas outside the South. In 1910, 73 percent of all blacks lived in rural areas; by 1960, 73 percent were in urban areas. Although by 1960, 40 percent of all blacks were living outside the South, they either were being prohibited from joining the exodus to suburbia or were being steered to certain suburban subdivisions.

The first piece of civil rights legislation in eighty-two years was signed into law on September 9, 1957, by President Eisenhower.[15] The Civil Rights Act of 1957 (71 STAT 634) mandated the establishment of a Commission on Civil Rights to appraise laws and policies of the federal government with respect to equal protection of the laws under the Constitution.

Despite civil rights protests, federal housing agencies and the majority of state governments either had endorsed openly or had ignored discriminatory practices, in direct opposition to the federal civil rights laws on the books. As a result, in November 1962, Executive Order 11063 was issued, prohibiting racial discrimination in housing financed by the federal government. However, the executive order lacked the teeth to bring about the kind of changes sought by civil rights activists. Executive Order 11063 applied only to housing contracted for after its effective date. It also exempted one- and two-family owner-occupied dwellings from its requirements and relied on complaints, rather than establishing a program to prevent discrimination.[16]

Additional civil rights legislation passed two years later. Title VI of the Civil Rights Act of 1964 prohibited discrimination on the basis of race, color, or national origin, against persons eligible to participate in and receive the benefits of any program receiving federal financial assistance. Unlike Executive Order 11063, this title covered all housing in urban renewal areas and all public housing.

Shortly after the assassination of Martin Luther King, Jr., the Civil Rights Act of 1968 was enacted, with its Title VIII establishing federal fair housing policy. Title VIII, however, limited the U.S. Department of Housing and Urban Development (HUD), the administering agency, to the receipt, investigation, and conciliation of complaints. When Title VIII became fully effective on January 1, 1970, it covered more than 80 percent of all housing. Passage of the 1968 Civil Rights Act also forced the four federal financial regulatory agencies—the Comptroller of the Currency, the Federal Deposit Insurance Corporation, the Federal Home Loan Bank Board, and the Federal Reserve System—to end their policies allowing discrimination against racial and ethnic minorities in mortgage lending.[17]

Two months after the 1968 Civil Rights Act was passed, the Supreme Court decided a case that reaffirmed the Civil Rights Act of 1866. In *Jones v. Alfred H. Mayer Co.* (392 U.S. 409), the Court decided that the 1866 Civil Rights Act precludes all discrimination on the basis of race in the sale or rental of real property, however private the transaction.

Since the Civil Rights Movement

The 1970s. Residential segregation did not become a central issue in the struggle for racial equality until the 1970s.[18] Only 1 percent of blacks viewed fair housing as a major goal in 1963, while 74 percent did by 1977. Although only 21 percent of whites surveyed in 1963 felt that fair housing was the main goal of the civil rights movement, 34 percent felt this way by 1977. A year later, however, in 1978, only 23 percent of whites in a Harris survey reported believing that blacks were discriminated against in the housing market. Growing suburbanization of middle-class minority group households may have fostered the false notion that housing discrimination was no longer a problem for blacks and Hispanics with sufficient money to purchase or rent housing in the private market. Numerous studies and court decisions in the 1970s and the 1980s debunk the notion that once the income problem has been solved, so is housing market discrimination.[19]

Court decisions in this decade seemed to support the concepts of fair housing and housing integration. In a 1974 federal court case—*Clark v. Universal Builders, Inc.*, 501 F. 2d 324 (7th Cir. 1974)—black homeowners in south Chicago successfully argued that the Civil Rights Act of 1866 prohibited price discrimination (the charging of higher prices for houses in black neighborhoods than for comparable houses sold to whites). Additionally, in separate cases, in 1969 and 1970, the federal courts decided that illegal discrimination existed when minority homebuyers had been given less favorable terms or had been charged higher prices than others who had placed contracts on comparable property.[20]

In 1972, the Supreme Court decided its first Title VIII case—*Trafficante v. Metropolitan Life Insurance Co.* (409 U.S. 205)—by affirming the thrust toward integration. A black and a white tenant living in a San Francisco apartment complex sued their landlord for discrimination against nonwhites in tenant selection. The Supreme Court decided that the landlord indeed had inflicted injury upon the tenants, and had deprived them of the social, business, and professional advantages of living with nonwhites.

In a landmark Supreme Court decision in 1976, *Hills v. Gautreaux* (425 U.S. 284), the Court approved a metropolitan-area-wide remedy for central city housing discrimination within federally subsidized housing. In this case, equal opportunity in housing for minorities was defined to require integrated occupancy.

Actions by the legislative branch were more mixed in intent than were the court cases cited here. On one hand, the 1974 Housing and Community Development Act, the legislation that ended the federal moratorium on housing assistance programs that had been established in 1973, enhanced the fair housing statutes. This act required that full credit be given the wife's income in all federally related mortgage transactions. It also conditioned receipt of Community Development Block Grants on the willingness of a community to provide low- and moderate- income housing within its borders. Finally, the 1974 Act amended Title VIII of the Civil Rights Act of 1968 by prohibiting discrimination on the basis of sex in the sale or rental of housing.

On the other hand, throughout the decade of the 1970s, the executive branch dragged its feet in implementing Title VIII. For more than twelve years following enactment of this law, the U.S. Department of HUD did not issue interpretive regulations or guidelines for the courts to use to determine Title VIII compliance. Although between 1969 and 1978 the Justice Department filed more than three hundred valid cases, the resolution of these cases changed housing and real estate practices and racial residential patterns very little.[21]

The 1980s. The decade of the 1980s was a mixed one for fair housing. It began with the Reagan administration withdrawing the interpretive regulations to accompany the 1968 Fair Housing Act that finally had been issued in 1980. Countervailing this was the 1982 Supreme Court ruling in *Havens v. Coleman* that clarified and sanctioned the standing of fair housing centers and testers in Title VIII court actions.

Testing or the use of testers throughout the nation has helped to illuminate the extent and varied forms of racially discriminatory behavior in the housing market. Testers are pairs of individuals of different races given nearly identical socioeconomic characteristics and requirements for residences to use when visiting housing providers (e.g., real estate agents and apartment management offices). These paired testers separately make visits, timed to be close together, to selected housing providers. Each inquires about availability and prices of residences. Responses given the testers at the various property offices are later compared.

In all cities where testers have been used, blacks and members of other minority groups were found to be discriminated against in a variety of ways. The most common techniques used by rental agents include being given fewer referrals, being shown fewer units, and being given a distant date of unit availability.[22] The National Association of Realtors and other industry groups have executed voluntary affirmative marketing agreements (VAMA) with HUD in an effort to lessen this more subtle, second-generation form of racial discrimination in the housing market.

A related legislative effort that may bolster the cause of fair housing was the passage over a veto by President Reagan of the Civil Rights Restoration Act of 1988. This Act overturns the effects of the Supreme Court ruling in the 1984 case of *Grove City v. Bell*. The Supreme Court held in this case that antidiscrimination laws involving recipients of federal funds applied only to the specific program or activity that received the money but not to the entire college, company, or other entity of which it is a part. The Civil Rights Restoration Act of 1988 broadens these antidiscrimination restrictions to the entire entity, any part of which receives funding, and provides coverage to minorities, women, the elderly, and the handicapped.

Another civil rights statute, the Fair Housing Amendments Act of 1988 (P.L. 100–430), was signed into law on September 13, 1988. This law expands the coverage of the 1968 Act to familial status and handicap.[23] In addition, the 1988 Fair Housing Amendments Act allows HUD to bring complaints before the federal courts or an administrative law judge at the request of either the plaintiff or the defendant. The final piece of civil rights legislation to be noted here is the Americans with Disabilities Act (P.L. 101–336) that was signed into law July 26, 1990. This statute broadened federal civil rights protections (beyond those afforded in the area of fair housing by P. L. 100–430) to disabled, or handicapped, citizens in areas such as public services, public accommodations, and telecommunications.

CHRONOLOGY: HOUSING STATUS

To what extent can the major developments in the legislative/judicial/ administrative history of fair housing be associated with changes in the housing status of black Americans? The housing status of black Americans can be characterized by:

- residence of a significant proportion of households in substandard units;
- price discrimination and low rates of ownership; and
- exclusion from selected areas—with the associated limited supply of units to rent or buy, and residence in racially segregated areas.

Although many measures can be proxies for substandardness, crowdedness is the only measure used here. This is primarily because crowdedness is a housing condition that inequality of opportunity in access to housing clearly could aggravate; if the supply of housing units available to a group of households is restricted, then doubling up with another household might be the best alternative.

Housing status for blacks is compared in the following sections to that for whites and for households of all races. To the extent that data are available, housing status with respect to fair housing is discussed separately in the major periods of economic and judicial/legislative history.

Industrialization

Although the federal government had paid little attention to housing conditions of blacks before the Depression, during the 1930s, the issue received attention while the new social welfare philosophy of the era was being developed. The federal government recognized the distressful housing conditions of blacks and examined them separately as part of the President's (Hoover) Conference on Home Building and Home Ownership (1932). In a volume issued as a result of this conference, three types of social pathology were associated with "Negro" residence areas—a high rate of delinquency, a high rate of mortality, and a distorted standard of living.[24]

By a distorted standard of living, the authors meant that blacks were required to spend a larger proportion of their incomes for rent than other groups.[25] Some of the implications of high rents and low wages were working mothers, lodgers to provide additional income, and overcrowding. Homeownership also was difficult for the financially strapped black household to achieve. Because the housing market was segmented by race, black households found a limited supply of units, along with the stringent mortgage terms of that period—short-term loans with only interest repayments due during the term, plus a balloon payment of principal due at the end of the term.[26]

Many landlords accommodated the growing demand in black neighborhoods (with their limited supply of dwellings) by partitioning rental housing into overcrowded quarters with insufficient supporting facilities. Speculators also often overpriced these units. Thus, exclusion and segregation fostered price discrimination and crowdedness; these, in turn, led to unit substandardness.

Decentralization of Industry

The Census of Housing for 1940 revealed several disparities between nonwhites and whites in housing status.[27] Only 24 percent of nonwhite households but 46 percent of white households owned their units. (See Table 1.) More nonwhite households also were crowded—that is, living in units with 1.01 or more persons per room—than were households of all races. Forty-two percent of nonwhite renter households but only 25 percent of households of all races occupied crowded units. A similar gap existed for owner households—32 percent of nonwhites but 14 percent of all races occupied crowded units.

TABLE 1
Housing Tenure and Crowdedness by Race, 1940–1987

	1940	1950	1960	1970	1980	1983	1987
TENURE a/							
Percent Owners							
Blacks b/	23.6	34.9	38.4	41.6	43.9	45.0	43.5
All Races c/	43.6 e/	55.0 e/	61.9 e/	62.9 e/	64.4 e/	64.7 e/	64.0 e/
Percent Renters							
Blacks b/	76.4	65.1	61.6	58.4	56.1	55.0	56.5
All Races c/	56.4 f/	45.0 f/	38.1 f/	37.1 f/	35.6 f/	35.3 f/	36.0 f/
INTERNAL CONDITIONS a/							
Crowded (Renters) d/							
Blacks b/	42.4	40.8	32.9	22.2	10.0	9.0	6.2
All Races c/	24.9	21.6	16.1	10.6	6.2	5.6	4.6
Crowded (Owners) d/							
Blacks b/	32.0	24.9	21.0	15.5	7.9	5.8	4.6
All Races c/	14.2	10.9	8.7	6.4	3.1	2.3	1.6

a. All figures are percentages indicating (by race) the proportion of units so characterized.
b. In 1940, 1950, and 1960, data for nonwhites are reported; in 1970, 1980, and 1983, data are for blacks.
c. All races includes blacks.
d. Crowded is defined as 1.01 or more persons per room.
e. Percent owners among whites is 45.7 (1940), 57.0 (1950), 64.4 (1960), 65.4 (1970), 67.8 (1980), 67.7 (1983), and 67.4 (1987).
f. Percent renters among whites is 54.3 (1940), 43.0 (1950), 35.6 (1960), 34.6 (1970), 32.2 (1980), 32.3 (1983), and 32.6 (1987).
Source: U.S. Censuses of Housing and the Annual (American) Housing Survey

The status of nonwhite households relative to white households or to households of all races did not improve appreciably over the decade 1940 to 1950. Overall, in 1950, 72 percent of nonwhite households but only 32 percent of white households were in substandard units. Ownership among nonwhites had increased from 24 percent to 35 percent, while it had risen from 46 percent to 57 percent for whites. The percentage of nonwhite renters and renters of all races living in crowded units had decreased slightly since 1940. The drop in crowding among owners was more striking than among renters—it fell from 32 percent to 25 percent for nonwhites and from 14 percent to 11 percent for all races.

Between 1940 and 1950, residential segregation—as measured for 109 cities using a dissimilarity index—increased.[28] This index computes the percentage of either population that would have to move in order for the percentage distribution by race on each block to equal that of the entire city. The mean index for all the cities increased from 85.2 in 1940 to 87.3 in 1950.

The Civil Rights Movement

Between 1954 and 1968, the years of the civil rights movement, the housing status of black (or nonwhite) Americans continued to compare unfavorably with that of other Americans along several dimensions— housing condition, housing price, and residential segregation.

Housing Condition. By 1960, despite some improvements in the quality of housing occupied by nonwhites, their housing remained inferior to that of whites and all races. Using an overall measure of substandardness, 41 percent of nonwhite renter households but only 21 percent of renter households of all races resided in such units. If blacks and whites alone are evaluated, 44 percent of all black households lived in substandard units versus 13 percent of all white households.

Crowdedness as an individual measure of substandardness presents a similar picture. Although the extent of crowdedness has lessened continually since the 1940s both for owners and renters, nonwhites remain disadvantaged relative to all races. Thirty-three percent of nonwhite renters (versus 16 percent of renters of all races) and 21 percent of nonwhite owners (versus 9 percent of owners of all races) continued to experience crowded living conditions in 1960. (See Table 1).

Price Discrimination. A substantial body of literature suggests that blacks pay more than similar whites for comparable housing.[29] In their studies using data from the 1960s and the 1970s, both Kain and Quigley, and Yinger found evidence of price discrimination against blacks. Kain and Quigley found discrimination markups for nine large metropolitan areas in 1960 that ranged from 3 percent to 20 percent—that is, for comparable units, nonwhites could expect to pay from 3 percent to 20 percent more than similar whites. Using multiple regression analysis, Yinger found that with any given racial composition, blacks paid about 15 percent more than whites for equivalent housing.

Related questions are: Can blacks choose among the same set of available units as whites? Do black and white households have access to the same housing market opportunities?[30] Other studies reveal that black households consume substantially less dwelling quality, neighborhood quality, and exterior space than white households of identical size, composition, and labor market attachment.[31] One example of this is the gap between the percentage of households that own. At the midpoint of the civil rights movement, 1960, the percentage of owners among nonwhites and whites had risen to 38 percent and 64 percent, respectively. (See Table 1.)

Exclusion and Residential Segregation. During the civil rights movement, the exclusion of blacks and the residential segregation of the races continued. Between 1950 and 1970, the number of blacks living in all-black census tracts increased from three out of ten to five out of ten. At the same time, the number of blacks living in mixed neighborhoods —neighborhoods in which blacks comprise 25 percent or less of the total population—declined from 25 percent to 16 percent.

Although there is no controversy over the continued existence of segregation, there is debate over its extent, as measured by the various indexes. For the years 1950–1970, the dissimilarity index and the exposure index are examined. As noted earlier, the dissimilarity index computes the percentage of either population that would have to move in order for the percentage distribution by race on each block to equal the percentage distribution by race for the entire city. The exposure index, on the other hand, is the ratio of actual exposure rates of blacks to whites divided by the exposure rate that would arise if blacks were evenly distributed throughout the metropolitan area. The black (white) exposure rate to whites (blacks) is defined by the proportion of whites (blacks) in the neighborhood of the average black (white).

The dissimilarity index, calculated for 109 cities, revealed decreases in segregation over the period 1950–1970, while the exposure index reflected increases. The mean dissimilarity index decreased—from 87.3 in 1950, to 86.1 in 1960, to 81.6 in 1970.[32] Every region except the South mirrored this pattern. Between 1950 and 1960, the mean for Southern cities increased from 88.5 to 90.8, reflecting greater segregation. The index subsequently declined to 88.0 in 1970 for the South.

The exposure indexes of *blacks to whites* reflected an increase in segregation in all regions and for the United States as a whole between 1960 and 1970.[33] Over the same period, the exposure indexes for *whites to blacks* indicated increased exposure of whites to blacks throughout the nation generally and in all regions except the South. These seemingly conflicting trends can be explained by the fact that blacks gained increased access to residential areas primarily through peripheral expansion of existing minority areas.[34] This expansion pattern, combined with more sluggish growth of white residential sectors than of black residential sectors, could account for the seeming contradiction.

Since the Civil Rights Movement

Since 1968, although the housing status of blacks has improved—as reflected in the measures of housing condition, housing price, and residential segregation—differentials remain between blacks and the majority population.

Housing Condition. Although a disparity remains in the overall housing conditions of the two groups, between 1970 and 1983 crowding lessened both for black and white owners and renters. In 1970, 22 percent of black renters and 11 percent of renters of all races lived in crowded units. By 1983, only 9 percent of black renters and 6 percent of renters of all races continued to live in crowded units. For owners in 1970, 16 percent of blacks and 6 percent of all races were crowded. By 1983, only 6 percent of blacks and 2 percent of all races were so housed. (See Table 1.)

Price Discrimination. Although data to assess whether blacks paid more for comparable housing than similar whites in the 1970s are scarce, data on homeownership differentials are readily available. Forty-two percent of black households owned in 1970, and 45 percent did in 1983. Among whites, 65 percent owned in 1970, and 68 percent owned in 1983. (See Table 1).

Two studies using 1970s data revealed that racial differentials in the probability of ownership also have diminished during the decade. Bianchi, Farley, and Spain concluded that, controlling for educational level, income, tenure, age, family type, region, or metropolitan status, the racial differential in the likelihood of ownership declined but did not disappear between 1960 and 1977. They used data for 1960 and sought differentials "before" and "after" the 1968 Fair Housing Act.[35]

Using the Panel Study of Income Dynamics, Silberman, Yochum, and Ihlanfeldt analyzed the *tenure choice* (decision between renting and owning) of blacks and whites in 1974 and 1978. They found that the gap between the probability of home purchases by black and by white households declined between 1974 and 1978, with newly formed black purchaser households experiencing a greater decline in this gap than all black purchaser households. The authors attributed the greater lessening of the gap among newly formed black purchaser households to a reduction in the legacy of discrimination in the "home purchase capital" of these households.[36]

Exclusion and Residential Segregation. In the years since the civil rights movement, exclusion and residential segregation have not disappeared. The 216 major metropolitan areas in the nation were 12 percent black in 1970. However, 21 percent of their central cities' populations, but only 5 percent of their suburban populations, were black. By 1980, the distribution had hardly changed. The major metropolitan areas were 13 percent black, their central cities were 22 percent black, and their suburbs 6 percent black. In 1971, the director of the Census Bureau stated that if blacks were to obtain income parity, the percentage residing in central cities would only drop to 78 percent (from the current level of 81 percent).[37] This indicates the pervasiveness of exclusion and segregation even when other factors are equalized.

Studies using different geographical measures reveal conflicting trends in the pattern of racial residential segregation between 1970 and 1980. Using data for counties throughout the United States with a population concentration index, Lichter found that racial residential segregation among blacks and whites had increased between 1970 and 1980.[38] McKinney and Schnare, on the other hand, using the exposure index with data for SMSAs, determined that racial residential segregation had declined between 1970 and 1980.[39]

Lichter used the population concentration index, which compares the distribution of population with the distribution of land area, with data for 3,070 counties in the United States to evaluate the difference in population distribution by race.[40] He found that in the 1970s, the black population continued to grow most rapidly in those counties with a disproportionate share (relative to land area) of the black population. During the same period, for the first time, the white population shifted to less densely populated counties. These divergent patterns are reflected in concentration indexes for whites of 62.84 in 1970 and 61.19 in 1980. Corresponding indexes for blacks are 78.45 in 1970 and 78.65 in 1980. When population concentration indexes are disaggregated into regional groups, all the indexes for whites decrease over the decade of the 1970s, while the indexes for blacks by region show opposing trends. In the West, the county-based concentration index for black population declined slightly between 1970 and 1980 (from 86.64 to 86.60), while in all the other regions it increased. The increase in the North Central is greatest—from 91.94 to 97.04 between 1970 and 1980—and indicates that 97 percent of the blacks in the North Central would have to move to another county in order to be evenly distributed across the counties within that region. Lichter concludes these diverging patterns, which led to increased segregation of the races by 1980, were rooted in racial differences in the patterns of suburbanization, metro vs. nonmetro growth, and shifts to rural areas.

In contrast, by calculating exposure indexes with Census data for 64 SMSAs, McKinney and Schnare found segregation to be lower in 1980 than in 1960 for the nation as a whole and for each of the census regions. They inferred that, although housing markets today are highly segregated, barriers to integration are breaking down. Tabulations of the dissimilarity index for these 64 SMSAs are consistent with these findings.[41] The mean dissimilarity index for 1960 was 87.99; for 1970, it was 87.0; and for 1980, it was 80.75. To retain perspective about the decline in segregation between 1970 and 1980, one need only note that at the rate of decline demonstrated by the drop from 87 to 81, it will take another half century to desegregate many cities and a century to desegregate cities such as Chicago, St. Louis, and Washington, DC.[42]

SYNTHESIS AND CONCLUSIONS

This article has described major legislative and judicial actions and economic events related to equal opportunity of access to housing for blacks prior to the civil rights movement. It also has provided a chronology of civil rights legislation and fair housing court cases from the civil rights movement up to the present and compared housing conditions or status for blacks, whites, and all races, using measures that might be influenced by equality of access to housing opportunities. Each of the trend lines that results from these investigations suggests potential impediments to the realization of equal opportunity in access to housing for blacks.

Taking the long historical view from the 1800s up to the civil rights movement it is possible to identify major economic events that have had some impact on equality of access to housing for blacks. However, that task is more difficult for the years since the civil rights movement, because of the increased number of potentially precipitous economic events and the second-generation nature of the housing market responses. For instance, most would probably agree that the following were major events in our national economy since 1968: Vietnam War build-up and aftermath; recession and oil crisis in the early 1980s; high interest rates and housing prices in the early 1980s; Reagonomics; rising budget deficits; and the stock market crash in October 1987. However, the chain of circumstances through which any of these events would affect the equality of access to housing for blacks over that same period are not easily identifiable.

Among these events, however, are portents of other forms of segregation that approximate the racial variety. For example, during the oil crisis in the early 1980s, a "back to the city" movement flourished in certain areas that resulted in complete racial turnover of neighborhoods as commuting whites sought to save fuel costs by moving closer to their white-collar jobs in the central cities. The increases in prices and property taxes on homes in urban neighborhoods forced out many longtime, minority residents. Such trends did not foster equal opportunity of access to housing for blacks in many localities, but they thwarted it along economic lines rather than along racial lines.[43]

The reduction in federal funding of assisted housing programs and the shift away from the construction of newly assisted projects during the 1980s also have limited the access to housing for blacks and other low-income households throughout the nation. In addition, since the early 1980s, the growing homelessness among family and minority households—resulting in part from evictions due to the inability to continue making rent payments— is another example of equal opportunity in access to housing for blacks being undermined, but for economic rather than racial reasons.[44]

When the Fair Housing Act became the "law of the land" as Title VIII of the 1968 Civil Rights Act, the Department of HUD was mandated to establish programs to foster fair housing. The widespread but subtle racial discrimination that continues to be practiced by housing providers and to be revealed by testing, however, suggests that those seeking to maintain "inequality" of access to housing for blacks have simply developed covert means to do so. The failure of HUD to promptly issue interpretive regulations for Title VIII may have been viewed by opponents of fair housing as a ''green light'' to try to maintain unequal access to housing opportunity by sub-rosa means.

In the years before the civil rights movement and before the 1968 Fair Housing Act, access to housing was one of many areas in which the rights of blacks were seriously proscribed. This was mirrored in the housing conditions of blacks. In both 1940 and 1950, over twice as great a percentage of black owners as owners of all races lived in crowded conditions. Twenty percentage points separated the share of black households that owned from the share of households of all races that owned in those years as well.

During the civil rights movement, housing status for blacks improved, although it still lagged behind the housing status of all races. In 1960, the percent of nonwhite owners equaled the percent of renters of all races. In that same year, the percentage of crowded nonwhite renter households was double the corresponding figure for renter households of all races; among owners, the percent of crowded nonwhite households was more than double the percent of crowded households of all races.

In the years since the civil rights movement, disparities in access to housing and in housing status have remained although the gaps have narrowed. The 22 percent of black renter households living in crowded units in 1970 (versus 11 percent of renter households of all races) reflected a 20 percentage point drop from 1940 for black renter households. However, it had been as long ago as 1950 when 22 percent of renter households of all races had lived in crowded units. It took 20 years for black renter households to ''improve'' to the level of crowdedness experienced by renter households of all races in 1950! Likewise, it was 1970 before the proportion of black owner households in crowded quarters roughly equaled that proportion among owner households of all races in 1940; 30 years were required for blacks to achieve that level! In 1970, 16 percent of black owner households were crowded in contrast to only 6 percent of owner households of all races. Some progress is evident, however, in the following 10-year lag—by 1980, the percentage of crowded black renter households nearly equaled the percentage of crowded renter households of all races in 1970!

Ownership rates for the races approached parity with a similar lag. The percentage of blacks who owned in 1980 approximated the percentage of whites who had owned in 1940. Blacks reached this 46 percent level with a 40-year lag!

Surveying the events in economic history, the trends in legislation and court cases, and the housing status of blacks versus other households as they relate to equal opportunity in access to housing reveals circumstances and behavior that suggest it will be difficult to create an environment in which equal opportunity prevails in access to housing. Where legislation and court cases have enhanced equality of opportunity in housing, increasing housing costs threaten to take it away. In addition, some members of society continue to act as if housing market racial discrimination is not illegal.

The 1968 Civil Rights Act brought us a long way. The 1988 Fair Housing Amendments Act has moved us a little closer to fair housing and other civil rights for black Americans and other protected classes. However, if and when we achieve full civil rights for all races and protected classes remains to be seen.

NOTES

The author is Principal Analyst, U.S. Congressional Budget Office (CBO). This analysis is the author's own and should not be attributed to the CBO.

1. In this article, the 1954 Supreme Court decision in *Brown v. Board of Education of Topeka, KS* (347 U.S. 483) is considered to mark the beginning of the civil rights movement and the Civil Rights Act of 1968 to mark its end. I date the beginning of the civil rights movement from the Brown decision because the watering down of this decision by the Pupil Placement Law demonstrated the need for something more than Supreme Court decisions to achieve progress and gave impetus to the initial civil rights activism. The Supreme Court decision in *Brown v. Board of Education of Topeka, KS* invalidated the doctrine of "separate but equal" for public education. The Pupil Placement Law counteracted the thrust of the Brown decision before it was implemented, because it allowed jurisdictions to determine where pupils should be placed on the basis of aptitude, family background, and other subjective criteria.

2. James Kushner, *Apartheid in America: An Historical and Legal Analysis of Contemporary Racial Segregation in the United States* (Frederick, MD: Associated Faculty Press, Inc., 1980), p. 67.

3. J. Greenberg, ed., "Blacks and the Law," *The Annals of the American Academy of Political and Social Science*, 407 (1973), p. 15.

4. Robert Weaver, "The Negro Ghetto," as cited in James Kushner, *Apartheid in America*, p. 6.

5. James Kushner, *Apartheid in America*, p. 11.

6. See Ibid., pp. 15–16 and R. Farley and W.R. Allen, *The Color Line and the Quality of Life in America* (New York, NY: Russell Sage Foundation, 1987), pp. 138–139.

7. E.S. Newman, *The Freedom Reader* (New York, NY: Oceana Publications, 1955), p. 206.

8. Ibid., p. 209.

9. Robert Weaver, "Housing Discrimination: An Overview," in U.S. Commission on Civil Rights, *A Sheltered Crisis* (Washington, DC: U.S. Government Printing Office, 1983), p. 1.

10. Federal policy in other housing assistance programs, such as the Low-Rent Public Housing program, also contributed to residential racial segregation. This additional type of segregation is not discussed here.

11. For further discussion on the federal role in establishing patterns of racial residential segregation, see "The Federal Government and Equal Housing Opportunity: A Continuing Failure," Chapter 18 in *Critical Perspectives on Housing*, ed. Rachel G. Bratt, Chester Hartman, and Ann Meyerson (Philadelphia, PA: Temple University Press, 1986), pp. 296–324.

12. E. S. Newman, *The Freedom Reader*, p. 181.

13. J.F. Kain, *Race and Poverty: The Economics of Discrimination* (New York, NY: Columbia University Press, 1969), p. 26.

14. Martin Sloane, "Federal Housing Policy and Equal Opportunity," in *A Sheltered Crisis*, pp. 136–37.

15. Here I count back to the Act of 1875 which had been invalidated by the 1883 Supreme Court decisions, rather than counting back to the 1866 Act.

16. Department of Housing and Urban Development, *Fair Housing—The Law In Perspective* (Washington, DC: U.S. Department of Housing and Urban Development, 1988), p. 6.

17. The FHA also revised its policies to encourage the inclusion of a wife's full income when reckoning mortgage eligibility. See U.S. Commission on Civil Rights, *Twenty Years After Brown* (Washington, DC: U.S. Commission on Civil Rights, 1975), p. 41. This is crucial for potential black homeowners who might not be eligible for mortgage loans without using the incomes of their wives.

18. D. Garth Taylor, "Housing, Neighborhoods, and Race Relations: Recent Survey Evidence, " in *Race and Residence in American Cities* (Annals of the American Academy of Political and Social Science) 441 (January 1979), pp. 27–28.

19. See Joe Darden, "Population Growth and Spatial Distribution," in *A Sheltered Crisis*, p. 13, for a discussion of this. He cites the following substantiating research: Farley, R., "Residential Segregation in Urbanized Areas of the United States in 1970: An Analysis of Social Class and Racial Differences," *Demography* 14 (November 1977), pp. 497–518; Langendorf, R., "Residential Desegregation Potential," *Journal of the American Institute Of Planners* 35 (March 1969), pp. 90–95; Massey, D., "Effects of Socioeconomic Factors on the Residential Segregation of Blacks and Spanish Americans in U.S. Urbanized Areas, "*American Sociological Review* 44 (December 1979), pp. 1015–1022; and Taeuber, K. "Residential Segregation," *Scientific American* 213 (August 1965), pp. 12–19.

20. Both cases were against F and F Investment—the first by the Contract Buyers League, 300 F. Supp. 210 (N.D., Ill. 1969) and the second by Baker, 420 F. 2d 1191 (7th Cir. 1970).

21. See Martin Sloane in *A Sheltered Crisis*, pp. 139–40.

22. For further information on the results of testing see: H. Newburger, *Recent Evidence on Discrimination in Housing* (Washington, DC: U.S. Department of Housing and Urban Development, 1984); R. Wienk, C. Reid, J. Simonson, and F. Eggers, *Measuring Racial Discrimination in American Housing Markets: The Housing Market Practices Survey* (Washington, DC: U.S. Department of HUD, 1979); and the article by V. Reed in this issue.

23. Terminally ill AIDS patients have been defined as handicapped and are covered by the protections of the 1988 Act as a result of *Association of Relatives and Friends of AIDS Patients v. Regulations and Permits Administration*, No. 90–1672, June 13, 1990.

24. J. Gries and J. Ford, *Negro Housing*, VI, *Report on the President's Conference on Home Building and Home Ownership* (Washington, DC: National Capital Press, 1932), p. 52.

25. Ibid., p. 58.

26. Ibid., pp. 71–72.

27. The availability of the data stratifications by race dictated the use of "nonwhites" and "all races" for certain years and certain variables. "All races" includes "nonwhites" or "blacks." Note that Table 1 reports data in its footnotes and in its body for as many groups for which data are available.

28. The dissimilarity index measures the divergence between two population distributions, such as for whites and blacks. If two populations are distributed identically over a geographical area, the index equals 0. If the two populations are distributed with no intersection, that is, no geographical unit has both black and white households, then the index equals 100.

29. For evidence on this issue, see: A. Thomas King and Peter Mieszkowski, "Racial Discrimination, Segregation, and the Price of Housing," *Journal of Political Economy* 81 (May/June 1973), pp. 590–605; John Yinger, "The Black-White Price Differential in Housing: Some Further Evidence," *Land Economics* 54 (May 1978), pp. 187–206; Robert Schafer, "Racial Discrimination in the Boston Housing Market," *Journal of Urban Economics* 6 (April 1979), pp. 176–196; and John Yinger, "Prejudice and Discrimination in the Urban Housing Market," in *Current Issues in Urban Economics*, ed. Peter Mieszkowski and Mahlon Straszheim (Baltimore: Johns Hopkins University Press, 1979), p. 463.

30. G. Galster models residential segregation and interracial economic disparities as a simultaneous-equation system, to control for as many relevant factors as possible. See Galster, "Residential Segregation and Interracial Economic Disparities: A Simultaneous Equations Approach, "*The Journal of Urban Economics* 21 (January 1987), pp. 22–44.

31. Kain and Quigley, *Housing Markets and Racial Discrimination: A Microeconomic Analysis*, pp. 255 and 282.

32. See Annemette Sorensen, Karl Taeuber, and Leslie Hollingsworth Jr., "Indexes of Racial Residential Segregation for 109 Cities in the United States, 1940 to 1970," *Sociological Focus* 8 (April 1975), pp. 125–133; and Karl Taeuber, "Appendix," in *A Decent Home: A Report on the Continued Failure of the Federal Government to Provide Equal Housing Opportunity*, Citizens Commission on Civil Rights (Washington, DC, 1983), pp. 1–7.

33. Ann Schnare, "Trends in Residential Segregation by Race: 1960–1970," *The Journal of Urban Economics* 7 (May 1980), pp. 293–301.

34. Schnare used the exposure and relative exposure indexes because, unlike the dissimilarity index used by Taeuber, the exposure indexes are independent of the distribution of blacks and whites between census tracts with above- and below-average concentrations of blacks. See Norman R. Cloutier, "The Measurement and Modeling of Segregation: A Survey of Recent Empirical Research," *Regional Science Perspectives* 14 (1984), pp. 15–32, for a critique of the dissimilarity index in this usage.

35. See S. Bianchi, R. Farley, and D. Spain, "Racial Inequalities in Housing: An Examination of Recent Trends," *Demography* 19 (1982), pp. 37–51.

36. See J. Silberman, G. Yochum, and K. Ihlanfeldt, "Racial Differentials in Home Purchase: The Evidence From Newly-Formed Households," *Economic Inquiry* 20 (1982), pp. 443–457.

37. James Kushner, *Apartheid in America*, p. 18.

38. See Daniel Lichter, "Racial Concentration and Segregation Across U.S. Counties," *Demography* 22 (November 1985), pp. 603–609.

39. See S. McKinney and A. B. Schnare, *Trends in Residential Segregation by Race: 1960–1980* (Washington, DC: The Urban Institute, Report 3627, 1986).

40. If the population concentration index equals 0, then population is distributed over all the counties in the nation in proportion to land area. As the index approaches, the

distribution of population across counties becomes increasingly concentrated. As calculated by Lichter, the index numbers represent the percentage of the black population that would have to move to another county for the black population to be evenly distributed across all the counties of the United States.

41. See Karl Taeuber, "Appendix"

42. Diana Pearce, "A Sheltered Crisis: The State of Fair Housing Opportunity in the Eighties," in *A Sheltered Crisis*, p. 144.

43. For further information on reinvestment displacement or gentrification, as it is sometimes called, see the following: Clay, P. L., "Managing the Urban Reinvestment Process," *The Journal of Housing* 36 (October 1979), pp. 453–458; Gale, D. E., "Middle Class Resettlement in Older Urban Neighborhoods," *APA Journal* 45 (July 1979), pp. 293–304; Hammer, Siler, George Associates, *The Role of the Real Estate Sector in Neighborhood Change* (Washington, DC: U.S. Department of Housing and Urban Development, 1979); and Zeitz, E., "Reinvasion: A Neglected Form of Residential Segregation in Urban Areas," *Black Scholar* 9 (September 1977), pp. 41–45.

44. See the following: General Accounting Office, *Homelessness: A Complex Problem and the Federal Response* (GAO/HRD-85-40, April 1985), pp. 17–31; General Accounting Office, *Homelessness: HUD's and FEMA's Progress in Implementing the McKinney Act* (GAO/RCED-89-50, May 1989), p. 32; Department of Housing and Urban Development, *A Report to the Secretary on the Homeless and Emergency Shelters* (Washington, DC: U.S. Department of Housing and Urban Development, May 1984), p. 27; U.S. Conference of Mayors, *A Status Report on Homeless Families in America's Cities* (Washington, DC: U.S. Conference of Mayors, 1987), pp. 19 and 21.

2

CIVIL RIGHTS LEGISLATION AND THE HOUSING STATUS OF BLACK AMERICANS: EVIDENCE FROM FAIR HOUSING AUDITS AND SEGREGATION INDICES

Veronica M. Reed

The Fair Housing Act of 1968 made discrimination against minorities in the sale or rental of housing illegal. Twenty years later the Act's coverage was expanded and its enforcement mechanisms strengthened in response to pressure from fair housing advocates and evidence of continued segregation and discrimination. Segregation indices and fair housing audits provide measures of the extent and nature of residential segregation and housing discrimination. High levels of residential segregation suggest that housing discrimination exists, and audits give a direct measure of the incidence of discrimination. To date, housing audits consistently show that black auditors encounter discriminatory treatment in the housing search process. Whether the strengthened enforcement mechanisms of the Act will have a substantial impact on housing market discrimination and, in turn, residential segregation, remains to be seen.

This article examines changes in fair housing legislation over time and patterns of residential segregation based on spatial variation. In addition, it reviews the results of fair housing audits.[1] The first section discusses the 1968 Fair Housing Act, in its original and amended form. The amendments, which were passed in 1988 in response to concern about continued segregation and discrimination in the housing market, expand the Act's protections and strengthen its enforcement mechanisms. The second section summarizes an analysis of residential segregation that includes five different dimensions of spatial variation. The analysis indicates that in some cities in the United States segregation is extreme to the point of isolation. The final section reviews selected results from rental and sales housing audit studies since the late 1970s. These studies show that black homeseekers will likely encounter discriminatory treatment during the housing search process. Housing discrimination limits the housing choices of black households. Limited housing choices perpetuate residential segregation. Future trends in the levels of residential segregation and housing discrimination, as measured by segregation indices and fair housing audits, will stand as evidence of the effectiveness of the strengthened enforcement mechanisms of the Fair Housing Act to reduce housing market discrimination.

FAIR HOUSING

Since 1968, it has been "the policy of the United States to provide, within Constitutional limitations, for fair housing throughout the United States." Title VIII of the Civil Rights Act of 1968 made discrimination in the rental or sale of housing on the basis of race, color, religion, or national origin a violation of federal law. It was the culmination of a long struggle to remove discriminatory barriers against minorities from the housing market and end residential segregation.[2] Women became a protected class under the law in 1974, and, in 1988, the Fair Housing Amendments Act expanded protection to handicapped persons and families with children.[3] Together, Title VIII of the Civil Rights Act of 1968 and the Fair Housing Amendments Act of 1988 comprise The Fair Housing Act.

Discriminatory housing practices prohibited in the Act include discrimination in terms and conditions, refusal to deal, discriminatory advertising, falsely representing availability, denying use of or participation in real estate services, and making representations regarding the entry or prospective entry of persons of a protected class into a neighborhood. These prohibitions apply to: (1) federally owned or operated dwellings; (2) dwellings supported in whole or part with the aid of federal loans, advances, grants, or contributions; (3) dwellings supported in whole or part by federally secured financing; and (4) dwellings purchased, rented, or otherwise obtained from public agencies receiving federal financial assistance. Single-family privately owned dwellings and multifamily dwellings of five units or less where the owner resides in one of the units are exempted, but these exemptions do not apply if the dwellings are sold or rented through a broker or agent or if discriminatory advertising is used.

In addition to expanding the protected classes under the Act, the Fair Housing Amendments Act strengthened enforcement mechanisms and increased penalties against parties found guilty of discrimination. Twenty years after the passage of the original legislation, discriminatory housing practices and high levels of residential segregation remained common-place in many U.S. cities. The American Civil Liberties Union, which supported passage of the Amendments, wrote that the Amendments "strengthened the Fair Housing Act by providing administrative enforcement and by giving it 'teeth.'"[4] Originally, HUD was charged with enforcing the Act. It was authorized to investigate complaints and seek the elimination and correction of discriminatory practices through conciliation. If a pattern or practice of discrimination was found, HUD referred the case to the Justice Department, which had the authority to enforce the law through judicial action. An individual or fair housing group could also elect to bring a private suit, in which a court could grant an injunction and restraining order and award actual damages, as well as up to $1,000 in punitive damages. Many private suits have been brought by individuals and fair housing groups in response to complaints from individuals or as a result of audits to test specifically for discrimination for litigation purposes. While courts awarded actual damages that grew increasingly larger, most fair housing advocates felt the 1968 Act was not an effective deterrent against discriminatory practices. The Fair Housing Council of Greater Washington, which also supported passage of the Amendments, said "the worst way to enforce the Fair Housing Act is to leave it to private plaintiffs, which is precisely what the existing law does."[5]

The Fair Housing Amendments Act of 1988 strengthened HUD's enforcement authority. Now, in addition to the authority to investigate and attempt to conciliate complaints, if there is "reasonable cause" to believe discrimination has occurred and no conciliation agreement can be reached, HUD can bring charges before an administrative law judge (ALJ) on behalf of the complainant. HUD can hold administrative hearings and issue subpoenas unless one of the parties elects to have the case heard in U.S. District Court. The ALJ has the authority to order a guilty party to cease its discriminatory activities, compensate the complainant, and pay civil penalties. If either party elects to have the case heard in court, the Department of Justice represents the complainant. The Justice Department can seek compensation, civil penalties, and punitive damages.

The 1988 Amendments also increased the penalties against those found guilty of discriminatory housing practices. An ALJ can impose penalties to be paid to the federal government ranging up to $10,000 for a first offense to up to $50,000 for third and subsequent violations. The Justice

Department can obtain penalties up to $50,000 for a first violation, and a maximum of $100,000 for any other. Also the $1,000 limit on punitive damages has been removed for individuals and private fair housing groups that bring a civil suit against a party engaged in discriminatory housing practices.

The Fair Housing Amendments Act has been in effect since March 1989. Whether the strengthened enforcement mechanisms and increased penalties provided will have a substantial impact on housing market discrimination remains to be seen. The system relies heavily on individuals to file complaints against suspected violators. But unless the discriminatory act is overt or blatant, individuals are not likely to realize they have been discriminated against. Fortunately, tests or audits to identify discrimination can increase the effectiveness of the Act, impacting on discriminatory housing practices and residential segregation.

RESIDENTIAL SEGREGATION

Elimination of residential segregation, a long-standing characteristic of U.S. housing markets, was one of the main goals of Title VIII of the Civil Rights Act of 1968. During the 1970s, however, there was on average throughout the nation only a modest decline in the segregation levels from the previous decade.[6] It is a myth that great strides have been made since 1968 in reducing the residential segregation of black Americans.[7] While results from the 1990 Census may refute these claims, to date most research suggests that racial residential segregation is the norm in American society.

Three main theories attempt to explain residential segregation along racial lines—the discrimination theory, the socioeconomic class theory, and the self-segregation theory.[8] The discrimination theory states that minorities are denied access to white neighborhoods because of discriminatory housing market practices. The root of segregation in the discrimination theory is racial prejudice. The class theory states that segregation is the result of the unequal socioeconomic distribution of racial groups and the distribution of neighborhoods in terms of housing quality and costs. The roots of segregation in the class theory are social and economic prejudices. Finally, the self-segregation theory states that all races prefer to live with members of their own kind. And, the root of segregation in the self-segregation theory is racial preference, not racial prejudice.

While all three theories have some validity, more evidence seems to show "that black residential segregation is best explained by exclusion and discrimination motivated by racial prejudice."[9] But no matter the cause, continued discriminatory actions by realtors and leasing agents toward minorities help maintain the status quo.[10]

Various indices have been developed to measure residential segregation. Among these indices is one that takes a multidimensional approach and "subsumes five distinct dimensions of spatial variation."[11] These dimensions are: (1) *evenness*, the degree to which the percentage of minority members within residential areas equals the citywide minority percentage; (2) *exposure*, the degree of potential contact between minority and majority members; (3) *clustering*, the extent to which minority areas adjoin one another in space; (4) *centralization*, the degree to which minority members are settled in and around the center of an urban area; and (5) *concentration*, the relative amount of physical space occupied by a minority group. These dimensions are measured using the index of dissimilarity, the isolation index, the index of spatial clustering (an index that reflects the extent to which a group is spatially distributed in distance from the central business district), and a relative concentration index, respectively.

Using 1980 Census data for sixty standard metropolitan statistical areas (SMSAs), these indices show that the level of residential segregation for blacks in some cities is extreme to the point of isolation.[12] Six SMSAs are "hypersegregated" or highly segregated on all five dimensions— Baltimore, Chicago, Cleveland, Detroit, Milwaukee, and Philadelphia. In addition, four SMSAs—Gary, Los Angeles, Newark, and St. Louis— are highly segregated on four dimensions. The black populations of these ten cities account for 23 percent of all blacks in the United States. In contrast, blacks in the nine cities with low segregation on at least four of the five indices—Albuquerque, Anaheim, El Paso, Greensboro, Salt Lake City, San Jose, Phoenix, Riverside, and Tucson—represent only 1.5 percent of all blacks in the United States.

The Fair Housing Act was passed in response to residential segregation, but a measure of residential segregation is at best an indirect measure of the extent and nature of discrimination blacks may face during a housing search. High levels of residential segregation suggest that discrimination exists; "auditing" or random testing for discrimination in housing market transactions gives a direct measure of the incidence of discrimination.

FAIR HOUSING AUDITS

A fair housing audit can be a controlled social science experiment or a targeted, non-scientific method of gathering evidence for a fair housing complaint or litigation. A scientific audit study, where randomly selected available housing units are "audited," can produce an objective evaluation of the extent and nature of racial discrimination for a city, a metropolitan area, or the nation. Carefully matched testers of different races enter into randomly selected housing transactions and record all treatment. Any difference in treatment is attributed to discrimination, because the testers differ only by race. The overall level of discrimination the testers encounter represents the extent of racial discrimination in the housing market. If housing discrimination is at the root of residential segregation, fair housing audits afford housing advocates and researchers a greater understanding of the nature of housing discrimination and subsequently of residential segregation.

Fair housing audits are also a method of enforcing fair housing laws. A pair of testers can uncover evidence of disparate treatment that effectively denies the minority tester access to the housing of choice. Initially, testing was designed primarily for litigation purposes. Multiple tests or audits with published statistical results date back to 1972.[13] These tests verify that blacks are likely to face discrimination when looking for housing, but it was not until 1977 that a nationwide study of discrimination against blacks in the sale and rental of housing fully developed the audit methodology in the United States.[14]

In 1977, the National Committee against Discrimination in Housing, under contract to HUD, conducted audits in forty metropolitan areas.[15] The Housing Market Practices Survey (HMPS) completed 1,609 rental audits and 1,655 sales audits. Apartment complexes and real estate agencies were selected for auditing by random sampling of real estate classified advertisements in the metropolitan areas' major newspapers. Auditors in each metropolitan area were paired in every relevant aspect—sex, age, income, and family size. Audit pairs followed identical procedures when conducting their audits and individually reported their experiences on audit report forms. Rental audit responses were summarized into five categories—availability, courtesy, terms and conditions, information requested, and information volunteered. Four categories were used for sales audits—availability, courtesy, service, and household information requested. Black auditor and white auditor responses were compared and the net difference of "white favored" and "black favored" treatment was attributed to racial discrimination. The HMPS found that nationally blacks encountered discriminatory treatment with regard to availability in 27 percent of the rental audits and 15 percent of the sales audits.

While these figures seem high, some researchers believe that they actually underestimate the discriminatory treatment shown black home-seekers.[16] The HMPS researchers calculated the percentage of discriminatory treatment as the net difference between "white favored" and "black favored" treatment. For example, using their findings that in 48 percent of the rental audits white auditors received favored treatment and in 21 percent of the cases blacks received favored treatment, the net difference is 27 percent. While some part of each of the percentages of favored treatment can be attributed to random factors, it can be said that in 48 percent of the rental audits, black auditors were treated less favorably than their white counterparts, rather than citing an incidence of discrimination in 27 percent of the audits. White auditors were favored—or the black auditors treated less favorably— in 39 percent of the sales audits.

Since HMPS, various black/white audit studies have been completed.[17] Table 1 lists selected results from seventy-six rental audit studies, including the results for the forty metropolitan areas audited in HMPS.[18] When available, the following are reported: (1) the year the audit took place, (2) the number of audits, (3) the overall incidence of discrimination, and (4) the incidence of discriminatory treatment with regard to the availability of units. Two measures of discrimination—an overall measure and an availability measure—are listed because individual studies use different means of reporting results. There are also different means of arriving at an "overall" measure of discrimination for an audit study.[19] For example, all results noted with an asterisk were calculated as the net difference in the percentage of audits where white auditors were favored over black auditors. In the other cases, it is not clear whether a comparable adjustment was made. So all of the reported numbers are not exactly comparable.

Nineteen of the seventy-six rental audit studies listed in Table 1 report an overall incidence of discrimination. The results range from a low incidence of 10 percent in South Bend to a high of 90 percent in Bakersfield, with an unweighted mean of 46 percent. Sixty-six studies report discriminatory treatment in the availability of units. Results in this category range from a low of –13 percent, which means black auditors were favored, in the metropolitan area of Albany-Schenectady-Troy to a high of 63 percent in Louisville. The unweighted mean is 30 percent.

TABLE 1
Summary of Rental Audit Studies:
Select Results, 1977 to 1988[a]

Location	Date	Number of Audits	Overall Incidence of Discrimination	Discriminatory Treatment in Availability
Akron, OH	1977	26	na	27*
Albany-Schen.-Troy, NY	1977	30	na	-13*
Asheville, NC	1977	29	na	24*
Atlanta, GA	1977	119	na	16*
Bakersfield, CA	1983	49	90	21
Baltimore, MD	1981-82	35	46	na
Boston, MA	1977	110	na	24*
	1981	156	na	29
Canton, OH	1977	29	na	38*
Carmichael-Citrus Hgts, CA	1982	18	50	na
Chicago, IL (south suburbs)	1981-82	na	na	45
	1982-83	na	na	57
	1983-84	na	na	59
	1984-85	na	na	21
	1985-86	na	na	31
	1986-87	na	na	34
Cincinnati, OH-KY-IN	1977	29	na	27*
Cleveland Hgts., OH	1985	29	14	na
Columbus, OH	1977	29	na	28*
Dallas, TX	1977	114	na	16*
Dayton, OH	1977	29	na	41*
Denver, CO	1982	na	na	5
Detroit, MI	1977	30	na	57*
Farmingham, MA	1987-88	22	63	na
Ft Lauderdale-Hollywood, FL	1977	28	na	36*
Fort Wayne, IN	1977	30	na	30*
Fort Worth, TX	1977	28	na	25*
Greenville, SC	1977	30	na	14*
Harrisburg, PA	1977	28	na	7*
Hartford, CT	1977	30	na	23*
Hayward, CA	1984-85	25	20*	16
Indianapolis, IN	1977	28	na	50*
Kentucky (state)	1981	na	na	46
	1985	na	na	17
Lawton, OK	1977	30	na	20*
Lexington, KY	1977	30	na	24*
	1980	na	na	56
	1985	na	na	14
	1987	na	na	53
Los Angeles-Long Beach, CA	1977	30	na	46*
Louisville, KY-IN	1977	30	na	30*
	1980	na	na	35
	1985	na	na	18
	1987	na	na	63
Macon, GA	1977	30	na	37*
Memphis, TN	1984	145	76	na
	1986	86	77	9
Milwaukee, WI	1977	108	na	14*
Monroe, LA	1977	29	na	52*
Nashville-Davidson, TN	1977	29	na	38*

TABLE 1 (continued)

Location	Date	Number of Audits	Overall Incidence of Discrimination	Discriminatory Treatment in Availability
New York, NY	1977	29	na	24*
Oklahoma (state)	1985	91	22	na
Oklahoma City, OK	1977	30	na	24*
Palo Alto, CA	1983	20	70*	10
Paterson-Clif.-Passaic, NJ	1977	29	na	-3*
Peoria, Il	1977	30	na	30*
Redwood City, CA	1982	35	69*	26
Sacramento, CA	1977	118	na	15*
	1985	32	25	na
Sasginaw, MI	1977	30	na	27*
San Bern.-Riverside-Ont., CA	1977	29	na	49*
Savannah, GA	1977	15	na	20*
Springfld-Chic.-Holy., MA-CT	1977	29	na	52*
South Bend, In	1984	na	na	11
	1985	35	34	na .
	1986-87	73	10	34
Stockton, CA	1977	28	na	25*
Sunnyvale, CA	1981	23	61*	na
Tampa-St. Petersburg, FL	1977	30	na	36*
Tulsa, OK	1977	30	na	40*
Vallejo-Napa, CA	1977	29	na	52*
Washington, DC	1986	280	48*	9
	1988	295	28*	na
Wisconsin (small cities)	1984-85	73	45	58
Wooster, OH	1985-86	15	20*	13
York, PA	1977	29	na	35*

Sources: Galster (1990), Newburger (1984), and Wienk, et. al., (1979).
 [a] Figures are percentages.
 na means not available.
 * means the net difference in the percentage of audits in which white auditors were favored over
   black auditors.
 — means black auditors favored.

Five locations with rental audit results reported in Table 1 are among the nation's ten most segregated cities.[20] They are Baltimore, Chicago, Detroit, Los Angeles, and Milwaukee. In Baltimore, the only one of the five to report an overall measure of discrimination, the incidence of discrimination is equal to the unweighted mean for that measure—46 percent. In Chicago, where there were six audit studies between 1981 and 1987, the incidence of discriminatory treatment in availability ranged from a low of 21 percent to a high of 59 percent. In Detroit, 57 percent of the audits reveal discriminatory treatment in availability, while in Los Angeles the incidence is 46 percent. Finally, in Milwaukee, 14 percent of the auditors experienced discrimination in availability. The unweighted mean for the availability measure is 30 percent. In seven of the ten audits completed in these five locations, the results are equal to or higher than the unweighted means for their measure. Thus, the segregation measure and the audit studies appear to support each other, although it would be helpful to also have audit results for the nine cities found to be the least segregated.

Table 2 lists selected results from sales audit studies. When available, an overall incidence of discrimination and discriminatory treatment in housing availability are reported. Five locations report an overall incidence of discrimination. The results range from a low of 10 percent, in South Bend, to a high of 29 percent in Cincinnati. The unweighted mean is 22 percent. The range of results for studies that report an incidence of discrimination in availability is from –30 percent in the metropolitan area of Springfield-Chicopee-Holyoke to 63 percent in Lexington, with an unweighted mean of 18 percent.

The nation's ten most segregated cities include four that have completed sales audit studies—Chicago, Detroit, Los Angeles, and Milwaukee.[21] These locations completed a total of six studies, all of which report the incidence of discriminatory treatment in availability. In Chicago, where there were three studies between 1980 and 1982, the reported results are 43 percent, 9 percent, and 34 percent. In Detroit, the incidence is 42 percent. In Los Angeles, the measure is 24 percent. And in Milwaukee, it is 33 percent. Five of the six studies report results above the unweighted mean—18 percent. As with the rental markets, the segregation measure and the audit studies appear to support each other, but again none of the least segregated cities have had any audit studies.

While a greater number of rental audit studies than sales audit studies have been completed—no doubt due to the relative simplicity of the former process—research shows that disparate treatment in both rental and sales audit occurs at a frequency that is too high to attribute to random differences in treatment.[22] Black auditors consistently encountered discrimination. And, according to the results of these studies, homeseekers in the rental market seem more likely to encounter discrimination than homebuyers.

The most recent audit studies reviewed were completed in 1988. During the summer of 1989, the Urban Institute, under contract to HUD, carried out approximately 3,800 rental and sales audits in twenty-five metropolitan areas throughout the United States. The Housing Discrimination Study (HDS) refined the audit methodology used in HMPS to reflect a three-stage housing search process: (1) the availability of a unit, (2) access to the unit, and (3) steering to other units.[23] In addition, unlike HMPS, HDS used the proportion of white favored audits as a gross

TABLE 2
Summary of Sales Audit Studies:
Select Results, 1977 to 1988

Location	Date	Number of Audits	Overall Incidence of Discrimination	Discriminatory Treatment in Availability
Akron, OH	1977	40	na	32*
Albany-Schen.-Troy, NY	1977	30	na	7*
Asheville, NC	1977	28	na	36*
Atlanta, GA	1977	78	na	11*
Boston, MA	1977	73	na	10*
	1981	118	na	24
	1983-84	na	na	10
Canton, OH	1977	30	na	30*
Chicago, IL (south suburbs)	1980	na	na	43
	1981	na	na	9
	1981-82	na	na	34
Cincinnati, OH-KY-IN	1977	48	na	50*
	1983	62	29	9
Cleveland Hgts., OH	1983-84	29	21	na
	1985	61	23	2
Columbus, OH	1977	40	na	48*
Dallas, TX	1977	80	na	7*
Dayton, OH	1977	43	na	14*
Denver, CO	1982	na	na	2
Detroit, MI	1977	51	na	42*
Ft Lauderdale-Hollywood, FL	1977	45	na	25*
Fort Wayne, IN	1977	25	na	-24*
Fort Worth, TX	1977	29	na	38*
Greenville, SC	1977	30	na	3*
Grand Rapids, MI	1981-82	100	24*	na
Harrisburg, PA	1977	30	na	3*
Hartford, CT	1977	30	na	0*
Indianapolis, IN	1977	50	na	34*
Lawton, OK	1977	30	na	-17*
Lexington, KY	1977	30	na	40*
	1987	na	na	63
Los Angeles-Long Beach, CA	1977	50	na	24*
Louisville, KY-IN	1977	39	na	13*
	1987	na	na	35
Macon, GA	1977	45	na	22*
Milwaukee, WI	1977	80	na	33*
Monroe, LA	1977	29	na	14*
Nashville-Davidson, TN	1977	39	na	13*
New York, NY	1977	50	na	38*
Oklahoma City, OK	1977	29	na	0*
Paterson-Clif.-Passaic, NJ	1977	30	na	26*
Peoria, Il	1977	30	na	0*
Sacramento, CA	1977	79	na	10*
	1985	32	25	na

TABLE 2 (continued)

Location	Date	Number of Audits	Overall Incidence of Discrimination	Discriminatory Treatment in Availability
Sasginaw, MI	1977	30	na	3*
San Bern.-Riverside-Ont., CA	1977	50	na	-7*
Savannah, GA	1977	30	na	30*
Springfld-Chic.-Holy., MA-CT	1977	30	na	-30*
South Bend, In	1987	16	10	3
Stockton, CA	1977	30	na	-7*
Tampa-St. Petersburg, FL	1977	44	na	12*
Tulsa, OK	1977	29	na	31*
Vallejo-Napa, CA	1977	29	na	15*
York, PA	1977	29	na	35*

Sources: Galster (1990), Newburger (1984), and Wienk, et. al., (1979).
 [a] Figures are percentages.
na means not available.
 * means the net difference in the percentage of audits in which white auditors were favored over black auditors.
 — means black auditors favored.

measure of the incidence of discrimination. While results of the HDS audits were not available during the preparation of this article, the findings are probably similar to the other studies reviewed here.[24] And as long as discrimination on the basis of race exists in the housing market, there is little hope for an end to racial segregation.

SUMMARY AND CONCLUSIONS

More than twenty years after the passage of the 1968 Fair Housing Act, blacks can still expect to encounter discriminatory housing practices when looking for a home to either rent or buy. In addition, based on 1980 Census data, racial segregation is as pervasive as ever.

Amendments to the Fair Housing Act have strengthened its enforcement mechanisms, but if the system continues to rely solely on private individuals to file complaints, the effectiveness of these enforcement tools also may be limited. Currently, knowledge of property owners and managers who fail to comply with the Fair Housing Act is brought to the attention of HUD by individuals. Most individuals may have no idea that they have been discriminated against, because of no comparable experience. Therefore the incidence of complaints to HUD is probably less than the incidence of discrimination, subsequently lessening the impact of the legislation's deterrents.

Many other federal departments test for compliance with their rules and regulations, in addition to responding to complaints from consumers. Fair housing audits are a proven method of identifying housing discrimination. A random system of audits would not only identify and hold accountable discriminators, but would also act as a deterrent against future discrimination. The Amendments to the Fair Housing Act gave it teeth; it is time for violators to feel a bite. A federally sponsored system of random fair housing audits would facilitate the type of impact needed for the Fair Housing Act to "remove discriminatory barriers against minorities from the housing market and end residential segregation."[25]

NOTES

1. In an audit study, teams of individuals matched in every characteristic except skin color identify "differences in quality, content, and quantity of information and service given to them by real estate firms and rental property managers" during their housing search process. See Clifford E. Reid, "The Reliability of Fair Housing Audits to Detect Racial Discrimination in Rental Housing Markets," *Journal of the American Real Estate and Urban Economics Association*, Volume 12, Number 1 (Spring 1984), pp. 86–96, and Ronald E. Wienk and John C. Simonson, "Everything You Ever Wanted to Know About Auditing But Didn't Bother to Ask," background paper prepared for a research colloquium given by the United States Department of Housing and Urban Development, on *Discrimination and the Audit: State of the Art* (Washington, D.C.: 1984).

2. See *The Fair Housing Act, Hearings Before the Subcommittee on Housing and Urban Affairs, the Committee on Banking and Currency*, United States Senate (90th Congress, 1st Session, Washington, D.C.: U.S. Government Printing Office, 1967).

3. See "Major Provisions of Fair Housing Legislation," *Congressional Quarterly*, Volume 46, No. 34 (August 20, 1988), pp. 2348–2350.

4. For a discussion of the debate surrounding passage of the Amendments see "Should Congress Approve The Fair Housing Amendments Act of 1987? Pros & Cons," *Congressional Digest*, Volume 67, Number 6–7 (June–July 1988).

5. *Congressional Digest*, p. 180.

6. For a discussion of segregation trends during the 1970s see John N. Farley, "Segregation in 1980: How Segregated are America's Metropolitan Areas?," *Divided Neighborhoods: Changing Patterns of Racial Segregation*, edited by Gary A. Tobin (Newbury Park, CA: Sage Publications, 1987), pp. 95–114.

7. See Gary A. Tobin, "Introduction: Segregation in the 1980s," *Divided Neighborhoods: Changing Patterns of Racial Segregation*, pp. 8–14.

8. For a discussion of the theories of residential segregation see: Joe T. Darden, "Choosing Neighbors and Neighborhoods: The Role of Race in Preference," *Divided Neighborhoods: Changing Patterns of Racial Segregation*, pp. 15–42; and George C. Galster and W. Mark Keeney, "Race, Residence, Discrimination, and Economic Opportunity: Modeling the Nexus of Urban Racial Phenomena," *Urban Affairs Quarterly*, Volume 24, Number 1 (September 1988), pp. 87–117.

9. Darden, p. 37.

10. See Harriet B. Newburger, "Discrimination by a Profit-Maximizing Real Estate Broker in Response to White Prejudice," *Journal of Urban Economics*, Volume 26, Number 1 (July 1989), pp. 1–19.

11. All information regarding this multidimensional segregation index is from Douglas S. Massey and Nancy A. Denton, "Hypersegregation in U.S. Metropolitan Areas: Black and Hispanic Segregation Along Five Dimensions," *Demography*, Volume 26, Number 3 (August 1989), pp. 373–391.

12. As a result of the 1980 Census, the designation for metropolitan area was changed, and the term SMSA is no longer used. The terms currently used are MSA (metropolitan statistical area), PMSA (primary metropolitan statistical area), and CMSA (consolidated metropolitan statistical area). See Wilhelmina A. Leigh, "Trends in the Housing Status of Black Americans Across Selected Metropolitan Areas" in this issue (footnote 1) for a more thorough discussion of the definitions of these terms.

13. For a list of 16 audit studies with published results conducted before HMPS, see Ronald E. Wienk and John C. Simonson (1984).

14. A nationwide audit study of discrimination against Asians and West Indians seeking housing and employment was conducted in England during the late 1960s and early 1970s. See Neil McIntosh and Davis J. Smith, *The Extent of Racial Discrimination* (London: The Social Science Institute, 1974).

15. All information regarding HMPS is from Ronald E. Wienk, Clifford E. Reid, John C. Simonson, and Fredrick J. Eggers, *Measuring Racial Discrimination in American Housing Markets: The Housing Market Practices Survey* (Washington, D.C.: U.S. Department of Housing and Urban Development, 1979).

16. See Raymond J. Struyk, "Race and Housing: Affordability and Location," paper presented at the conference on *New Perspectives on Racial Issues: Middle-Sized Metropolitan Areas* (Madison, WS: 1989).

17. Numerous Hispanic/anglo audits, Native American/white, and Asian/anglo studies have also been completed. See Harriet Newburger, *Recent Evidence on Discrimination in Housing* (Washington, D.C.: U.S. Government Printing Office, 1984) and George Galster, "Racial Discrimination in Housing Markets During the 1980s: A Review of the Audit Evidence," *Journal of Planning Education and Research*, Volume 9, Number 3 (1990), pp. 165–175.

18. The majority of these studies were conducted independently of one another, except for the forty SMSAs audited in HMPS in 1977.

19. See Galster (1990).

20. See Massey and Denton (1989).

21. See Massey and Denton (1989).

22. See Galster (1990) and Wienk, et. al. (1979).

23. The Urban Institute, "Proposal to Conduct a Housing Discrimination Study" (Washington, D.C.: 1988).

24. Only if the new fair housing legislation has had an immediate impact on the behavior of actors in the rental and sales housing markets is this likely to be untrue.

25. See footnote 4.

II

General Housing Conditions and Special Populations

3

TRENDS IN THE HOUSING STATUS
OF BLACK AMERICANS
ACROSS SELECTED METROPOLITAN AREAS

Wilhelmina A. Leigh

This article examines housing data for a set of metropolitan areas and their central cities, and explores the major issues that arise when considering the impacts by race of federal housing assistance programs. Housing market conditions and characteristics vary widely by race across the areas covered—Birmingham, AL; Buffalo, NY; Cleveland, OH; Indianapolis, IN; Memphis, TN; Milwaukee, WI; Newport News, VA; Oklahoma City, OK; Providence, RI; Salt Lake City, UT; and San Jose, CA. Issues related to racial impacts of federal housing assistance emanate from two major policy goals—to help low-income households and to provide equal housing opportunity.

Each of the chapters in Section III examines the housing status of black Americans in a U.S. city or metropolitan area and also explores the disparities between the housing status of black Americans and white Americans in these places. This introductory article sets the stage for these subsequent more detailed analyses by (1) examining aggregated housing data for a set of metropolitan areas and their central cities, and (2) exploring the major issues that arise when considering the impacts by race of federal housing assistance programs.

The cities and metropolitan areas covered here are: Birmingham, AL; Buffalo, NY; Cleveland, OH; Indianapolis, IN; Memphis, TN; Milwaukee, WI; Newport News, VA; Oklahoma City, OK; Providence, RI; Salt Lake City, UT; and San Jose, CA. The data for cities featured in this article are primarily from the 1984 American Housing Survey (AHS) and the 1986 State and Metropolitan Area Data Book. Because each wave of the AHS for metropolitan areas provides data for a geographically representative set of places, the cities examined here are dispersed throughout the United States. Likewise, the cities studied in detail in the articles that follow also are geographically diverse. Only one city, Buffalo, NY, is analyzed both in this overview article and in a separate article as well.

The first section of this article analyzes the housing-related data for the eleven cities featured herein. (The expanded city synopses themselves are found in the Appendix.) The second section discusses some of the major issues related to race that arise within the federal housing programs noted in the chapters in Section III. The final section provides a summary. (Details on the relevant federal housing programs are provided in the glossary at the back of this issue.)

FINDINGS FROM HOUSING-RELATED DATA

Although the eleven metropolitan areas studied in the 1984 American Housing Survey (AHS) are geographically diverse, the trends reflected in the data for these places are quite similar. In most cases, however, at least one metropolitan area or central city provides ''the exception that proves the rule.'' Trends for the eleven areas are discussed in the following sections.

First, in a majority (seven) of these places, both the central cities and metropolitan areas reflected the same trends in population change over the periods 1970–1980 and 1980–1984.[1] (See Tables 1 and 3). In Buffalo, Cleveland, and Milwaukee, the shared population trend was a decrease over the entire period, while in Memphis, Newport News, Oklahoma City, and San Jose, the common trend was an increase. In Birmingham, Indianapolis, Providence, and Salt Lake City, however, the metropolitan areas and their central cities reflected different patterns of population change between 1970 and 1984. In Birmingham and Providence, while the metropolitan area populations grew during the entire period, the central city populations declined. The metropolitan areas of Indianapolis and Salt Lake City, on the other hand, also grew throughout the 1970–1984 period, while their central city populations first declined (between 1970 and 1980) and then increased (between 1980 and 1984).

Second, although the differences vary considerably, in ten of the eleven places, notably larger percentages of minority households are found in the central cities than throughout the metropolitan areas. (See Tables 1 and 3). The single exception to this is the Norfolk-Virginia Beach-Newport News, VA Metropolitan Statistical Area (MSA), where the percentages

TABLE 1
Demographic Characteristics of Selected Metropolitan Areas, 1980

	Population							Households	
			Percent Change		Percent	Percent			Percent
					Black	Sp. Origin			Change
	1970	1980	1970-80	1980-84	(1980)	(1980)		1980	1970-80
Birmingham, AL MSA	794,083	884,014	11.3	1.3	27.2	0.7		316,381	27.0
Buffalo, NY CMSA a/	1,349,200	1,242,800	-7.9	-3.1	9.2	1.3		445,475	6.5
Cleveland, OH PMSA	2,063,700	1,898,800	-8.0	-1.7	18.2	1.4		694,401	6.8
Indianapolis, IN MSA	1,111,400	1,166,600	5.0	2.4	13.5	0.8		418,485	20.6
Memphis, TN MSA b/	834,103	913,472	9.5	2.3	39.9	0.9		311,996	27.8
Milwaukee, WI PMSA	1,403,900	1,397,000	-0.5	-0.2	10.8	2.5		500,684	15.7
Newport News, VA MSA c/	1,058,800	1,160,300	9.6	8.7	28.1	1.6		385,929	29.0
Oklahoma City, OK MSA	718,737	860,969	19.8	11.8	9.1	2.2		321,546	36.3
Providence, RI (2 PMSAs) d/	913,056	925,917	1.0	1.0	2.7	2.1		330,632	N/A
Salt Lake City, UT MSA e/	683,913	910,222	33.1	12.6	0.9	4.9		289,379	47.7
San Jose, CA PMSA	1,065,313	1,295,071	21.6	5.9	3.4	17.5		458,519	42.0

Source: State and Metropolitan Area Data Book 1986
Note: MSA is metropolitan statistical area; PMSA is primary metropolitan statistical area; and CMSA is consolidated metropolitan statistical area. N/A means not available.
a. Full name is Buffalo-Niagara Falls, NY CMSA.
b. Full name is Memphis, TN-Arkansas-Mississippi MSA.
c. Full name is Norfolk-Virginia Beach-Newport News, VA MSA.
d. Represents two PMSAs: Providence, RI PMSA and the Pawtucket-Woonsocket-Attleboro, RI-MA PMSA.
e. Full name is Salt Lake City-Ogden, UT MSA.

of both blacks and persons of Spanish origin are virtually identical in both the central cities of the area (29 percent) and in the entire metropolitan area (28 percent). Although the geographic irregularities of the Tidewater area of Virginia plus creative annexation of areas could explain this trend, in part, this finding may simply reflect lesser geographic concentration of minority group members in the central cities of this MSA than in the 10 others surveyed by the AHS in 1984.

Third, in nine of the eleven places, in both the metropolitan areas and their central cities, blacks are the dominant minority group. (See Tables 1 and 3). As would be expected, the exceptional places are in the West— the Salt Lake City-Ogden, UT MSA and the San Jose, CA Primary

TABLE 2
Housing Characteristics of Selected Metropolitan Areas, 1980

								Median
			Percent Built			Percent	Median	Gross
		Percent	-------------------		Percent	With 1.01+	Value of	Rent of
	Number	Change	1970 to	Prior	Owner-	Persons	Owned	Rented
	in 1980	1970-80	March 1980	to 1940	Occupied	Per Room	Units	Units
Birmingham, AL MSA	341,006	29.6	28.5	18.9	68.1	4.3	$38,500	$208
Buffalo, NY CMSA a/	474,247	8.9	11.9	43.3	63.7	1.9	$39,700	$216
Cleveland, OH PMSA	734,110	8.5	14.1	32.8	64.5	2.0	$56,100	$238
Indianapolis, IN MSA	451,319	22.0	23.9	24.9	65.2	2.9	$40,300	$228
Memphis, TN MSA b/	332,079	29.9	29.1	12.2	60.3	6.4	$38,100	$201
Milwaukee, WI PMSA	521,505	16.1	18.1	32.1	60.1	2.5	$61,900	$252
Newport News, VA MSA c/	413,364	30.9	30.2	12.6	58.6	3.7	$46,100	$250
Oklahoma City, OK MSA	352,321	37.8	31.0	14.1	67.7	3.3	$41,400	$238
Providence, RI (2 PMSAs) d/	357,977	17.3	N/A	N/A	59.4	N/A	N/A	N/A
Salt Lake City, UT MSA e/	306,639	51.3	36.6	16.6	69.9	4.5	$61,800	$244
San Jose, CA PMSA	473,817	40.7	31.8	7.4	59.7	5.3	$109,400	$334

Source: State and Metropolitan Area Data Book 1986
Note: MSA is metropolitan statistical area; PMSA is primary metropolitan statistical area, and CMSA is consolidated metropolitan statistical area. N/A means not available.
a. Full name is Buffalo-Niagara Falls, NY CMSA.
b. Full name is Memphis, TN-Arkansas-Mississippi MSA.
c. Full name is Norfolk-Virginia Beach-Newport News, VA MSA.
d. Represents two PMSAs: Providence, RI PMSA and the Pawtucket-Woonsocket-Attleboro, RI-MA PMSA.
e. Full name is Salt Lake City-Ogden, UT MSA.

Metropolitan Statistical Area (PMSA). Persons of Spanish origin are the dominant minority group in these two places.

Fourth, in a majority of places (six out of the ten for which data are available), a higher percentage of the housing stock in the central cities than in the entire metropolitan areas was old in 1980—that is, built prior to 1940. (See Tables 2 and 3.) In all the exceptional places other than Memphis, the more interesting trends seem to be: the near equality of the shares of older units in the central cities and their corresponding metropolitan areas; and the near equality of the shares of newer (1970 to March

TABLE 3
Demographic and Housing Characteristics of Central Cities in Selected Metropolitan Areas, 1980

| | Population | | | | | | Households | Units | | | |
	1970	1980	Percent Change 1970-80	Percent Change 1980-84	Percent Black (1980)	Percent Sp. Origin (1980)	1980	Number in 1980	Percent Built 1970 to March 1980	Percent Built Prior to 1940	Percent Owner-Occupied
Birmingham, AL MSA	334,188	316,142	-5.4	-1.7	55.2	0.8	118,445	126,362	14.5	27.5	53.7
Buffalo, NY CMSA a/	548,217	429,254	-21.7	-5.6	24.3	2.4	168,226	185,974	3.4	69.5	46.6
Cleveland, OH PMSA	751,076	573,822	-23.6	-4.8	43.8	3.1	218,297	239,416	4.4	57.7	48.2
Indianapolis, IN MSA	736,916	700,807	-4.9	1.4	21.8	0.9	260,167	283,176	19.6	25.9	58.9
Memphis, TN MSA b/	649,802	674,494	3.8	0.3	47.1	0.8	239,724	253,943	20.8	13.3	56.4
Milwaukee, WI PMSA	756,925	686,531	-9.3	-2.1	21.4	4.2	259,462	271,779	11.6	40.5	47.8
Newport News, VA MSA c/	859,507	948,896	10.4	8.1	29.3	1.8	318,265	339,995	28.4	13.2	55.7
Oklahoma City, OK MSA	445,205	497,739	11.8	9.8	12.3	2.6	195,167	215,256	28.2	16.2	62.5
Providence, RI (2 PMSAs) d/	303,011	273,922	-9.6	-0.7	7.5	4.4	105,632	115,657	8.3	62.1	39.3
Salt Lake City, UT MSA e/	245,351	227,440	-7.3	2.5	1.9	8.2	91,561	98,429	15.0	37.2	52.9
San Jose, CA PMSA	515,951	684,667	32.7	8.4	4.5	20.8	232,634	240,339	36.2	8.6	61.4

Source: State and Metropolitan Area Data Book 1986
Note: MSA is metropolitan statistical area; PMSA is primary metropolitan statistical area; and CMSA is consolidated metropolitan statistical area.
N/A means not available.
a. Full name is Buffalo-Niagara Falls, NY CMSA.
b. Full name is Memphis, TN-Arkansas-Mississippi MSA.
c. Full name is Norfolk-Virginia Beach-Newport News, VA MSA.
d. Represents two PMSAs: Providence, RI PMSA and the Pawtucket-Woonsocket-Attleboro, RI-MA PMSA.
e. Full name is Salt Lake City-Ogden, UT MSA.

1980) units in the central cities and their corresponding metropolitan areas. In two of these three places—Newport News and Oklahoma City—the percentage of newer units greatly exceeds the percentage of older units both in the central cities and the entire metro areas. In Indianapolis, the nearly equal shares of older units in both the central city (26 percent) and the metropolitan area (25 percent) exceed the shares of newer units in these places. Finally, in Memphis, although the shares of older units in the central city and metropolitan area are nearly equal, only 21 percent of the units in the central city are relatively new versus the 29 percent in the entire metropolitan area.

Fifth, with only one exception, the rate of owner-occupancy throughout each metropolitan area exceeded this rate in each central city. (See Tables 2 and 3.) In the central city of the San Jose, CA PMSA, 61 percent of units in 1980 were owner-occupied, compared to nearly 60 percent of all the units throughout the metropolitan area. This very slight differential suggests greater vitality in the central city of the San Jose, CA PMSA than in many other of the areas treated herein.

Finally, the share of black households increased in the categories of renter households considered to reflect increasing neediness and eligibility for housing assistance in 1984. (See Tables 4 and 5). Specifically, in all eleven metropolitan areas, the share of black households among all renter households with very low incomes and with a HUD program subsidy exceeded the share of black households among all renter households merely with very low incomes. (This latter share exceeded the share of black households among all renter households.) Because federal housing assistance generally targets households with very low incomes, one would expect the percentages of black households among very low income renter households and the percentages of black households among very low income renter households that get HUD program subsidies to be nearly equal in all these metro areas, if black renter households are assisted in proportion to their eligibility. Instead, the latter figure consistently exceeds the former by from 3 percent to 33 percentage points.

ISSUES RELATED TO FEDERAL HOUSING PROGRAMS

The federal government first intervened in the nation's housing markets in the 1930s and has continued to intervene since, for a variety of reasons. One of the goals for this intervention has been to help meet the needs of those households whose incomes are so low as to render their demand ineffective to procure housing that meets minimum standards of

TABLE 4
All Renter Households and Renter Households With Very Low Incomes in Selected Metropolitan Areas by Race, 1984

	All Renter Households			Renter Households With Very-Low Incomes		
	Number	Percent Black a/	Percent White a/	Number	Percent Black a/	Percent White a/
Birmingham, AL MSA	328,147	25	74	72,658	50	48
Buffalo, NY CMSA b/	446,948	9	89	73,180	24	71
Cleveland, OH PMSA	701,279	18	79	133,664	39	56
Indianapolis, IN MSA	441,285	12	87	72,389	27	72
Memphis, TN MSA c/	329,153	35	64	64,950	71	28
Milwaukee, WI PMSA	512,598	11	87	80,197	29	64
Newport News, VA MSA d/	429,648	26	71	53,978	59	38
Oklahoma City, OK MSA	370,921	8	87	56,061	18	74
Providence, RI (2 PMSAs) e/	357,319	2	94	47,465	5	84
Salt Lake City, UT MSA f/	333,672	1	92	44,187	2	84
San Jose, CA PMSA	482,874	3	74	49,511	4	55
All Eleven Metro Areas	4,733,844	13	82	748,240	32	60

Source: American Housing Survey
Note: Very-low-income households have incomes less than or equal to 50 percent of the median incomes in their metropolitan areas. MSA is metropolitan statistical area; PMSA is primary metropolitan statistical area; and CMSA is consolidated metropolitan statistical area. N/A means not available.
a. Percents do not add to 100 because households of other racial and language groups, such as Asians, Hispanics, and Indians, are not included.
b. Full name is Buffalo-Niagara Falls, NY CMSA.
c. Full name is Memphis, TN-Arkansas-Mississippi MSA.
d. Full name is Norfolk-Virginia Beach-Newport News, VA MSA.
e. Represents two PMSAs: Providence, RI PMSA and the Pawtucket-Woonsocket-Attleboro, RI-MA PMSA.
f. Full name is Salt Lake City-Ogden, UT MSA.

safety and adequacy.[2] Another goal for intervention has been to provide equal opportunity in access to housing for all racial and ethnic groups.

TABLE 5
Renter Households With Very Low Incomes in Selected Metropolitan Areas and Living in HUD-Subsidized Housing, By Household Type and Race, 1984

	Renter Households Of All Races With Very-Low Incomes And HUD Program	Black Renter Households				White Renter Households		
		Percent a/ Subsidy	Percent a/ Elderly Children	Percent with Children	Percent Nonelderly Without Children	Percent a/ Elderly Children	Percent with Children	Percent Nonelderly Without Children
Birmingham, AL MSA	13,078	81	12	52	17	17	8	6	3
Buffalo, NY CMSA b/	8,050	45	7	25	13	48	11	19	17
Cleveland, OH PMSA	20,050	72	25	39	9	27	15	9	2
Indianapolis, IN MSA	9,411	42	10	30	2	56	23	23	10
Memphis, TN MSA c/	11,691	82	12	56	14	16	10	3	3
Milwaukee, WI PMSA	12,832	35	8	21	6	65	39	19	7
Newport News, VA MSA d/	14,034	80	10	57	13	19	5	9	5
Oklahoma City, OK MSA	5,045	36	6	24	6	56	17	31	8
Providence, RI (2 PMSAs) e/	9,018	11	5	4	3	76	41	19	16
Salt Lake City, UT MSA f/	4,419	6	2	1	3	72	25	37	10
San Jose, CA PMSA	5,941	7	3	3	0	40	23	13	3
All Eleven Metro Areas	113,569	55	11	34	9	38	18	14	7

Source: American Housing Survey

Note: Very-low-income households have incomes less than or equal to 50 percent of the median incomes in their metropolitan areas. MSA is metropolitan statistical area; PMSA is primary metropolitan statistical area; and CMSA is consolidated metropolitan statistical area. N/A means not available.

a. Percentages for black and white households do not add to 100 because households of other racial and language groups—Indians, Asians, and Hispanics—are not included. Percentages by household types do not sum to 100 because of rounding.

b. Full name is Buffalo-Niagara Falls, NY CMSA.

c. Full name is Memphis, TN-Arkansas-Mississippi MSA.

d. Full name is Norfolk-Virginia Beach-Newport News, VA MSA.

e. Represents two PMSAs: Providence, RI PMSA and the Pawtucket-Woonsocket-Attleboro, RI-MA PMSA.

f. Full name is Salt Lake City-Ogden, UT MSA.

Each of these reasons for federal intervention in the housing market is discussed here, along with several conceptual issues that arise when trying to evaluate how successful federal programs have been in achieving these goals. The section concludes with a discussion of the impacts of selected federal programs.

Intervention for Low-Income Households

According to Struyk and Tuccillo, the housing policy goal to help meet the needs of low-income households translates into the desire to ensure the availability of adequate and affordable housing, especially to low-income households. John Maynard Keynes provided theoretical support for government intervention to lessen poverty on the grounds that only activist but carefully calculated "government demand" could counteract deficiencies in aggregate demand.[3]

Around the same time in the 1930s that the federal government first intervened in the private market because of the private sector's failure to house most Americans adequately, President Hoover convened the President's Committee on Home Building and Home Ownership. This Committee isolated "Negro housing" as a topic of inquiry, due to evidence that the units occupied by "Negroes" were undermaintained, overpriced, and crowded.[4] The Hoover Committee also found that "Negroes" paid a higher percentage of income for shelter than other population subgroups.

Eligibility for federal rental housing programs is based on income, although these programs are not entitlements—that is, all the households with qualifying incomes do not receive assistance. In fact, only about 28 percent of all eligible households throughout the nation receive this assistance.[5] Households accepted into most of these programs pay 30 percent of income toward rent.

The most common rubric for a household's income eligibility for housing assistance programs is some fraction of the median income for the metropolitan statistical area (MSA) that contains a locality. Thus, federal rental assistance programs are open to households with incomes that are a certain percentage of area median income. For instance, the Section 8 voucher program serves households with incomes less than or equal to 50 percent of the local area median, while the Section 8 existing-housing certificate program serves households with incomes less than or equal to 80 percent of the area median. In the Section 8 existing-housing certificate program, households pay a maximum of 30 percent of income toward rent, while in the voucher program, households pay a minimum of 30 percent of income toward rent.

Because the income distribution of blacks has lower ranges and a lower median than that of whites, blacks might dominate the federal rental housing assistance programs in certain localities. In 1988, black median household income was about $16,400 while white median household income was about $28,800.[6]

Intervention for Equal Housing Opportunity

One of the seven major goals of federal housing policy is to provide equal opportunity in housing.[7] Equal opportunity in access to housing means the ability of households of all racial and ethnic groups to move into any neighborhood of their choice constrained only by whether they have the income to purchase or rent a unit there. The Civil Rights Act of 1866 first codified this goal, when it guaranteed to all citizens in every state and territory the same right as is enjoyed by white citizens to inherit, purchase, lease, sell, hold, and convey real and personal property. The 1964 and 1968 Civil Rights Acts reaffirmed this goal. Title VI of the 1964 Civil Rights Act prohibits racial discrimination in all programs that receive federal funding, while Title VIII of the 1968 Civil Rights Act prohibits discrimination in housing on the basis of race, color, religion, and national origin.[8] HUD administers Title VIII by investigating complaints of housing discrimination and attempting to resolve them with conciliation. Also under Title VIII, the Justice Department is able to bring suit against parties believed to violate the statute.

The Fair Housing Amendments Act of 1988 (P.L. 100–430) expanded the protected classes to include families with children and the handicapped. This Act also authorizes the Secretary of HUD to file complaints with administrative law judges on behalf of complainants who contact the agency. This new authority complements the authority of the Justice Department to file suits for violation of the nation's fair housing legislation.

HUD has tried to achieve equal opportunity in access to federally subsidized housing by three major means—enforcing fair housing and antidiscrimination laws, choosing sites for housing projects to enhance the racial integration of neighborhoods, and providing vouchers for rental housing.[9] Court challenges to the operation of federally subsidized housing programs have helped, somewhat, to foster the goal of equal opportunity within these programs.

Conceptual Issues

Two major conceptual issues confound one's ability to determine whether federal policy and programs have enhanced equal opportunity in access to housing for minority group members. The first of these is the difficulty in determining the effectiveness of any program, given the range of measures of equality of access or racial disparity generally considered. Albeit gratuitously, any given program may lessen the racial disparity by one measure but not by another.

The other major issue is the fact that equality of access to housing also can be affected by policies and programs that enhance the employment of and/or increase the incomes of black households. In fact, it may not be possible to eliminate racial disparities in housing conditions by attacking them as housing problems.

To illustrate some of the questions that must be answered when seeking to evaluate whether selected housing programs enhance equality of access to housing for members of minority groups, consider the following. Would you expect equal proportions of blacks and whites among federal housing program recipients? Or would you expect the proportion of blacks served out of the universe of all eligible blacks to equal the proportion of whites served out of the universe of all eligible whites? Or would you expect the proportions of each racial group served by federal programs to be unequal in order to redress the inequities in housing experienced both historically and currently by blacks in the private market?

Another consideration is: Should we think of eliminating racial disparities in housing the same way we think of reaching full employment? Would we agree we had eliminated the disparities when we had narrowed the differentials to less than or equal to 3 percent, say, for each parameter?

Selected Program Impacts

Looking at just the Low-Rent Public Housing program and the various Section 8 subprograms (e.g., New Construction, Existing-Housing Certificates, Vouchers), reveals different impacts on the access to housing for members of minority groups. (See Glossary for details on these programs).

For instance, the Low-Rent Public Housing program seems to decrease equality of access for minority group members. Many public housing projects are located in predominantly low-income and/or minority areas, and 59 percent of all program units are occupied by minority house-holds.[10] The policy of locating projects in predominantly black/minority areas has contributed to segregation within projects and within city neighborhoods. In some communities, projects within the jurisdiction of a single local housing authority (LHA) are completely segregated—that is, the white projects are in one part of town, and the black projects are in another. If, in addition, the waiting lists for public housing are comprised mainly of members of minority groups, LHAs have limited ability to integrate projects, even if they want to.

On the other hand, reliance on the Section 8 Existing-Housing Certificate program, which places assisted households in units scattered among the existing stock, could improve both the quality of housing occupied by blacks and their opportunities for enhanced access to the housing stock in an area. However, if the Section 8 New Construction program built units in predominantly white suburbs that were hostile to blacks (or that blacks were unwilling to move to), then blacks would seldom obtain housing or equal access to nonsegregated neighborhoods through this subprogram. Data for the Section 8 New Construction program show that 80 percent of its assistance recipients are elderly, and minorities are only 11 percent of these elderly. Thus, minority elderly are 8.8 percent, and all minority group members are 15 percent of New Construction program tenants.[11]

Although extensive evidence is not yet available, the voucher demonstration program also may not provide blacks equal access to residential areas. Proponents of the voucher concept say it could enhance residential integration more than could public housing, but the same fears and hostilities that might prevent Section 8 Existing-Housing certificate holders from seeking units in predominantly white suburbs also could constrain voucher holders. In 1982, 72 percent of minority, versus 52 percent of non-minority enrollees in the Section 8 program failed to become recipients within sixty days.[12] Some of this dropping out may have been due to discrimination that has limited the choices of minority households and made it impossible to find units in some markets.

SUMMARY AND CONCLUSIONS

The overview material on eleven metropolitan areas plus the discussion of issues related to federal housing programs was intended to set the stage for the city-specific chapters in Section III. The overview data for the eleven metropolitan areas featured herein was intended to show the limits to understanding the workings of local housing markets using aggregated data. In addition, the paucity of race-specific data for these metropolitan area markets should appear in vivid contrast to the contents of the city-specific articles that follow. Analyses of the city of Buffalo here and in the chapter by Price clearly reflect the difference between what one knows from the most commonly available aggregated data versus what one knows from a detailed investigation conducted at the local level.

The discussion of issues related to federal housing programs was intended to provide a generic backdrop against which to view the discussions of federal programs as implemented in the cities profiled in the chapters in Section III. The questions raised take varying twists and even assume new meanings in the context of specific places, inhabited by specific groups of people.

NOTES

The author is Principal Analyst, U.S. Congressional Budget Office (CBO). This analysis is the author's own and should not be attributed to the CBO.

1. The simplest configuration for a metropolitan area is a Metropolitan Statistical Area (MSA) with at least one of the following: (a) one city with 50,000 or more inhabitants (known as a central city), or (b) a Census Bureau-defined urbanized area of at least 50,000 inhabitants and a total MSA population of at least 100,000 (75,000 in New England). If a MSA has 1 million or more inhabitants, and meets the criteria for separate component areas of it to be defined, then that MSA is called a Consolidated Metropolitan Statistical Area (CMSA) and its component areas are known as PMSAs (or Primary Metropolitan Statistical Areas).

2. Raymond J. Struyk and John A. Tuccillo, "Defining the Federal Role in Housing: Back to Basics," *Journal of Urban Economics* 14 (September 1983): 206–223.

3. Rawle Farley, "Theoretical Foundations for Government Subsidies to Low-Income People," *The Review of Black Political Economy* 11 (Fall 1980): 20.

4. J.M. Gries and J. Ford, eds., *Report on the President's Conference on Home Building and Home Ownership*, vol. 6, *Negro Housing* (Washington, DC: National Capital Press, 1932).

5. William C. Apgar Jr. and H. James Brown, *The State of the Nation's Housing 1988* (Cambridge, MA: Joint Center for Housing Studies of Harvard University, 1988), 17.

6. Department of Commerce, Bureau of the Census, *1990 Statistical Abstract of the United States* (Washington, DC: GPO, 1990) Table No. 717.

7. See Struyk and Tuccillo, *Defining the Federal Role*.

8. The 1974 Housing and Community Development Act added sex to the list of protected statuses.

9. C. Theodore Koebel, "Effects of Housing Assistance on Integration: Evidence from the Section 8 Existing Housing Program in Jefferson County, Kentucky," Paper presented at the Mid-Year Meeting of the American Real Estate and Urban Economics Association (Washington, DC, 29–30 May 1984), p. 1.

10. U.S., President's Commission on Housing, *Report* (Washington, DC, 1982), p. 37.

11. Ibid., p. 20.

12. Ibid., p. 41.

APPENDIX
CITY AND METROPOLITAN AREA SYNOPSES

BIRMINGHAM, AL MSA

Between 1970 and 1984, the population in the Birmingham, AL MSA grew—by 11.3 percent between 1970 and 1980 (from about 794,000 to 884,000) and by an additional 1.3 percent between 1980 and 1984. (See Table 1.) The total 1980 population was constituted as 316,381 households and was 27 percent black. The units available to the 316,381 households in the area had increased by 30 percent between 1970 and 1980, and, in 1980, nearly 30 percent of the units in the MSA had been built between 1970 and March 1980. (See Table 2.) Sixty-eight percent of the units were owner-occupied, and the median value of owned units was $38,500 in 1980.

In the central city of the Birmingham, AL MSA, on the other hand, population decreased by over 5 percent between 1970 and 1980 (to a total slightly greater than 316,000) and decreased by nearly an additional 2 percent between 1980 and 1984. (See Table 3.) Blacks were the majority of the population in the Birmingham central city in 1980—55 percent—while persons of Spanish origin represented nearly identical shares of the population in both the central city and the entire metropolitan area (0.8 percent and 0.7 percent, respectively). Close to 30 percent (28 percent to be exact) of all units in the central city in 1980 had been built prior to 1940, almost exactly the same as the share of units in the entire metropolitan area built between 1970 and March 1980. A smaller share of the units in the central city—nearly 54 percent—than in the entire metropolitan area were owner-occupied.

The Birmingham, AL MSA had over 328,000 renter households in 1984—a quarter of them were black and the remainder were white. (See Table 4.) The percentage of black households doubled to one-half among renter households with very low incomes. Among renter households with very low incomes who received HUD program subsidies, blacks were even more dominant—81 percent of the 13,078 such households in the Birmingham MSA. (See Table 5.) Representation of black renter households in each of the categories noted above increased with the measure of neediness.

BUFFALO-NIAGARA FALLS, NY CMSA

The population in the Buffalo-Niagara Falls, NY CMSA declined steadily between 1970 and 1984—between 1970 and 1980, it fell by nearly 8 percent and between 1980 and 1984, it fell by an additional 3 percent. (See Table 1.) In 1980, the population, which was constituted as 445,475 households, was 9 percent black and over 1 percent of Spanish origin.

Over two-fifths (43.3 percent) of the units in the metropolitan area in 1980 had been built prior to 1940, and nearly 64 percent were owner-occupied. (See Table 2.) The median value of owned units in 1980 was $39,700, while the median gross rent of rented units was $216.

Population trends in the central cities of the Buffalo-Niagara Falls, NY CMSA are similar to but more marked than the trends noted above for the entire metropolitan area. (See Table 3.) In the central cities of the Buffalo metropolitan area between 1970 and 1984, population fell—by nearly 22 percent (from 548,217 to 429,254) between 1970 and 1980, and by nearly 6 percent more between 1980 and 1984. The percentages of blacks and persons of Spanish origin among the population—24 percent and 2 percent, respectively—also are larger than for the entire metropolitan area. A larger percentage of the units in the central cities in 1980 (than in the entire metropolitan area) were old—about 70 percent had been built prior to 1940—while a smaller percentage were owner-occupied (47 percent).

Among renter households in the Buffalo-Niagara Falls, NY CMSA in 1984, only 9 percent of the nearly 447,000 total were black, while among renter households with very low incomes, nearly three times as great a percentage (24 percent) were black. When the focus is very low income households that also receive a HUD subsidy, the split between blacks (45 percent) and whites (48 percent) is nearly even. As the neediness of the category of renter households increases, so does the proportion of these households that are black. (See Tables 4 and 5.)

CLEVELAND, OH PMSA

Population in the Cleveland, OH PMSA fell from over 2 million in 1970 to about 1.9 million in 1980, an 8 percent decline. (See Table 1.) Between 1980 and 1984, the metropolitan area population declined by another 1.7 percent. Blacks were 18 percent and persons of Spanish origin more than 1 percent of the 1980 population that had arrayed itself in about 694,400 households. These households were living in a stock one-third of which had been built before 1940. (See Table 2.) Nearly two-thirds of all units in the area were owner-occupied, and the median value of owned units was $56,100 in 1980.

In the central city of the Cleveland, OH PMSA, population also declined

steadily between 1970 and 1984. (See Table 3.) Between 1970 and 1980, population declined about 24 percent while between 1980 and 1984, it declined
nearly an additional 5 percent. The percentages of blacks and persons of Spanish
origin in the central city population—44 percent and 3 percent, respectively—are
more than double these shares in the metropolitan area as a whole. In addition,
a higher percentage of the units in the central city (58 percent) than in the entire
metropolitan area in 1980 are older, having been built prior to 1940. A lower
percentage (48 percent) of central city residents than of residents in the entire
metropolitan area were owners in 1980.

Although blacks were 18 percent of all renter households in 1984, they were
more than double that share (39 percent) of all renter households with very low
incomes. The doubling was nearly repeated when we look at renter households
with very low incomes who receive a HUD program subsidy—blacks are 72
percent of this group. The representation of blacks among categories of renter
households increases as does the neediness reflected in the measure of the category. (See Tables 4 and 5.)

INDIANAPOLIS, IN MSA

Population grew steadily in the Indianapolis, IN MSA from 1970 to 1984—by
5 percent between 1970 and 1980 and by 2.4 percent between 1980 and 1984.
(See Table 1.) The 1980 population of about 1.7 million was nearly 14 percent
black and 1 percent of Spanish origin. Housing stock in 1980 was nearly equally
likely to be new as to be old—24 percent of the 451,319 units in the metropolitan
area had been built between 1970 and March 1980, while 25 percent of the total
units had been built prior to 1940. (See Table 2.) Sixty-five percent of the units
were owner-occupied, and all owned units had a median value of $40,300 in
1980.

In the central city of the Indianapolis, IN MSA, on the other hand, population
declined between 1970 and 1980, although it increased (by 1.4 percent) from
1980 to 1984. (See Table 3.) Between 1970 and 1980, central city population
decreased by nearly 5 percent, from 736,916 to 700,807. The 1980 population
in the central city was 22 percent black, a 50 percent increase over the share in
the entire MSA. The population of Spanish origin in the central city was 0.9
percent of the total, while it had been nearly identical, at 0.8 percent of the total,
in the MSA. The spread between the shares of the units that were relatively new
(i.e., built between 1970 and March 1980, inclusive) and relatively old (i.e.,
built prior to 1940) in 1980 is greater in the central city than for the entire
metropolitan area. Nearly 26 percent of the central city stock was built prior to
1940, while nearly 20 percent of this stock was built between 1970 and March
1980. A smaller share of units in the central city was occupied by owners (59
percent) than in the metropolitan area.

In 1984, black households were 12 percent of all renter households and 27 percent of all renter households with very low incomes. Among renter households with very low incomes that received a HUD subsidy, blacks were an even greater share—42 percent. As the neediness of the categories of renter households increased, the proportion of blacks in each likewise increased. (See Tables 4 and 5.)

MEMPHIS, TN-ARK-MS MSA

The Memphis, TN-ARK-MS MSA experienced steady population growth between 1970 and 1984. (See Table 1.) Population in the area grew by nearly 10 percent between 1970 and 1980, and by an additional 2 percent between 1980 and 1984. The 1980 population was 40 percent black and nearly 1 percent of Spanish origin. A larger proportion of the units in the metropolitan area in 1980 was built between 1970 and March 1980 (29 percent) than was built before 1940 (12 percent). (See Table 2.) Three-fifths of the units in the metropolitan area were occupied by owners, and the median value of owned units was $38,100 in 1980.

Population trends in the central city were similar, although the percentage increases were smaller. (See Table 3.) Between 1970 and 1980, population increased by nearly 4 percent, while increasing by only 0.3 percent between 1980 and 1984. When comparing the metropolitan area to its central city in 1980, one finds that the percent black among the population increased from two-fifths to nearly one-half (47 percent). Also in 1980, a higher proportion of units in the central city had been built between 1970 and March 1980 (21 percent) than before 1940 (13 percent). Over 56 percent of the units in the central city of the metropolitan area were owner-occupied.

When renter households alone are examined in 1984, one finds that 35 percent of their total of 329,153 was black. Among renter households with very low incomes, this proportion had doubled to 71 percent. The share of blacks increases even more—to 82 percent—among all renter households with very low incomes that get HUD subsidies. Thus, as the categories of renter households increase in neediness, the proportion of blacks among them also increases. (See Tables 4 and 5.)

MILWAUKEE, WI PMSA

From 1970 to 1984, the Milwaukee metropolitan area experienced slight population declines in both the 1970–1980 period (a 0.5 percent decline) and the 1980–1984 period (a 0.2 percent decline). (See Table 1.) The 1980 population was 11 percent black and 2.5 percent of Spanish origin. Nearly a third (32 percent) of the units in the metropolitan area in which the 500,684 households lived in 1980 had been built prior to 1940, and only 18 percent of these units had been built between 1970 and March 1980. (See Table 2.) Three-fifths of all units were owner-occupied, and owner-occupied units had a median value of $61,900. Population declined more dramatically in the central city of the Milwaukee, WI PMSA than in the entire metropolitan area. (See Table 3.) Between 1970 and 1980, central city population declined 9 percent, while between 1980 and 1984, it declined an additional 2 percent. Twenty-one percent of the 1980 central city population was black, and 4 percent was of Spanish origin. In 1980, a higher percentage of units in the central city—41 percent—than in the entire metropolitan area had been built prior to 1940. The share of owners in the central city was 48 percent, lower than the three-fifths of owners found in units throughout the metropolitan area.

Among all renter households, blacks constituted 11 percent, although blacks were 29 percent of all renter households with very low incomes in 1984. The proportion of black households increases again, to 35 percent, out of all renter households with very low incomes that received a HUD program subsidy. Representation of blacks among renter households steadily increased as the categories were defined more narrowly by need. (See Tables 4 and 5.)

NORFOLK-VIRGINIA BEACH-NEWPORT NEWS, VA MSA

The Norfolk-Virginia Beach-Newport News, VA MSA showed an increasing rate of growth between 1970 and 1984. (See Table 1.) During the 1970–1980 period, population grew by nearly 10 percent, and increased beyond that by nearly 9 percent between 1980 and 1984. In 1980, the population was 28 percent black and nearly 2 percent of Spanish origin. The population of over 1.16 million arrayed itself in 385,929 households in 1980. Over 30 percent of the units in the metropolitan area in 1980 were built between 1970 and March 1980, and nearly three-fifths of all units were owner-occupied. (See Table 2.) The median value of owned units in 1980 was $46,100, and median gross rent of rented units was $250.

Population growth in the central cities was nearly identical to that for the entire metropolitan area, as were the percent black and of Spanish origin. (See Table 3.) Between 1970 and 1980, the population of the central cities grew by over 10 percent, while growing an additional 9 percent in the 1980–1984 period. The percent black in 1980 was 29 percent while the percent of Spanish origin was about 2 percent. The share of units built between 1970 and March 1980 and the percent of owner-occupied units in the central cities in 1980 also were close to the figures for the entire metropolitan area. Over twenty-eight percent of the units in the central cities had been built between 1970 and March 1980, while 56 percent of the units were owner-occupied.

Among renter households in 1984, 26 percent were black. More than double that share, or 59 percent, were black renter households with very low incomes. The proportion of blacks among renter households with very low incomes that received a HUD subsidy was greatest of all—80 percent. Thus, the representation of blacks among subcategories of renter households increased as did the neediness reflected in each subcategory. (See Tables 4 and 5).

OKLAHOMA CITY, OK MSA

The rate of population growth in the Oklahoma City, OK MSA has decreased since 1970, from the 20 percent rate of growth between 1970 and 1980 to the 12 percent rate of growth between 1980 and 1984. (See Table 1). The 1980 MSA population of 860,969 was 9 percent black and 2 percent of Spanish origin and had arrayed itself in 321,546 households.

Housing stock in the Oklahoma City, OK MSA could be characterized as relatively young with nearly a third (31 percent) of the 352,321 units in 1980 built between 1970 and March 1980. (See Table 2.) Over two-thirds (68 percent) of these units were owner-occupied, and the median value for all owner-occupied units was $41,400 in 1980.

Although the levels of the population growth rates in the central city were less than the population growth rates for the entire metropolitan area, in the central city as in the entire metropolitan area, population growth had increased since 1970. (See Table 3.) Between 1970 and 1980, central city population grew by nearly 12 percent—from 445,205 to 497,739.Between 1980 and 1984, central city population grew by an additional 10 percent. At 12 percent and nearly 3 percent, respectively, the percentages of black residents and residents of Spanish origin in the central city in 1980 are somewhat greater than the corresponding figures in the metropolitan area. The housing stock in the central city is slightly older, and there are somewhat proportionately fewer homeowners in the central city than in the metropolitan area. Twenty-eight percent of the 215,256 units in the central city were built between 1970 and March 1980, while about 63 percent of the units were owner-occupied in 1980.

The proportion that blacks constituted of all renter households (8 percent) in the MSA was less than their share of all renter households with very low incomes (18 percent) in 1984. Black households constituted an even greater share (36 percent) among renter households with very low incomes that received a HUD program subsidy. Thus, the representation of blacks among these groups of renter households increased with the neediness of each group. (See Tables 4 and 5.)

PROVIDENCE, RI PMSA AND PAWTUCKET-WOONSOCKET-ATTLEBORO RI-MA PMSA

Although these two PMSAs have experienced low population growth since 1970, the rate in the early 1980s seems to have doubled the rate from the 1970s. (See Table 1.) The 1980 population of 925,917 represents a 1 percent increase over the 1970 figure; in addition, between 1980 and 1984, population also increased by 1 percent. Blacks are nearly 3 percent of the residents of the area, while persons of Spanish origin are 2 percent. The 1980 population had arrayed itself in 330,632 households. Between 1970 and 1980, the number of units available to these households had increased by 17 percent to 357,977. (See Table 2.) Owners occupied over 59 percent of the units in these areas.

The central cities of these PMSAs experienced population decline between 1970 and 1984, although the rate of decline slowed in the 1980–1984 period. (See Table 3.) Between 1970 and 1980, population declined nearly 10 percent while between 1980 and 1984, it declined by less than 1 percent (0.7 percent). The 1980 populations of these central cities were nearly 8 percent black and 4 percent of Spanish origin. Over three-fifths (62 percent) of the 115,657 units in these central cities in 1980 had been built prior to 1940, with only 8 percent built between 1970 and March 1980.Nearly two-fifths (39 percent) of all units in 1980 were owner-occupied.

Although the proportion of black households out of all renter households was low (2 percent), it more than doubled to 5 percent of all renter households with very low incomes. The figure for black households more than doubled again to 11 percent of renter households with very low incomes that received HUD program subsidies in 1984. Black households increased their share of renter households as the neediness of each subcategory increased. (See Tables 4 and 5.)

SALT LAKE CITY-OGDEN, UT MSA

Population in the Salt Lake City-Ogden, UT MSA grew over the entire 1970–1984 period, although at a somewhat lower rate in the 1980–1984 period than in the 1970–1980 period. (See Table 1.) Population grew by 33 percent—from 683,913 in 1970 to 910,222 in 1980—before increasing by nearly 13 percent between 1980 and 1984. Blacks were a smaller share (0.9 percent) of the population in the MSA than were persons of Spanish origin (nearly 5 percent) in 1980. Also in 1980, the population had distributed itself in 289,379 households.

The housing stock in the MSA is relatively new—in 1980, close to two-fifths of the units (37 percent) had been built between 1970 and March 1980—and is dominated by owner-occupants (70 percent). (See Table 2.) The median value of owned units in 1980 was $61,800, and the median gross rent of rented units was $244.

In the central cities of this MSA, population trends differed from those in the MSA as a whole. Population declined by 7 percent during the 1970–1980 period but increased in the 1980–1984 period by 2.5 percent. (See Table 3.) Residents of Spanish origin outnumbered blacks in the central cities (as they had in the entire MSA), although here it is by a ratio of 4 to 1. Blacks were about 2 percent of the population, while persons of Spanish origin were over 8 percent. Exactly opposite the finding for the metropolitan area as a whole in 1980, units built prior to 1940 dominated the stock in the central cities. Nearly two-fifths (37 percent) of the 98,429 units in the central cities in 1980 had been built prior to 1940. The ownership rate of 53 percent in the central cities was lower than the figure reported for the entire MSA.

Although small, the share of black renter households increased as did the degree of neediness reflected by each renter subcategory. (See Tables 4 and 5.) For example, blacks were only 1 percent of all renter households but double that percentage (2 percent) of all renter households with very low incomes. Blacks trebled their share —to 6 percent—among all renter households with very low incomes that received a HUD program subsidy in 1984.

SAN JOSE, CA PMSA

Population in the San Jose, CA PMSA grew between 1970 and 1984— dramatically between 1970 and 1980 (by 22 percent) and somewhat less between 1980 and 1984 (by 6 percent). (See Table 1.) Like the Salt Lake City-Ogden, UT MSA, but moreso, persons of Spanish origin dominated blacks as the major minority group; here persons of Spanish origin and blacks were in the ratio of 6 to 1. In 1980, blacks were somewhat over 3 percent, while persons of Spanish origin were nearly 18 percent, of the total PMSA population. The 1,295,071 people in the San Jose, CA PMSA resided in 458,519 households in 1980.

The housing stock in San Jose is relatively young, with nearly a third (32 percent) of the units available in 1980 built between 1970 and March 1980. (See Table 2.) Nearly three-fifths of the units were owner-occupied. In 1980, the PMSA had both the highest median value of owned units ($109,400) and the highest median gross rent of rented units ($334) of all the metropolitan areas featured in this analysis.

Population growth in the central city of the San Jose, CA PMSA outstripped that of the entire metropolitan area. (See Table 3.) Between 1970 and 1980, central city population increased by a third, while between 1980 and 1984, population grew by an additional 8 percent. As in the metropolitan area as a whole, the black population was outnumbered by the Spanish origin population in the central city. Here the black population was 5 percent, and the Spanish origin population was 21 percent. An even larger share (36 percent) of the units in the central city than those throughout the metropolitan area in 1980 were relatively new, having been built between 1970 and March 1980. The owner-occupancy rate (61 percent) in the central city also slightly exceeded that in the PMSA.

Although the percentage of blacks among subcategories of renter households increased with the degree of neediness, the increases are not as marked as in some of the other metropolitan areas covered in this article. (See Tables 4 and 5.) In 1984, blacks were 3 percent of all renter households; 4 percent of all renter households with very low incomes; and 7 percent of all renter households with very low incomes that received a HUD program subsidy. The gap between 4 percent and 7 percent suggests the extent to which the black renter households were overrepresented among renter households that received HUD program subsidies in 1984.

4

THE EFFECTS OF EXTENDED FAMILIES AND MARITAL STATUS ON HOUSING CONSUMPTION BY BLACK FEMALE-HEADED HOUSEHOLDS

David Macpherson and James B. Stewart

This study examines factors affecting the housing consumption of households headed by black women. The investigation focuses particular attention on the extent to which marital status and household composition, especially extended family configurations, influence the quality of housing consumed. The specific measure of housing quality used in the study is crowdedness, proxied by the number of persons per room.

Analysis of data taken from the 1980 U.S. Census Public Use Sample reveals that female-headed extended households experience crowding disproportionately in comparison to other female-headed households. Marital status, age and location also significantly affect housing consumption. Young black female household heads who are separated and live in the South are particularly likely to reside in crowded conditions.

Improved labor market outcomes for household heads are found to be more effective in generating improvements in housing quality than increased transfer payments.

A comprehensive assessment of the housing status of black Americans should examine the extent to which particular subpopulations face special constraints. This analysis examines selected factors affecting the quality of housing consumed by black female-headed households.

A detailed analysis of the determinants of housing consumption by extended and nonextended black female-headed households can provide useful information regarding trade-offs associated with housing, labor market, and schooling choices. More complete information about the factors affecting these economic decisions can enable the design and implementation of policies that optimize the consumption options of those receiving various forms of public assistance.

The present analysis uses data from the Public Use Sample of the 1980 Census to compare the relative importance of various factors hypothesized to affect the number of persons per room in extended and nonextended households headed by black women. Age, geographic location, levels and sources of income, tenure, household composition, marital status, and type of housing are all hypothesized to affect the number of persons per room.

The following section reviews literature relevant to the analysis of the determinants of the quality of housing consumed by black female-headed households. Differences in economic functioning between extended and nonextended households are discussed. The third section describes the data and specifies the empirical model. The fourth section presents the results. Policy implications and suggestions for further research are considered in the final section.

HOUSING QUALITY AND ECONOMIC FUNCTIONING IN BLACK FEMALE-HEADED HOUSEHOLDS

The growing disparity between the economic circumstances of never-married and formerly married black female heads of households is a special concern in this investigation. In 1984 the poverty rate for black children in married couple families was approximately 25 percent. However, in families headed by formerly-married black women the rate was 61 percent, while the rate for children in households headed by never-married women was 77 percent.[1]

Leigh notes, "Female-headed family households and single person nonfamily households are most likely to experience a diminished quality of life, as reflected by the condition of their housing."[2] Within the population of female-headed households differences may exist in the quality of housing consumed relative to marital status because "The costs of household separation (psychic and monetary) as a result of death or divorce, for example, are directly correlated with household incidence and, therefore, with housing consumption."[3]

A variety of measures could provide information about the quality of housing consumed by female-headed black families. These include measures of quantity and structural quality. The measure of housing quality used in this investigation, number of persons per room, is a measure of crowdedness. While the frequency of overcrowdedness has declined monotonically over time for all populations, the rate of overcrowding is twice as great for black households as for white households. Renters experience a greater extent of overcrowding than owners for all population groups.[4] In the case of black households, housing consumption may be disproportionately affected by discriminatory behavior of landlords unwilling to rent to female-headed households.

One of the principal concerns of this investigation is how black female-headed households cope with housing affordability problems.[5] The demand for housing is determined to a large extent by the labor market attachment of household members. Pooling multiple wage earner incomes of current household members, stretching existing resources, and improving existing housing in lieu of moving to higher cost housing are all coping mechanisms typically used to ameliorate housing affordability problems. However, as it has been noted, "Black households are limited in the extent to which they can employ all of these coping mechanisms."[6]

One of the coping mechanisms used extensively and disproportionately by black households to respond to housing affordability problems and other adverse economic circumstances is the formation or maintenance of extended households. Various research indicates that members of extended households undertake special patterns of economic adjustment involving substantial resource sharing.[7] One study suggests that in extended households headed by black females, adaptations are made that enable young mothers to both participate in the labor force and attend school.[8]

The disadvantaged circumstances of many black female-headed households are likely to make household merger a viable option to counteract deterioration in economic circumstances. The feasibility of such mergers is, of course, affected by the size of affordable housing units and by occupancy regulations. In addition, the phenomenon of oscillation between receipt of public assistance and labor market attachment introduces an instability to economic decisionmaking that influences both housing choices and the attractiveness of extended household configurations.[9]

Household merger can facilitate economizing on total housing costs and potentially increase the efficiency of some activities that directly affect total income, e.g., child care. At the same time, however, merger also can reduce the quality of housing consumed, for example, by increasing crowdedness. Differences between the number of persons per room in extended and nonextended households can serve as one indicator of differences in housing quality associated with these alternative household configurations.

Comparison of the determinants of the degree of crowdedness in extended and nonextended black female-headed households can shed light on whether the use of particular coping mechanisms varies across household arrangements. Hill and Shackelford report that the number of black children living in an extended household arrangement increased from 23 percent to 33 percent between 1969 and 1974.[10] They argue that this increase was due to a deterioration in the economic circumstances of single parent families. The proportion of all blacks living in extended households increased from 23 percent to 28 percent between 1970 and 1980 while the proportion of whites living in extended arrangements was 11 percent in both years.[11]

If an extended configuration does not result from the merger of two previously separate households, there may be greater flexibility than in a merger situation to respond to changes in important factors like housing prices and new educational and labor market opportunities. Births to teenagers contribute significantly to the subpopulation of extended households not resulting from household merger. Over 85 percent of black unwed teenage mothers continue to live in the homes of their parents after the birth of their children.[12] The availability of in-kind child care in parents' households and limited labor market options both contribute significantly to this pattern. In general, provisions for child care are likely to be different for extended and nonextended households. Although 42 percent of black working mothers obtain care for their youngest child in the homes of relatives or nonrelatives, 18 percent have their children cared for in their own homes by relatives or nonrelatives.[13]

The foregoing discussion suggests it is reasonable to expect that gross differences exist in the number of persons per room between extended and nonextended households headed by black females, *ceteris paribus*. In particular, we would anticipate more crowding in extended households. The discussion indicates, however, the need to control for the marital status of the family head in examining housing consumption patterns. The data and empirical model used to explore these issues are described as follows.

DATA AND EMPIRICAL MODEL

The data base for the present investigation is the 1980 1/100 U.S. Census Sample. This data set has the advantage of providing a large sample. Its disadvantages are the absence of information about changes in household configurations and resource sharing with nonhousehold members.

The sample consists of households headed by black females of two types; (1) those in which a daughter with children resides in the household and (2) those in which there is no subfamily present. The second group is subdivided into households with heads less than thirty years old and those headed by women thirty and older. This bifurcation serves two purposes. First, previous research indicates that the labor market behavior of younger, black female heads of households is significantly different from that of older heads of either extended or nonextended households.[14] As noted previously, the economic situation of households headed by never-married black women is particularly burdensome. Segmenting the sample allows us to focus specific attention on this subpopulation. Second, the demographic characteristics of the older group of heads of nonextended households are similar to those of the population of heads of extended households. This allows a reasonably direct comparison of how extendedness affects housing consumption and economic decisionmaking.

Table 1 presents the means and standard deviations of the basic variables for the entire sample and Table 2 contains similar information for the three subsamples. Inspection of the two tables indicates that of the 25,879 women in the total sample, 2,255 head extended households. The number of heads under thirty years old in the sample is 6,598. Definitions of the variables are provided in the Appendix.

The average number of persons per room for the entire sample is approximately .78. This means that, using the standard of one person per room (1.0) established by the U.S. Census Bureau, the average household in the sample was not living in crowded conditions at the time of the survey. About 47 percent of the sample reside in the South and 84 percent of the sample reside in an SMSA.[15] Approximately 9 percent of the entire sample are in extended households. While the mean age of women in the sample is approximately forty-two, 26 percent are less than thirty years old. The overall sample is fairly evenly divided by marital status, with about 31 percent never-married, 22 percent widowed, 24 percent divorced, and 23 percent separated. Approximately 34 percent of the sample own their residences. About 21 percent of the sample live in two-family residences, 10 percent live in residences that accommodate three or four households, and 29 percent live in units in complexes designed for five or more households.

TABLE 1
Variable Means and Standard Deviations

Variable	Mean	Std. Dev.
Dependent Variable		
AVGROOM	.78	.44
X_i		
WAGEINC	4892.92	6562.44
SELFINC	105.41	1693.50
OTHERINC	498.49	2076.10
OTHERFAM	3367.58	6402.41
OTHERHH	707.30	3021.88
TRANSFER	1254.45	1877.68
TRANSKID	436.77	873.95
SOUTH	.47	.50
SMSA	.84	.36
HT_i		
OWNER	.34	.47
MOBILE	.02	.13
N2FAM	.21	.41
N3-4FAM	.10	.30
N5FAM	.29	.45
OWNEREXT	.04	.20
MS_i		
SEP	.23	.42
DIV	.24	.43
WID	.22	.41
HC_i		
EXTEND	.09	.28
AGE_i		
AGE30	.26	.44
ACTAGE	41.66	15.71
ACACESQ	1982.01	1522.64
Y_i		
SMSASEP	.20	.40
SMSADIV	.21	.41
SMSAWID	.16	.37

TABLE 1 (continued)

Variable	Mean	Std. Dev.
Z_i		
TRANEXT	111.32	648.41
TRANKEXT	36.79	291.35
OTHRFEXT	691.24	3456.71
$MSHT_i$		
OWNRRSEP	.06	.23
OWNRRDIV	.10	.29
OWNRRWID	.13	.33
$AGEINT_i$		
AGE30SEP	.05	.21
AGE30DIV	.04	.19
AGE30WID	.005	.07
AGE30EXT	.007	.08
N		25,879

T-tests indicate that there are statistically significant differences between the means for virtually all the variables in each two-way comparison. The exceptions are income from self-employment and the probability of residing in a two-family dwelling.[16]

The most significant comparison to note in Table 2 is that the mean persons per room is larger in extended households (1.05) than in either nonextended households headed by women thirty or older (.74) or under thirty (.80). This suggests that persons living in extended households are experiencing crowdedness to a more significant degree than residents living in nonextended households.

The model used to examine the determinants of the number of persons per room in the household takes the general form:

(1) Persons/room$_i$ = f(X_i, HC_i, MS_iHT_i, AGE_i, Y_i, Z_i, $MSHT_i$, $AGEINT_i$)

In this formulation X_i refers to a vector of control variables that are designed to capture the effect of economic and geographical constraints on housing consumption. Income sources are disaggregated to enable an assessment of the comparative sensitivity of housing consumption choices

TABLE 2
Variable Means and Standard Deviations
Three Subsamples

Variable	NONEXTENDED HOUSEHOLDS HEAD<30		NONEXTENDED HOUSEHOLDS HEAD30>		EXTENDED HOUSEHOLDS	
	Mean	Std. Dev.	Mean	Std. Dev.	Mean	Std. Dev.
AVGROOM	.80	.42	.74	.42	1.05	.49
X_i						
WAGEINC	4107.59	5603.22	5251.96	6910.24	4479.97	6238.24
SELFINC	64.28	1409.90	125.25	1857.54	75.95	1018.77
OTHERINC	361.99	1427.84	560.50	2335.58	429.70	1492.46
OTHERFAM	1066.77	3698.31	3654.56	6446.58	7932.86	8928.13
OTHERHH	836.33	2956.59	694.26	3130.97	428.20	2254.85
TRANSFER	1173.99	1808.04	1282.57	1909.78	1277.57	1826.59
TRANSKID	421.86	727.22	444.47	921.09	422.25	900.94
SOUTH	.44	.50	.47	.50	.54	.50
SMSA	.88	.33	.84	.37	.77	.42
HT_i						
OWNER	.11	.32	.40	.49	.49	.50
MOBILE	.02	.15	.02	.13	.02	.12
N2FAM	.21	.41	.21	.41	.21	.41
N3-FAM	.14	.34	.09	.28	.06	.25
N5FAM	.41	.49	.25	.43	.18	.39
OWNEREXT	N.A.		N.A.		.49	.50
MS_i						
SEP	.18	.38	.25	.43	.22	.42
DIV	.15	.36	.28	.45	.22	.42
WID	.02	.14	.28	.45	.37	.48
HC_i						
EXTEND	N.A.		N.A.		N.A.	

TABLE 2 (continued)

Variable	NONEXTENDED HOUSEHOLDS HEAD<30		NONEXTENDED HOUSEHOLDS HEAD30>		EXTENDED HOUSEHOLDS	
	Mean	Std. Dev.	Mean	Std. Dev.	Mean	Std. Dev.
AGE_i						
AGE30	N.A.		N.A.		.08	.27
ACTAGE	24.83	3.01	47.05	14.02	50.13	14.25
ACACESQ	625.36	145.71	2410.58	1501.97	2715.67	1484.09
Y_i						
SMSASEP	.15	.36	.21	.41	.19	.39
SMSADIV	.13	.34	.25	.43	.19	.39
SMSAWID	.02	.12	.21	.41	.25	.43
ZH1Y						
TRANEXT	N.A.		N.A.		1277.57	1826.59
TRANKEXT	N.A.		N.A.		422.25	900.94
OTHRFEXT	N.A.		N.A.		7932.86	8928.13
$MSHT_i$						
OWNRRSEP	.02	.14	.07	.25	.08	.27
OWNRRDIV	.03	.17	.12	.32	.11	.31
OWNRRWID	.005	.07	.16	.37	.23	.42
$AGEINT_i$						
AGE30SEP	N.A.		N.A.		.01	.11
AGE30DIV	N.A.		N.A.		.01	.09
AGE30WID	N.A.		N.A.		.0004	.02
AGE30EXT	N.A.		N.A.		.08	.27
N	6,598		17,026		2,255	

N.A.-Not Applicable

to changes in transfer payments, earned income of the head, self-employment income, and income of other household members. HC_i is a variable indicating whether a household is extended or not (1 = Yes; 0 = No). HT_i is a vector of indicators of housing characteristics and tenure including the interaction of owner status with HC_i. MS_i is a vector of dummy variables indicating marital status and AGE_i is a vector, one element of which is a dummy variable indicating whether the household head is thirty years old or older (1 = Yes; 0 = No). The other elements of AGE_i are the head's actual age and its squared value. These elements replace the dummy indicator in the subsample estimations. Y_i is a vector of interaction terms created by multiplying the variable SMSA by the elements of MS_i. In a parallel manner Z_i is a vector of interaction terms created by multiplying selected elements of X_i by HC_i. $MSHT_i$ is a vector of interaction terms created by multiplying the elements of MS_i by the indicator of owner status in HT_i. $AGEINT_i$ is a vector of interaction terms created by multiplying the dummy variable from AGE_i by the elements of MS_i and HC_i.

In addition to estimating the general model using the full sample, modified models are estimated for subsets of the sample partitioned by age of the household head (less than thirty or thirty and older) and household configuration (extended or nonextended). Separate estimates are generated including one of two variants of the measure of transfer payments. One set of estimations uses total transfer payments and the other set uses total transfer payments deflated by the number of children in the household.[17] OLS regression analysis is used to estimate the models.

RESULTS

Table 3 includes only the coefficients of control variables. Results for indicators of marital status and extended household composition are reported separately.[18]

The number of persons per room that would be expected independent of the effects of the various controls is reflected by the intercept of .89. Thus, excluding the impacts of age, geographic location, family composition, and economic activity the situation of the average household would not be characterized as crowded. As is evident from Table 3 the number of persons per room for households located in the South is higher than in the non-South but the differential effect does not increase the average persons per room in the South above 1.0.[19] Residence in an SMSA decreases persons per room *ceteris paribus*. This result may reflect the

TABLE 3
Partial Regression Results
Income, Transfer Payments, Geographic Location,
Housing Tenure, Housing Type, and Age

Variable	Coefficient	T-Value
INTERCEPT	.894*	57.41
X_i		
WAGEINC	-.000009*	-21.56
SELFINC	-.0000016*	-1.07
OTHERINC	-.000005*	-3.95
OTHERFAM	.000006*	12.66
OTHERHH	.00001*	16.40
TRANSKID	-.00003*	-10.20
SOUTH	.0564*	9.94
SMSA	-.0767*	-5.57
HT_i		
OWNER	-.1713*	-13.23
MOBILE	.0919*	4.66
N2FAM	-.0250*	-3.36
N3-4FAM	.0244*	2.48
N5FAM	.0707*	9.33
AGE30	-.0309*	-3.25

R^2 =   .13

F = 128.93

* Significant at the 95 percent level of confidence or better

effects of higher incomes in urban areas and larger family sizes in rural areas. Persons per room is also slightly lower in households headed by women under thirty. This is the likely effect of smaller family size. The childbearing experiences of women in this age group have not been completed.

As would be expected, persons per room varies systematically across housing tenure and housing type. Persons per room in owner-occupied residences is .17 lower than in renter-occupied residences. Persons per room for mobile home occupants is .09 greater than is the case in other

TABLE 4
Partial Regression Results
Coefficients Indicating Variation in Persons/Room by Marital Status*

COEFFICIENTS
Marital Status

Effect	Separated	Divorced	Widowed
Status Effect	.05	-.04	-.15
Age Effect (less than 30)	---	---	.15
SMSA Effect	---	---	.04
Owner Effect	---	.04	.03

* Only coefficients significant at the 95 percent level of confidence or better are presented.

types of structures. Interestingly, persons per room is slightly higher in single family than in two-family dwellings. This is not the case, however, for other dwelling types. For all other dwelling types, persons per room is greater than for single family residences. In no case, however, is the incremental effect large enough to produce a value of persons per room greater than 1.0.[20]

Persons per room decreases with increasing wage income of the head, increases with increasing nonwage income, and decreases with increasing transfer payments to children. The coefficient of the deflated transfer payment variable is extremely small relative to the coefficient of wage income. This result is particularly significant because it suggests that increased support for children does not enable households to improve the quality of housing consumed as effectively as improvements in labor market outcomes. Notably, persons per room increases as income of other family members and other residents of the household who are not family members increases.

The basic results described above are useful for contextualizing those obtained for the marital status variables, the indicator of whether a household is extended, and the relevant interaction terms. Table 4 summarizes the results for marital status and Table 5 presents similar results focusing on extended households.

The coefficient values in Table 4 indicate the joint effects of differing marital statuses and other factors. The coefficients quantify the differential in persons per room in comparison to the effects for never-married

TABLE 5
Partial Regression Results
Coefficients Indicating Impacts of Extended
Household Arrangements on Person/Room*

	Coefficient
Basic Effect	.33
Age Effect (less than 30)	.11
Owner Effect	-.04
Transfer Payments/Child Effect	---
Other Family Member Effect	-.000002

* Only coefficients significant at the 95 percent level of confidence or better are presented.

heads over thirty years old who do not own their residences and do not live in an SMSA. The results show that the most complex incremental effects occur for young widows. However, in contrast to the conclusions of studies of relative economic jeopardy discussed previously, separated women have a greater chance of living in crowded conditions than never-married women. Interestingly, the incremental owner effect increases persons per room for divorced and widowed heads in contrast to the general effect of reducing persons per room indicated by the coefficient of OWNER in Table 3. This is probably an artifact related to differences in family size. In general, then, the results confirm that marital status has significant effects on the housing consumption of black female-headed households. However, the incremental effects are insufficient to generate significant variations in the extent of crowdedness experienced across differing marital statuses.

As indicated in the first line of Table 5, living in an extended household, per se, increases persons per room by .33. The magnitude of this basic effect when added to the intercept (.89) provides additional evidence that individuals living in an extended household experience crowding. Note the fact that the subsample mean of 1.05 is the first piece of evidence of crowding. This crowding is worse in the case of households headed by women under thirty (see Table 5). Crowding is reduced somewhat by an owner effect that is slighter larger than the basic owner effect indicated in Table 3. In contrast to the basic results in Table 3, the effect of income of other family members in extended households shown in

Table 5 is to reduce the number of persons per room. Thus the presence of multiple earners in extended households enhances the quality of the housing consumed unlike the situation in nonextended households.

The results for the entire sample suggest that the dynamics of housing consumption differ between extended and nonextended black female-headed households. These conclusions are supported by the results obtained from the separate estimations for each subsample.[21] Age, income, transfer payment, housing type, and marital status effects are less significant in the regression for extended households than for either the young or old nonextended subsamples.

From the results presented in Tables 3–5 it is possible to describe profiles of households that are most likely to experience crowded conditions, i.e., households where the expected persons per room is greater than 1.0. Extended households are in greatest jeopardy of living in crowded conditions. Extended households headed by widows (See Table 4) who are over thirty (See Tables 4 and 5), reside in an SMSA (See Tables 3 and 4), and who reside in a one- or two-unit dwelling (See Table 3) that they own (See Tables 3, 4, and 5) are the most likely to avoid crowding. Extended households headed by women less than thirty years old who are not widows would need approximately $20,000 in additional wage income to have the same expected persons per room as older widows heading extended households, *ceteris paribus.*[22] The figure is even higher for heads who are separated. In the case of nonextended households the results indicate that approximately $9,100 of additional wage income is required for nonwidows to have the same expected persons per room as widows, *ceteris paribus.*[23]

In general, for all household types, living outside the South in an SMSA significantly reduces the probability of living in crowded housing. The value of this combination in terms of equivalent wage income is approximately $13,500.[24]

SUMMARY AND CONCLUSION

This analysis has examined the factors affecting the housing consumption of households headed by black females. The principal objective was to determine how housing consumption is affected by marital status and extended household configurations. In general, based on the average number of persons per room, the housing status of the average nonextended black female-headed household is not appropriately characterized as crowded. For extended households this is not the case. The results indicate that marital status, age, and location significantly affect housing consumption. Young black female heads who are separated and live in the South appear to be particularly likely to reside in crowded housing.

The finding that housing consumption patterns differ by marital status suggests the usefulness of detailed reviews of housing policies and programs. Such reviews should be focused on identification of strategies to ameliorate the extent to which changes in marital status lead to a worsening of housing status.

Individuals living in extended households are in the greatest jeopardy of being crowded. Policies to address this problem should examine not only extended households per se but also the extent to which networks of relatives and friends residing in separate households can be strengthened to approximate some of the benefits of extended household arrangements. As noted earlier, these benefits include in-kind provision of child care and facilitation of labor market attachment. In this context Leigh observes that "The proximity of relatives is relevant to household incidence because, without relatives nearby, the likelihood of heading one's own separate household is much greater."[25]

The finding that improvements in labor market outcomes for the household head are more effective in enabling improvements in housing quality than are increases in transfer payments signals the need for a comprehensive approach to the design of housing and employment and training policies. This would require additional research that explicates the linkages between the two policy areas. The requisite research designs should disaggregate broadly defined population groups by marital status, household composition, and other criteria to produce a more accurate picture of how housing markets and nonmarket mechanisms are functioning. Through such an approach, perhaps policy makers can design programs that meet the housing and employment needs of diverse types of low-income households without imposing inequitable burdens of adjustment on particular subpopulations.

NOTES

1. Cynthia Rexroat, "The Declining Economic Status of Black Children: What Accounts for the Change?" Monograph prepared for the Joint Center for Political and Economic Studies, 1989.

2. Wilhelmina A. Leigh, "The 'Housing Quotient' of Black Families," in Harold E. Cheatham and James B. Steward (eds.), *Black Families: Interdisciplinary Perspectives* (New Brunswick, N.J.: Transaction Publishers, 1990), p. 71.

3. Wilhelmina A. Leigh, *Shelter Affordability For Blacks. Crisis or Clamor?* (New Brunswick, N.J.: Transaction Books, 1982).

4. Leigh, "The 'Housing Quotient' of Black Families," p. 72.

5. The question of shelter affordability as it relates to blacks is addressed in Leigh, *Shelter Affordability for Blacks. Crisis or Clamor?*

6. Leigh, *Shelter Affordability for Blacks. Crisis or Clamor?* p. 72.

7. See for example Joyce Aschenbrenner, "Extended Families Among Black Americans," *Comparative Family Studies* (1973), pp. 257–268; Andrew Billingsley, *Black Families in White America* (Englewood Cliffs, N.J.: Prentice-Hall, 1968); and Carol Stack, *All Our Kin* (New York: Harper and Row, 1974).

8. David A. Macpherson and James B. Stewart, "The Labor Supply and School Attendance of Black Women in Extended and Nonextended Households," *AEA Papers and Proceedings*, May, 1989, pp. 71–74.

9. See Sar Levitan, Martin Rein, and David Marwick, *Work and Welfare Go Together* (Baltimore: John Hopkins University Press, 1972).

10. Robert Hill and Lawrence Shackelford, "The Black Extended Family Revisited," *Urban League Review* 1 (1975).

11. See Walter R. Allen, "Class, Culture and Family Organization: The Effects of Class and Race on Family Structure in Urban America," *Journal of Comparative Family Studies* 10 (1979), pp. 301–313; and Walter R. Allen and Reynolds Farley, "The Shifting Social and Economic Tides of Black America, 1950–1980," *American Sociological Review* 12 (1986), pp. 277–306.

12. Robert Hill, et al. *Research on African-American Families: A Holistic Perspective.* Assessment of the Status of African-Americans, Volume II (Boston: The William Monroe Trotter Institute, University of Massachusetts at Boston, 1989), p. 14.

13. Ibid, p. 15. Approximately 12 percent of black working mothers placed their children in formal day care centers.

14. Macpherson and Stewart, "The Labor Supply and School Attendance of Black Women in Extended and Nonextended Households."

15. As a result of the 1980 Census, the designations for metropolitan areas were changed. The SMSA has been replaced by the Metropolitan Statistical Area (MSA), Primary Metropolitan Statistical Area (PMSA), and Consolidated Metropolitan Statistical Area (CMSA). For detailed definitions see Wilhelmina A. Leigh, "Trends in the Housing Status of Black Americans Across Selected Metropolitan Areas" (this issue), note 1.

16. Complete data are available from the authors upon request.

17. The deflated measure is an attempt to reflect the sensitivity of transfer payments to the presence of young children. There is obviously some imprecision since not all transfer payments are provided based on number of children in the household.

18. Only the results obtained from estimating the complete model using the deflated measure of transfer payments are presented. Results using the alternative measure can be obtained from the authors upon request.

19. This can be seen by adding the value of the intercept (.894) to the coefficient of SOUTH (.0564), generating a sum of .9504.

20. Adding the value of the intercept (.894) to the coefficients of N2FAM, N3-4FAM, and N5FAM yields values, respectively, for persons per room of .869, .9184, and .9647.

21. Complete results can be obtained from the authors upon request.

22. The results are computed using a modified model that includes only interaction terms involving the indicator that a household is extended. As a result, the coefficients for several of the controls are slightly different from those generated using the complete model. Only the results generated from the complete model are reported in the tables. The method used to calculate these gross estimates is simply to find the amount of wage income that, when multiplied by its coefficient, equals the value of the coefficient of the factor to be offset. To compute the income needed to offset being under thirty and not

widowed it is necessary to combine the coefficient of the variable AGE30EXT (.107) and the coefficient of AGE30 (–.015) with the negative value of the coefficient of WID (–.099), producing a sum of .191. Dividing this sum by the coefficient of WAGEINC (–.0000092) yields an additional income requirement of $20,760.

23. This figure is computed using the same supplemental results referred to in note 22. In this case the coefficient of AGE30EXT is irrelevant. The sum of the other two coefficients is .084. Dividing this figure by the coefficient of WAGEINC (–.0000092) yields an income deficit of $9,130.

24. Using the same supplemental results referred to in notes 22 and 23 the same procedure can be used for computing the income value of non-South SMSA residence. The coefficient of SMSA is –.068 and that of SOUTH is –.056. The coefficient of WAGEINC is –.0000092. The amount of income required to offset non-SMSA residence in the South is then (.068 + .056)/.0000092 = $13,478.

25. Leigh, *Shelter Affordability*, p. 18.

APPENDIX
Variable Designations and Definitions

Designation	Description
AVGROOM	Number of persons per room in residence
WAGEINC	Earnings from employment of the household head
SELFINC	Earnings from self-employment of head
OTHERINC	Other income of household head
OTHERFAM	Income of family members other than head
OTHERHH	Income of non-family household members
TRANSFER	Total Transfer payments of all household members
TRANSKID	Total transfer payments divided by number of children under 18 years old
SOUTH	Dummy variable assigned the value 1 if the household resides in the South, 0 otherwise
SMSA	Dummy variable assigned the value 1 if the household resides in a metropolitan statistical area, 0 otherwise
OWNER	Dummy variable assigned the value 1 if the head owns the residence, 0 otherwise
MOBILE	Dummy variable assigned the value 1 for households residing in mobile homes, 0 otherwise
N2FAM	Dummy variable assigned the value 1 for households living in 2-family dwellings, 0 otherwise
N3-4FAM	Dummy variable assigned the value 1 for households in buildings designed for 3 or 4 occupants, 0 otherwise
N5FAM	Dummy variable assigned the value 1 for households in buildings designed for 5 or more occupants, 0 otherwise
SEP	Dummy variable assigned the value 1 if the head is separated, 0 otherwise
DIV	Dummy variable assigned the value 1 if the head is divorced, 0 otherwise
WID	Dummy variable assigned the value 1 if the head is widowed, 0 otherwise
EXTEND	Dummy variable assigned the value 1 if a sub-family headed by a daughter of the head lives in the residence, 0 otherwise
AGE30	Dummy variable assigned the value 1 if the head is under thirty years old, 0 otherwise
ACTAGE	Age of the household head
ACAGESQ	Squared value of ACTAGE
SMSASEP	SMSA multiplied by SEP
SMSADIV	SMSA multiplied by DIV
SMSAWID	SMSA multiplied by WID
TRANEXT	TRANSFER multiplied by EXTEND

Designation	Description
TRANKEXT	TRANSKID multiplied by EXTEND
OTHRFEXT	OTHERFAM multiplied by EXTEND
OWNEREXT	OWNER multiplied by EXTEND
OWNERSEP	OWNER multiplied by SEP
OWNERDIV	OWNER multiplied by DIV
OWNERWID	OWNER multiplied by WID
AGE30SEP	AGE30 multiplied by SEP
AGE30DIV	AGE30 multiplied by DIV
AGE30WID	AGE30 multiplied by WID
AGE30EXT	AGE30 multiplied by EXTEND

III

Case Studies

5

RACIAL DISPARITY IN THE ATLANTA HOUSING MARKET

Carla J. Robinson

Atlanta has the reputation of being a city of opportunity for blacks.
However, in Atlanta, as well as in other cities across the nation, the
nexus of racism and economic discrimination has resulted in disparities between the housing status of blacks and whites. This article
examines racial disparities in the Atlanta housing market. It begins by
tracing recent trends in the Atlanta-area economy and by providing
background information on the local housing market. It then discusses
the roles of the federal Home Mortgage Disclosure Act of 1975 and
Community Reinvestment Act of 1977 in the efforts of local groups to
reduce racial disparities in the housing market. The final section discusses recent local developments that might lead to improvements in
the housing status of black Atlantans.

It is a land of the Mercedes and the mall, the hungry and the
homeless. It is the nation's third-fastest-growing metropolitan area;
it is the nation's second-poorest core city. It is a magnet for exec-
utives on the make and for the poor from the country. It is "Hot-
lanta": capital city of the South.[1]

Atlanta is a city of contrasts. One of the most striking contrasts involves the housing status of black and white residents. This article examines those disparities. It also discusses ways in which local organizations have utilized two federal laws, the Home Mortgage Disclosure Act
of 1975 and the Community Reinvestment Act of 1977, in their efforts to
eliminate racial disparites in housing status. The article begins with an
overview of recent developments that have taken place in the Atlanta-area
economy. It then provides background information on the local housing
market and on housing assistance programs. This is followed by a discussion of racial disparities in home mortgage lending and of the utili-

zation of the two federal laws. The final section discusses recent developments within city government and housing organizations that might eliminate some of the disparities in the housing status of blacks and whites in the Atlanta housing market.

THE "TWO ATLANTAS"

For most of the 1980s, the eighteen-county Atlanta area was one of the fastest growing metropolitan areas in the country (Map 1).[2] Between 1980 and 1986, its population growth rate of nearly 20 percent outpaced those of all other metropolitan areas except Phoenix and Dallas-Fort Worth, which grew at rates of 26 percent and 25 percent, respectively. Between 1982 and 1987, its 5.7 percent rate of job growth exceeded those of all other metropolitan areas. But not all population subgroups, geographic sections, and economic sectors in the area have benefited equally from the economic good fortune. Some analysts describe recent development trends in the area in terms of "two Atlantas," one characterized by growth and prosperity and the other characterized by decline and despair.

The rate of job growth within the seven-county Atlanta region varies from county to county (Table 1). During the 1980 to 1988 period, employment in the region grew at an average annual rate of 6 percent. On the high end, employment grew by 20 percent in Gwinnett County and by 12 percent in Cobb County. DeKalb and Fulton counties, which contain the city of Atlanta, had the lowest growth rates. Employment in the city of Atlanta grew by only 1.5 percent. In addition to trailing in job growth, DeKalb and Fulton counties also tend to be among the counties with the highest unemployment rates in the region. In 1980, Fulton County led the region with an unemployment rate of 6.7 percent, followed by Clayton County with a rate of 5.5 percent and DeKalb County with a rate of 5.1 percent.[3] By 1986, the overall Fulton County rate had fallen slightly to 6.3 percent and the Clayton and DeKalb county rates had each fallen to 4.3 percent.[4] In 1980, black unemployment rates in Fulton and DeKalb counties were 10.2 percent and 8.5 percent, respectively.

The Atlanta region has been classified as a "diversified advanced services center," based on the variety of business services and headquarters facilities located there.[5] This classification reflects Atlanta's role as the economic and administrative capital and transportation hub of the Southeast. The region is also the nation's third largest center for conventions and trade shows. The Atlanta-area economy has a relatively small

MAP 1
The Atlanta Metropolitan Area

Square Mileage:
City limits 136
Seven-county (Clayton,Cobb, DeKalb, Douglas, Fulton, Gwinnett, Rockdale) 2,065
18-county area 5,147
Source: Atlanta Chamber of Commerce

manufacturing base. Manufacturing employment accounted for only 11 percent of total employment in 1989.[6] Services, retail trade, and construction have been the fastest growing sectors of the economy in recent years.[7] Within the services sector, business and health services are the largest employers.

The uneven pattern of recent development trends in the Atlanta region can be seen by examining the pattern of population growth within the seven-county region (Table 2). The outlying counties of Gwinnett, Rockdale, and Cobb posted the highest average annual growth rates between

TABLE 1
Atlanta Region Employment: 1970, 1980, 1988

County	1970	1980	1988	1970-1980 Average Annual Change		1980-1988 Average Annual Change	
				Number	Percent	Number	Percent
Clayton	27,753	52,841	99,200	2,509	9.04	5,795	10.97
Cobb	60,887	96,685	190,800	3,580	5.88	11,764	12.16
DeKalb	120,554	218,142	311,400	9,759	8.10	11,657	5.34
Douglas	3,891	9,075	17,200	518	13.31	1,016	11.20
Fulton	386,988	445,341	544,000	5,835	1.51	12,332	2.77
Gwinnett	14,532	48,514	126,100	3,398	23.38	9,698	19.99
Rockdale	5,088	10,834	19,300	575	11.30	1,058	9.77
Region	623,693	881,432	1,308,000	25,774	4.13	53,321	6.05
City of Atlanta*	338,054	355,526	398,141	1,747	0.52	5,327	1.50

*Compiled from census tract data, not the exact boundaries of the city.
Sources: Atlanta Regional Commission, Regional Development Plan, 1985, 1985; and Employment, 1988, 1989.

1980 and 1989, with rates of 10.90 percent, 5.49 percent, and 5.37 percent, respectively. The population of these counties was overwhelmingly white in 1989. Blacks and others were only 6.3 percent of the Gwinnett County population, 9.8 percent of the Rockdale County population, and 6.8 percent of the Cobb County population.[8] In contrast, blacks and others represented significantly higher proportions of the population in counties posting the lowest growth rates during this period. With average annual growth rates of 1.62 and 1.53, respectively, DeKalb and Fulton counties posted the lowest growth rates within the region. Blacks and others were 32.2 percent of the DeKalb County population and 51.1 percent of the Fulton County population.

The city of Atlanta experienced an average annual population growth rate of only 0.24 percent between 1980 and 1989, increasing from 426,215 to 435,474 (Table 3). The city's population actually declined by nearly 70,000 residents during the previous decade. Within the city, population growth rates have been highest in the central business district (CBD), the affluent and predominantly white Buckhead section, and the predominantly black southwestern section (Map 2).[9] By 1989, blacks and others accounted for 70 percent of all residents in the city and 61 percent of the 185,564 households in the city. Regionally, blacks and others accounted for only 26 percent of the population and 39 percent of all households. Nearly half of the region's black and other population resides in Atlanta, compared to only 8 percent of the white population.

Household income provides another indicator of the uneven pattern of recent development trends in the Atlanta region. In 1988, just over 20 percent of the households in the region had incomes below $15,000, and nearly 23 percent had incomes of $50,000 or more (Table 4). Nearly 35 percent of the households in Fulton County and close to 20 percent of the households in DeKalb County had incomes below $15,000. (Fulton and DeKalb counties also had the highest shares of population with incomes of $75,000 or more, suggesting that the counties contain pockets both of the very poor and of the very rich.) At the other extreme, 26 percent of the households in both Cobb and Gwinnett counties had incomes of $50,000 or more.

Within the city, nearly half of the households had incomes below $15,000 (Table 5). Large proportions of the households in both the CBD and southeast superdistricts also had incomes at that level. Only 10 percent of the households in the city had incomes of $50,000 or more. Nearly 25 percent of these households resided in the affluent Buckhead section.

TABLE 2
Atlanta Region Population: 1970, 1980, 1989

County	1970	1980	1989	1970-1980 Average Annual Change		1980-1989 Average Annual Change	
				Number	Percent	Number	Percent
Clayton	98,126	150,357	181,800	5,223	5.32	3,494	2.32
Cobb	196,793	297,718	441,700	10,093	5.13	15,998	5.37
DeKalb	415,387	483,024	553,300	6,764	1.63	7,808	1.62
Douglas	28,659	54,573	75,700	2,591	9.04	2,347	4.30
Fulton	605,210	589,904	671,300	-1,531	-0.25	9,044	1.53
Gwinnett	72,349	166,808	330,300	9,446	13.06	18,166	10.90
Rockdale	18,152	36,747	54,900	1,860	10.25	2,017	5.49
Atlanta Region	1,434,676	1,779,131	2,309,000	34,446	2.40	58,874	3.31

Sources: Atlanta Regional Commission, *Regional Development Plan, 1985*, 1985; and *1989 Population and Housing*, 1989.

MAP 2
City of Atlanta Superdistricts

Source: Atlanta Regional Commission

As these figures suggest, poverty is spatially concentrated within the region. In 1980, nearly 27 percent of the city's population fell below the poverty line, while only 12 percent of the population in the seven-county Atlanta region fell below the poverty line. Over 57 percent of the city's poverty population lived in census tracts in which a third or more of the population was poor. The city's poverty rate was the second highest in the country, behind only that of Newark, New Jersey. As Keating and Creighton point out:

Poverty in the Atlanta region is concentrated in a belt which extends

TABLE 3
City of Atlanta Population: 1970, 1980, 1989

Superdistrict	1970	1980	1989	1970-1980 Average Annual Change		1980-1989 Average Annual Change	
				Number	Percent	Number	Percent
Buckhead	45,332	41,966	48,126	-337	-0.74	684	1.63
Northwest	119,833	93,283	93,549	-2655	-2.22	30	0.03
Northeast	72,763	54,637	56,747	-1813	-2.49	12	0.02
Southwest	97,859	104,224	107,294	637	0.65	341	0.33
Southeast	107,503	88,867	85,289	-1864	-1.73	-398	0.45
CBD	5,762	5,955	6,888	19	0.33	104	1.74
Atlanta-DeKalb	46,687	37,283	37,581	-940	-2.01	33	0.09
City of Atlanta*	495,739	426,215	435,474	-6952	-1.40	1029	0.24

*Compiled from census tract data, not the exact boundaries of the city.
Sources: Atlanta Regional Commission, Regional Development Plan, 1985, 1985; and 1989 Population and Housing, 1989.

TABLE 4

Atlanta Region Household Income Distribution: 1988

(percent)*

County	Number of Households	Less than $15,000	$15,000-$24,999	$25,000-$34,999	$35,000-$49,999	$50,000-$74,999	Over $74,999
Clayton	63,552	16.0	24.0	25.0	19.0	10.5	5.5
Cobb	166,287	15.4	16.6	19.0	23.3	19.2	6.8
DeKalb	205,689	18.0	23.0	17.0	16.9	16.1	9.0
Douglas	24,174	15.8	21.2	21.0	22.5	17.0	2.5
Fulton	265,670	34.7	18.8	13.0	13.5	12.0	8.0
Gwinnett	120,803	10.3	15.7	20.0	28.0	20.8	5.2
Rockdale	17,875	14.0	18.0	25.5	21.5	16.5	4.5
Atlanta Region	864,050	21.3	19.4	17.5	19.0	15.7	7.2

*Detail in table may not add to total because of rounding.
Source: Atlanta Regional Commission, *1988 Household Income*, 1989.

TABLE 5
City of Atlanta Household Income Distribution: 1988
(percent)*

Superdistrict	Number of Households	Less than $15,000	$15,000-$24,999	$25,000-$34,999	$35,000-$49,999	$50,000-$74,999	Over $74,999
Buckhead	23,357	19.1	14.8	13.6	14.2	17.5	2.0
Northwest	36,654	49.9	21.7	12.0	8.6	5.1	2.6
Northeast	27,458	48.0	21.7	11.8	9.2	6.1	3.0
Southwest	37,030	45.9	24.1	14.5	9.7	4.7	1.3
Southeast	29,533	60.3	22.5	10.7	4.7	1.3	0.5
CBD	2,436	85.5	7.9	3.8	2.2	0.5	0.0
Atlanta-DeKalb	13,399	46.2	28.7	11.3	6.6	5.3	2.0
City of Atlanta**	169,867	46.5	21.8	12.5	8.8	6.2	4.4

*Detail in table may not add to total because of rounding.
**Compiled from census tract data, not the exact boundaries of the city.
Source: Atlanta Regional Commission, 1988 Household Income, 1989.

across the southern sector of the city and into DeKalb County. Seventy-two percent of the 214,517 persons in the region who were poor in 1980 lived in this area.[10]

In addition to having a spatial dimension, the pattern of income inequality in the Atlanta region also has a racial dimension. In 1960, median family income in census tracts that were over 90 percent white was 2.66 times higher than median family income in tracts that were over 90 percent black.[11] This ratio decreased to 2.13 by 1970, but then increased dramatically to 3.34 by 1980. Interestingly, between 1960 and 1980 income inequality also *increased* among tracts that were over 90 percent black, while it *decreased* among tracts that were over 90 percent white.[12] The racial dimension of income inequality in Atlanta is also illustrated by the fact that blacks are more likely than whites to be poor. While the poverty rate for black families in the city was 31.4 percent in 1980, the rate for white families was only 7.3 percent.[13]

THE ATLANTA HOUSING MARKET

The housing stock in the Atlanta region increased by 42 percent during the 1980s, from 681,520 units in 1980 to 969,673 units in 1989 (Table 6). During this same period, the housing stock in Gwinnett County more than doubled, increasing by 134 percent, and leading all counties in the region. DeKalb and Fulton counties had the lowest growth rates (26 percent and 21 percent, respectively).

The spatial pattern of housing development is highly uneven within the city. The city's housing stock grew by only 4 percent between 1980 and 1989 (Table 7). Slightly over half of the 7,648 units added were located in the Buckhead superdistrict, which led all sections with a growth rate of 21 percent. The southeast superdistrict saw a 3 percent decrease in the number of housing units. In their study of the Atlanta housing market, Keating and Creighton point out that 92 percent of the new housing units built in the city between 1978 and 1986 were located in just 22 percent of the city's census tracts.[14] Over half of the 7,648 units added during that period were located in the Buckhead area.

Housing units in the city were split nearly equally between single-family and multifamily units in 1987.[15] In contrast, nearly two-thirds of the units in the region were single-family, while only a third were multifamily. Within the city, just over two-thirds of the units were renter-occupied.

TABLE 6
Atlanta Region Housing Units: 1980, 1989

			Change	
	1980	1989	Number	Percent
County				
Clayton	52,989	71,261	18,272	34.48
Cobb	113,271	188,428	75,157	66.35
DeKalb	181,803	229,859	48,056	26.43
Douglas	17,746	27,092	9,346	52.67
Fulton	245,585	296,894	51,309	20.89
Gwinnett	57,982	135,860	77,878	134.31
Rockdale	12,144	20,279	8,135	66.99
Atlanta Region	681,520	969,673	288,153	42.28

Source: Atlanta Regional Commission, 1989 Population and Housing, 1989.

According to Atlanta Bureau of Planning estimates, the average sales price for new and existing homes in the city was $73,000 in 1987.[16]Averages for subareas of the city ranged from $27,624 in the west-central section to $179,900 in the northernmost section. The median contract rent in 1986 was $376.[17] City estimates indicate that the average rent for one-bedroom units ranged from $275 in the west-central section to $505 in the northernmost section. The average rent for two-bedroom units ranged from $370 in the west-central and south-central sections to $620 in the northernmost section.

The suburban northside housing submarkets experienced substantial overbuilding during the 1980s. This resulted primarily from the oversupply of multifamily and high-cost single-family units. Vacancy rates for multifamily units in some of these areas exceeded 20 percent in early 1987.[18] By 1989, the vacancy rate for all units in the region was 7.7 percent, while the rate for the city was 8.1 percent.[19] City census tracts that were 90 percent or more black had a vacancy rate of 8.7 percent, while tracts that were 90 percent or more white had a vacancy rate of 9.7 percent.

In examining the housing problems of households in the Atlanta region, Keating and Creighton focused on lack of complete plumbing,

TABLE 7
City of Atlanta Housing Units: 1980, 1989

Superdistrict	1980	1989	Change Number	Percent
Buckhead	21,202	25,656	4,454	21.01
Northwest	39,224	40,618	1,394	3.55
Northeast	29,598	30,799	1,201	4.06
Southwest	38,084	39,457	1,373	3.61
Southeast	33,775	32,613	-1,162	-3.44
CBD	2,705	2,721	16	0.59
Atlanta-DeKalb	14,009	14,381	372	2.66
City of Atlanta*	178,597	186,245	7,648	4.28

*Compiled from census tract data, not the exact boundaries of the city.
Source: Atlanta Regional Commission, 1989 Population and Housing, 1989.

overcrowding, and payment of more than 30 percent of income for housing costs.[20] They found that 53 percent of the renters in the region and 20 percent of the homeowners had at least one of these problems in 1989. In the city, 45 percent of the renters and 38 percent of the owners had at least one problem. In both the city and the region, nearly 90 percent of the households with housing problems paid at least 30 percent of their incomes for rent.

HOUSING ASSISTANCE PROGRAMS

Among the government programs that have had significant impacts on the city's housing market are the federal housing assistance programs and a local housing enterprise zone program. The Atlanta Housing Authority (AHA), which administers the federal housing assistance programs, is the fifth largest public housing authority in the nation.[21] AHA operates the Low-Rent Public Housing Program, the Section 8 Housing Assistance Payments program, and a local homebuyers' program that assists participants in making the transition from renting their homes to owning them. In 1988, these programs involved 20,454 units, accounting for 11 percent of the city's housing stock and housing 11 percent of the population. Of these units, 14,804 were in public housing developments, 5,505 were subsidized through the Section 8 program, and 145 were part of the homebuyers' program.

The Atlanta Housing Enterprise Zone Program is an outgrowth of the Atlanta Urban Enterprise Zone Act of 1983, which allowed the creation of commercial and industrial enterprise zones within the city. Tax abatements are used to attract additional investment to the designated zones. A 1986 amendment to the act allowed the creation of housing enterprise zones. This component of the program encourages private investment in housing construction and rehabilitation in selected sections of the city. The program is not limited to the development of housing for low- and moderate-income households. However, each zone must be located in a census tract in which either the household poverty rate or unemployment rate is twice that of Fulton County or which has fewer than 1,000 residents.

In addition, each zone must contain a minimum of five acres, with certain exceptions. If the zone is within 1,000 feet of a pedestrian entrance to a transit station or encompasses a historic, muti-family structure capable of providing at least four housing units, it can be less than five acres in size.[22] All taxes are abated during the first five years, 80 percent during the sixth and seventh years, 60 percent during the eighth year, 40 percent during the ninth year, and 20 percent during the tenth year. After the tenth year, the tax abatement ceases and the zones are abolished.

Housing development under the enterprise zone program has been concentrated in two census tracts, although 45 tracts satisfy the program criteria. The Bedford Pine urban renewal area near the CBD was eligible for the program because it had fewer than 1,000 residents.[23] Of the 940 units built under the program, 790 have been located in this area. Of these, 598 are condominiums and 192 are garden apartments. They primarily serve middle- and upper-income households. Prices in one of the condominium developments still under construction range from around $75,000 to $125,000.[24]

The remainder of the units that have been developed under the program are in the North Grant Park area, which is adjacent to a gentrifying neighborhood. This area qualified because its poverty rate is at least twice that of Fulton County. A total of 114 units (45 new and 69 rehabilitated) are located here. New capital investment in both areas totals around $63 million and will involve an estimated $3 million in tax abatements annually during the first five years.[25] The two projects cover nearly 70 acres of land.

RACIAL DISPARITIES IN HOME MORTGAGE LENDING IN ATLANTA

During the last two years, the existence of racial disparities in the pattern of home lending in the Atlanta region has been raised by the local press, politicians, and community-based organizations. In this section, the roles of the federal Home Mortgage Disclosure Act of 1975 and the Community Reinvestment Act of 1977 in allowing this issue to be raised are examined. Ways in which local groups have used the two federal laws to press for the development of more equitable lending practices also are discussed.

Federal Legislation on Home Lending Practices

The purpose of the Home Mortgage Disclosure Act of 1975 (HMDA) is:

> to provide the citizens and public officials of the United States with sufficient information to enable them to determine whether depository institutions are [ful]filling their obligations to serve the housing needs of the communities and neighborhoods in which they are located.[26]

The HMDA requires financial institutions to produce annual reports documenting the number and dollar volume of residential loans made in each census tract in the communities they serve. Reports must be filed by all federally regulated depository institutions that have $10 million or more in assets and at least one branch in a metropolitan statistical area. These reports must be made available for public inspection. A 1980 revision to the HMDA requires the U.S. Department of Housing and Urban Development to report information on the volume and location of loans insured by the Federal Housing Administration (FHA).[27] Another 1980 revision requires the Federal Reserve Board to computerize all of the reports and to designate a central depository for each metropolitan area. Each computer tape costs $250 and contains the annual reports for all the metropolitan areas.

The Community Reinvestment Act of 1977 (CRA) is designed to

> encourage regulated financial institutions to fulfill their continuing and affirmative obligation to help meet the credit needs of their communities, including low-and moderate-income neighborhoods, consistent with safe and sound operation of such institutions.[28]

Under the CRA, financial institutions are required to prepare reports that delineate the communities they serve, list the types of credit they intend to extend within the areas, indicate the efforts made to meet community credit needs, and assess their performance in meeting those needs. These reports also must be available for public inspection. Citizens have the right to add written comments to the CRA files of financial institutions and to examine the comments submitted by other citizens. They also have the right to make their credit needs known to the institutions. Federal regulatory agencies rate financial institutions on the basis of their performance in meeting community credit needs. The CRA performance of the vast majority of financial institutions has received favorable ratings. More than 97 percent of the institutions rated before March 1989 received a rating of 1 or 2, based on a scale in which 5 is the least favorable rating.[29]

Financial institutions' CRA ratings and performance records are taken into consideration when regulatory agencies review applications for mergers, acquisitions, branches, and relocations. Citizens who are dissatisfied with institutions' CRA records can file formal protests with the regulatory agencies and can request public hearings as part of the review of the institutions' applications. According to Shlay, "a successful CRA challenge occurs when a community acquires bargaining power vis-a-vis a lender."[30] Prior to 1989, only eight of the fifty thousand applications submitted by financial institutions were turned down due to CRA noncompliance.[31] Thus, in practice, the bargaining power provided by CRA results more from the community's ability to delay rather than to halt bank actions, such as mergers.

By providing access to information on the mortgage lending patterns of financial institutions and by providing a process through which the records of specific institutions can be challenged, the HMDA and the CRA can serve as powerful tools for communities interested in redirecting credit flows. Studies using HMDA data for several major cities have shown lending disparities between central cities and suburbs and between white and minority areas. As Shlay points out:

Pressure on financial institutions to demonstrate progress in meeting community credit needs has intensified as communities publicly link neighborhood deterioration, housing abandonment, and low rates of black homeownership to unequal credit flows.[32]

Use of the HMDA and the CRA to Highlight Lending Disparities in Atlanta

Although the effort to highlight lending disparities in the Atlanta region was spearheaded primarily by a coalition of community organizations called the Atlanta Community Reinvestment Alliance (ACRA), activities designed to draw attention to lending disparities began in the summer of 1986, prior to the formation of ACRA.[33] Early activities included a series of community hearings sponsored by the Georgia Housing Coalition, another coalition of housing-oriented community organizations. During the hearings, blacks provided testimony concerning their dealings with banks; maps indicating the spatial lending patterns of local financial institutions were presented; and the CRA was discussed. Speakers commented on the tendency of financial institutions to close branches in areas in which the population shifts from predominantly white to predominantly black. Many speakers held negative perceptions of financial institutions, and as a result did not conduct business with them. Others told of problems they encountered in applying for loans.

The number of organizations interested in lending issues grew as a result of the hearings, leading to the formation of ACRA. The new coalition received technical assistance from the National Training and Information Center, a Chicago-based organization that assists community groups in organizing, conducting research, developing tactics, and negotiating with government and other institutions.

ACRA decided to focus its initial efforts on Trust Company Bank, since several people who testified at the community hearings had complained about the bank and since its parent company, SunTrust Banks, was about to ask the Federal Reserve Board for permission to merge with another bank. ACRA's complaints against the bank's policies concerned disparities in the bank's lending patterns in black and white neighborhoods with similar income levels, as well as its failure to finance the development of low-income and multifamily housing, to assist nonprofit housing development organizations, to provide low-fee "lifeline" checking accounts, and to process mortgage applications at branches located in black neighborhoods. ACRA also asked Trust Company to fund a non-profit community development corporation and to conduct a survey to determine the credit needs of low- and moderate-income households. Negotiations between ACRA and Trust Company began in September 1986, and lasted over a year.

Because ACRA believed that progress was being made in the negotiations, the organization decided not to file a formal CRA protest against Trust Company's proposed merger. Trust Company had agreed to: investigate the possibility of offering a lifeline checking account, conduct the credit needs survey, market its low-interest House Money mortgage program more effectively in black neighborhoods, and provide loan assistance to groups associated with ACRA.

However, by 1987 when SunTrust sought permission for another merger, ACRA had grown dissatisfied because many of the issues raised in the negotiations associated with SunTrust's earlier merger request still had not been resolved to its members' satisfaction. By that time, the bank had decided there was little demand for lifeline checking accounts and that the accounts probably would not be profitable. The bank had conducted the community needs survey, but it disagreed with ACRA over the interpretation of the results. The bank had expanded its advertising to the *Atlanta Daily World*, the city's largest black newspaper, in October 1986, but it did not advertise in that paper again until it filed the merger application a year later. The House Money low-interest loan program had provided only approximately nine loans between 1985 and 1987.

ACRA filed a formal CRA protest against Trust Company's proposed merger in 1987. Shortly thereafter, Trust Company and a number of other local banks discussed the formation of a loan pool that would provide below-market rate mortgages for low- and moderate-income households. These discussions, along with the year-long negotiations between Trust Company and ACRA, favorably impressed Federal Reserve officials. As a result, the officials refused to hear ACRA's CRA challenge to the proposed merger. In commenting on the case, a Federal Reserve official wrote:

> The record in this case reflects that Trust Company has made efforts to serve the low- and moderate-income and minority communities in Atlanta through its House Money program and through its participation in a loan consortium that will provide below-market rate financing of single-family homes.[34]

ACRA was more successful in its negotiations with Georgia Federal Bank, which was more responsive to the organization's concerns. Georgia Federal agreed to institute a lifeline checking account, to provide free checking services to customers utilizing the automatic deposit service, to advertise in black neighborhoods, and to open some of its branches in black neighborhoods on Saturdays.

Following the Federal Reserve Board's refusal to hear ACRA's CRA challenge against Trust Company, Dennis Goldstein, an Atlanta Legal Aid Society housing attorney representing some of the members of ACRA, decided that the racial disparities in the lending patterns of local financial institutions should be publicized. Goldstein gave a copy of the CRA protest that ACRA had filed against Trust Company to *The Atlanta Journal and Constitution*. Staff writer Bill Dedman was eventually given permission to research the story for a special series. Based on HMDA data, he documented the pattern of mortgage lending in black and white neighborhoods in the Atlanta area.[35]

The four-part series, titled "The Color of Money," ran in *The Atlanta Journal* and *The Atlanta Constitution* on May 1-4, 1988. The series, which won a Pulitzer Prize as well as other awards, uncovered the discriminatory effects of the mortgage lending practices of financial institutions in the Atlanta region. The study on which much of the series was based covered 64 middle-income census tracts in the Atlanta region. Median household income in these tracts ranged between $12,894 and $22,393 in 1980, or between 70 percent and 122 percent of the 1980 Atlanta-area median household income of $18,355. Of the 64 tracts, 39 with populations that were at least 80 percent white were classified as white, 14 with populations that were at least 80 percent nonwhite were classified as black, and the remaining 11 were classified as integrated.

The study's findings pointed to marked disparities in the pattern of lending activity in black and white neighborhoods (Map 3). Banks and savings and loan institutions made 4.0 times as many loans per 1,000 single-family structures in white neighborhoods as in comparable black neighborhoods in 1984, 4.7 times as many in 1985, and 5.4 times as many in 1986. A separate analysis was made of real estate records from all 1986 home sales in 16 of the 64 middle-income census tracts. This analysis showed that although banks and savings and loan institutions provided 35 percent of the home loans in white areas, they provided only 9 percent of the home loans in black areas.[36] Furthermore, banks and savings and loan institutions provided 31 percent of the home loans in lower-income white neighborhoods in which the median household income was less than 70 percent of the area median. In contrast, in upper-middle-income black neighborhoods in which the median income was greater than the area median, banks and savings and loan associations provided only 17 percent of the home loans.

Dedman summarized other key findings of the study as follows:

- Banks and savings and loans return an estimated 9 cents of each dollar deposited by blacks in home loans to black neighborhoods. They return 15 cents of each dollar deposited by whites in home loans to white neighborhoods.
- The offices where Atlanta's largest banking institutions take home loan applications are almost all located in predominantly white areas. Most savings and loans have no offices in black areas.
- Several banks have closed branches in areas that shifted from white to black. Some banks are open fewer hours in black areas than in white areas.
- Meanwhile, a black-owned bank in Atlanta, which makes home loans almost exclusively in black neighborhoods, has had the lowest default rate on real estate loans of any bank its size in the country.[37]

Nine days after the series ran in the newspapers, Atlanta's major banks announced a set of programs that would provide a total of $65 million for home purchase and home improvement loans in specific black and low- and moderate-income sections of the Atlanta region.[38] One of the programs was a $20 million loan pool formed by nine local banks.[39] The pool, called the Atlanta Mortgage Consortium, was initiated by Trust Company Bank following the 1987 CRA protest filed by ACRA. The consortium provides below-market interest rate loans to households with annual incomes below $33,500. The thirty-year, fixed rate loans are for amounts of up to $60,000 and must be used to purchase single-family, owner-occupied homes in certain low- and moderate-income sections of the region. The consortium exhausted the first $20 million in loans by the end of October 1989. The second phase of the program will involve an additional $30 million provided by ten local financial institutions.

FUTURE PROSPECTS

This article has highlighted the housing status of blacks in Atlanta. It has shown that although Atlanta has the reputation of being a city of opportunity for blacks, it is a city in which marked differences exist between the housing status of blacks and whites. Recent initiatives by local organizations and the major newspapers have drawn attention to some of the disparities. These efforts were facilitated by information and protest procedures provided under the Home Mortgage Disclosure Act of 1975 and the Community Reinvestment Act of 1977.

MAP 3
Mortgage Lending Patterns in the Atlanta Region

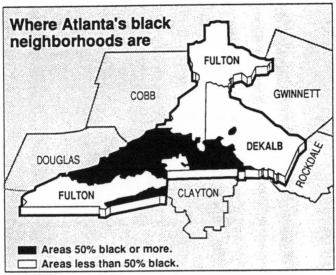

Source: 1980 U.S. Bureau of the Census figures

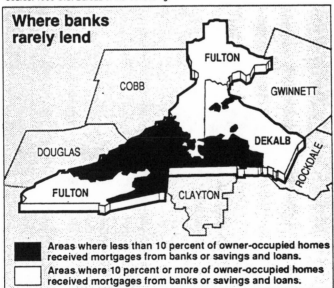

Reprinted by permission of *The Atlanta Journal and Constitution*.

Recent developments indicate that the future prospects for more equitable housing conditions in Atlanta might be good, however. Mayor Maynard Jackson has indicated that housing will be a high-priority policy area for his administration. Since taking office in January 1990, he has proposed several housing initiatives. Among them is the creation of a separate department of housing within the city government structure. This department will establish policy guidelines for city participation in housing matters and will coordinate the city's housing development efforts. City-sponsored housing initiatives will emphasize the provision of affordable housing for selected population subgroups, including low- and moderate-income households and residents of areas with high concentrations of substandard housing.[40] The Atlanta Home Ownership Program will provide a revolving fund that can be used to finance the construction of homes for low- and moderate-income households. The city and several major banks have joined forces to form the Atlanta Equity Fund, which will provide a mechanism through which corporations can invest in multifamily housing projects for low-income households and receive federal tax credits. The city also intends to bring back on line the approximately 2,000 public housing units that are currently vacant. Mayor Jackson's housing record to date differs significantly from that of his predecessor, Andrew Young, who was widely criticized for neglecting issues related to affordable housing.[41]

A second recent development that might result in improvements in the housing status of black Atlantans is the provision of financial resources by several national and local organizations. The Ford Foundation, through its Local Initiatives Support Corporation, has given a grant to the Atlanta Economic Development Corporation (a quasipublic organization that functions as the city's development arm) for the development of low-income housing.[42] Also, the Atlanta Chamber of Commerce is using a $100,000 grant from the U.S. Department of Housing and Urban Development to support a Housing Resource Center. The center will serve as a clearinghouse for information and resources that can be used by nonprofit organizations involved in housing development. In addition, the United Way is considering sponsoring a $5 million revolving loan fund for the development of nonprofit rental housing.

Another recent development is the continued mobilization of local nonprofit housing development organizations.[43] Recent changes in the CRA, combined with increased support among key members of Congress for community reinvestment issues, should provide additional support for the groups' efforts.[44] Past experience in Atlanta and elsewhere has shown that these activities tend to make banks more responsive to community concerns.[45] In addition to confronting local banks about their lending records in black neighborhoods, housing organizations are also expanding their capacity to develop affordable housing. Recently passed state and city laws streamlining the process of acquiring tax-delinquent land will assist these groups in their efforts by reducing red tape and costs.[46]

The pattern of racial disparity within the Atlanta housing market results from the nexus of racism and economic discrimination, which has been a part of American society ever since Africans were first brought here against their will. History has shown that, in the area of housing as well as in other areas, the forces of racism and economic discrimination are not easily neutralized. Despite this, the recent initiatives undertaken by the Jackson administration and local housing organizations have the potential to improve the housing conditions of some black households in Atlanta and thereby reduce disparity in the local housing market. The initiatives are still too recent to have had significant impacts. However, their results should be closely monitored to determine the extent to which they promote the elimination of racial disparity in the Atlanta housing market.

NOTES

1. John Helyar, "The Big Hustle: Atlanta's Two Worlds: Wealth and Poverty, Magnet and Mirage," *The Wall Street Journal*, (February 29, 1989), p. 1
2. The Atlanta Metropolitan Statistical Area, shown in Map 1, consists of eighteen counties. This study is based on the smaller seven-county region served by the Atlanta Regional Commission (ARC), one of eighteen regional planning agencies established by the Georgia legislature. The counties served by ARC are Clayton, Cobb, DeKalb, Douglas, Fulton, Gwinnett, and Rockdale. These counties are shaded in Map 1. An eighth county, Henry, was added to the Atlanta region in 1989. This study focuses on the seven counties in the region prior to that time, since ARC has not yet compiled a complete set of time-series data for Henry County.
3. U.S. Department of Commerce, Bureau of the Census, *County and City Data Book, 1984* (Washington, DC: U.S. Department of Commerce).
4. U.S. Department of Commerce, Bureau of the Census, *State and Metropolitan Area Data Book, 1986* (Washington, DC: U.S. Department of Commerce).
5. Thierry Noyelle, "The Rise of Advanced Services: Some Implications for Economic Development in U.S. Cities," *Journal of the American Planning Association*, Vol. 49, No. 3 (Spring 1983), pp. 283–284.
6. Atlanta Regional Commission, *Atlanta Region Outlook* (Atlanta, GA: Atlanta Regional Commission, May 1990), pp. A-16–A-22.
7. Frank Hughes, *Economic and Spatial Transformations in Atlanta: A Political Economy Approach* (Master's thesis, Georgia Institute of Technology, 1989).
8. ARC groups blacks and others in the data it provides on the racial and ethnic characteristics of the population. Data from the 1980 Census of Population indicate that most of the people in this group are black. Of the 509,555 people classified as "black and

other'' in 1980, 92 percent were black, 4 percent were of Spanish origin, and 2 percent were Asian or Pacific Islanders. In recent years, the Spanish origin and Asian populations have grown rapidly. However, blacks remain the predominant group within the black and other category.

9. ARC has designated 33 subcounty planning areas, called superdistricts, within the region. Each superdistrict consists of a group of 1980 census tracts. Seven of the superdistricts are in the city of Atlanta. However, the boundaries of these superdistricts and those of the city are not identical, since the superdistricts contain entire census tracts and the city's boundaries cut through census tracts in some cases.

10. Larry Keating and Max Creighton, *Nonprofit Housing Supply: Atlanta Case* (Atlanta, GA: Community Design Center, 1989), p. 19.

11. David M. Smith, *Geography, Inequality, and Society* (Cambridge, England: University of Cambridge Press, 1987), pp. 56–57.

12. Ibid., p. 58. Smith used coefficients of variation to measure the degree of income inequality within groups of black and white census tracts. The coefficient of variation provides a measure of dispersion and is calculated by dividing the standard deviation of a distribution by the distribution's mean. The coefficient of variation for median family income in black tracts in Atlanta increased from 23.83 in 1960 to 29.24 in 1970, and then to 49.08 in 1980. The coefficient for median family income in white tracts increased from 47.93 in 1960 to 48.21 in 1970, but then decreased to 38.49 in 1980.

13. David L. Sjoquist, *The Economic Status of Black Atlantans* (Atlanta, GA: The Atlanta Urban League, Inc., 1988), Table 3.

14. Keating and Creighton, *Nonprofit Housing Supply*, pp. 34–36.

15. City of Atlanta, Department of Community Development, Bureau of Planning, *Mayor's Proposed Housing Plan* (July 1989), p. 20. Single-family includes single-unit detached, single-unit attached, and duplex structures.

16. Ibid., p. 59.

17. Ibid., p. 72.

18. Keating and Creighton, p. 37.

19. Atlanta Regional Commission, *1989 Population and Housing* (Atlanta, GA: Atlanta Regional Commission, 1989).

20. Keating and Creighton, pp. 24–33.

21. City of Atlanta, pp. 34–38, 113.

22. City of Atlanta, Department of Community Development, Bureau of Planning, *Urban Enterprise Zone Program* (June 1989).

23. See Keating and Creighton for discussions of efforts to promote the development of high-income housing near the CBD and the history of urban renewal in the Bedford Pine community.

24. Maria Saporta, ''Intown Housing No Longer on the Outside,'' *The Atlanta Journal and Constitution* (May 20, 1990), p. H–1.

25. Keating and Creighton, p. 90.

26. *Home Mortgage Disclosure Act of 1975* (Washington, DC: U.S. Government Printing Office, 1975), p. 501.

27. Anne B. Shlay, ''Financing Community: Methods of Assessing Residential Credit Disparities, Market Barriers, and Institutional Reinvestment Performance in the Metropolis,'' *Journal of Urban Affairs*, Vol. 11, No. 3 (1989), pp. 204–206.

28. *Federal Register*, Vol. 43, No. 198 (October 12, 1978), pp. 47144–47155.

29. Francis X. Grady, ''Setting Out a Workable Program for Generating Community Reinvestment,'' *Office of Thrift Supervision Journal* (March 1990), pp. 16–19.

30. Shlay, p. 203.

31. Grady, p. 17.

32. Shlay, p. 203.

33. Much of the information in this section was obtained from an April 24, 1990 interview with Dennis Goldstein, a housing attorney with the Atlanta Legal Aid Society, Inc., which represented members of ACRA.

34. Bill Dedman, *The Color of Money*, series reprint, *The Atlanta Journal and Constitution*, (May 1–4, 1988), p. 26.

35. Ibid. The analysis relied on a methodology developed by researchers at the Hubert A. Humphrey Institute of Public Affairs at the University of Minnesota, Johns Hopkins University, and Temple University. Research assistance was provided by Stan Fitterman, a graduate student in city planning at the Georgia Institute of Technology. Fitterman had conducted some of the preliminary analysis used earlier by ACRA.

36. The remaining loans in both types of areas were provided primarily by mortgage companies. Some of these companies are owned by banks, while others are unaffiliated. Approximately half of all home loans made in middle-income black areas during 1986 were guaranteed by the Federal Housing Administration or the Veterans Administration. In comparable white areas, only 13 percent of the loans were guaranteed by the government.

37. Dedman, pp. 1–2.

38. Ibid., p. 43.

39. Michelle Murff, "The Atlanta Mortgage Consortium, Inc.," unpublished paper, City Planning Program, Georgia Institute of Technology, 1989.

40. "New Directions in Atlanta Housing Policies," presentation by John Reid, Executive Officer, Office of the Mayor, City of Atlanta. Delivered at the Spring Conference of the Georgia Planning Association, May 18, 1990, Atlanta.

41. Amy Wallace, "Housing Plan Met with Skepticism," *The Atlanta Journal and Constitution*, August 28, 1989, p. A-1.

42. "Nonprofits and Low-Income Housing," *Research Horizons*, Vol 18, No. 1 (Spring 1990), pp. 28–29.

43. Robert Luke, "Community Groups Challenge Proposed C and S – Sovran Merger," *The Atlanta Journal and Constitution*, (January 24, 1990), p. B-1.

44. *Federal Register*, Vol. 55, No. 84, (May 1, 1990), pp. 18163–13175 and Grady, p. 17. As of July 1, 1990, regulatory agencies will be required to make public their ratings of the CRA performance of financial institutions. They will also be required to replace the five-tiered numerical rating system with a four-tiered descriptive rating system. The four ratings to be used in assessing the extent to which financial institutions meet community credit needs are "outstanding," "satisfactory," "needs to improve," and "substantial noncompliance." The performance areas to be assessed are the determination of community credit needs, the marketing and types of credit offered and extended, the geographic distribution and record of opening and closing offices, discrimination and other illegal practices, and community development. Congressional support for community reinvestment issues has been provided by Representative Henry Gonzalez, chairman of the Banking, Finance, and Urban Affairs Committee of the U.S. House of Representatives.

45. Mark Sherman, "City and C & S Set to Launch Program to Create More Low-Cost Housing," *The Atlanta Journal and Constitution*, (May 6, 1990), p. D-3.

46. "Nonprofits and Low-Income Housing," p. 28.

6

THE ROLE OF HOUSING VOUCHERS IN BALTIMORE CITY, MARYLAND

Sheila Ards

In Baltimore City, the relative well-being of black and white families
using Section 8 housing vouchers versus Section 8 housing certificates is compared. Logistic regression is used to examine whether the
social and economic characteristics of a regional planning district play
a significantly different role in the likelihood that a district will have
voucher or certificate recipients. A second analysis examines the average monthly rent paid by blacks and whites for housing in the
certificate and voucher programs. The results suggest that whites
receive greater economic benefits in the voucher program than in the
certificate program while blacks do not.

After years of providing public housing in tenant complexes, many of
which became rat-infested, crime-ridden and deteriorated, and after re-
alizing that building new houses would not meet the needs of all the poor,
public officials sought alternative forms of housing assistance for lower-
income households. They sought a form of assistance that encouraged the
rental of existing housing stock. Two new forms of housing assistance
were tried: Section 8 housing certificates and Section 8 housing vouchers.
Although the programs are very similar, they differ in important ways.
This study examines the effects of these differences on black families in
Baltimore City, Maryland.

Two approaches are pursued in this investigation. One explores whether
blacks are better off in the housing voucher program than in the certificate
program. The other examines black and white relative differences in both
programs in Baltimore City.

This analysis is organized as follows: 1) a description of Baltimore City and its housing market conditions is given; 2) the major program features of housing vouchers and housing certificates are discussed; 3) the methods of analyses are detailed; and 4) the major findings are summarized.

BALTIMORE CITY AND ITS HOUSING MARKET

Baltimore City has the largest black population of any locality in Maryland.[1] Fifty-five percent of Baltimore City's population is black, compared to 23 percent for the state and 12 percent for the nation. In addition, Baltimore City has the lowest owner-occupancy rate, median household income, and median gross rent of renter-occupied units of any locality in Maryland. Only 47 percent of the housing units in Baltimore City are owner-occupied, compared to 62 percent for the state and 64 percent for the nation. The median gross rent in Baltimore City is $214, while the median gross rent for Maryland and the rest of the nation is $243. The unemployment rate for Baltimore City is almost twice that of the state.

SECTION 8 VOUCHERS AND CERTIFICATES

Program Descriptions

Vouchers and Existing-Housing (EH) certificates are forms of rent subsidies that are part of the Section 8 Housing Assistance Program. These programs are designed to encourage low-income families to actively seek better quality housing by providing them with a greater choice of units in a local housing market, due to enhanced purchasing power.[2] The rent subsidy is given to an eligible family for the purpose of offsetting its housing costs. The amount of the subsidy is the difference between a fair market rent (FMR) for housing in the locality and a specified percentage of the family's income.

There are three major differences between the housing voucher program and the certificate program. One difference is the amount that the tenant can pay for housing. In both programs, there is a locally determined Fair Market Rent (FMR). This FMR is determined by the existing rental prices within the locality, varying by unit size (i.e., number of bedrooms).

In the Housing Voucher program, the actual rent paid to the landlord can exceed the FMR. The housing assistance payment, however, is the difference between the FMR and 30 percent of adjusted income, regardless of the rental price of the unit actually chosen by the family. If the rental price is higher than the FMR, the tenant pays the difference. In the certificate program, the assisted tenant also pays 30 percent of adjusted income toward rent, but unit rent can not exceed the FMR. (See Glossary of Federal Housing Subsidy Programs for more details on the two programs.)

The second difference between the voucher and the certificate programs is that the Housing Voucher subsidy is not tied to the geographic boundary of the housing authority administering the program. In the voucher program, the tenant can move to a unit within the same MSA or in an MSA contiguous to the one in which the public housing authority (PHA) that issued the voucher is located.[3] The certificate program does not allow recipients to move into units outside the jurisdiction of the local public housing authority.

The third difference is whether the assistance contract is tied to the family or to the housing unit. In the EH certificate program, the assistance contract is variously assigned to the family and to the unit. In the housing voucher program, however, the subsidy is tied to the family and not the rental unit. This demand power of the family is thought to encourage bargaining between the tenant and the landlord, allegedly resulting in better quality housing for the tenant.

The enhanced purchasing power engendered by these demand subsidies also was believed to enhance the integration of neighborhoods. This follows from the assumptions that neighborhoods are segregated because minorities are unable to afford housing within white neighborhoods, and that assistance payments, therefore, enable minorities to move into the more integrated areas.[4]

Earlier Studies

Two studies, conducted during the 1970s, played a major role in the present design of the housing voucher program. One was the Experimental Housing Allowance Program (EHAP). The major findings of the EHAP experiments were: 1) Participation rates were much lower than rates in existing income transfer programs; 2) Most of the allowance payment was spent on nonhousing items; and 3) Rent burdens decreased from 40 to 25 percent. Although the first two findings do not support the subsidy strategy, the third does, although it results from the program design.

The second study was an evaluation of the New Construction and Existing Housing (NCEH) certificate subprograms of the Section 8 Housing Assistance Payments Program. This study compared participating households in sixteen metropolitan areas of the U.S. with the eligible population in those areas. The bases of comparison were: 1) the degree of improvement in the housing of participants; 2) the reduction in housing costs; and 3) the extent to which increased mobility and changes in the racial or economic concentration of neighborhoods resulted.[5] The primary participants in the NC program were the elderly, although relatively few of these elderly were minorities. In contrast, the participants in the EH Program were representative of the entire eligible population. Thus the EH program had a high minority participation rate.

What do we learn from these two studies that may apply to Baltimore City? Are blacks better off in the housing voucher program than in the certificate program in Baltimore? Are there differences in outcomes between blacks and whites in the voucher program in Baltimore? Because the programs were established by two separate pieces of legislation, one passed in 1974 and the other in 1983, they were implemented in Baltimore at different times. The first assistance payment in the certificate program was made in 1976. The first voucher payment was made in 1985. The difference in implementation dates may contribute to differences in the characteristics of program participants.

Characteristics of the Recipient Population in Baltimore

Characteristics of the participants in the Section 8 EH and Voucher programs differ somewhat, when compared by race, age/disability status, family structure, and socioeconomic characteristics. For example, 95 percent of the housing voucher recipients are black, compared to 83 percent of the certificate recipients.[6] Correspondingly, the participation rate of whites in the voucher program (5 percent of all assisted households) is much lower than their participation rate in the certificate program (17 percent). The reason for the difference in participation rates by race in the two programs is unknown.[7]

A large fraction of certificate holders are elderly and/or disabled, while the voucher program has some handicapped recipients. The number of handicapped voucher recipients is negligible when compared to the numbers of non-elderly, non-disabled and non-handicapped persons also receiving vouchers.

The family structure, on the other hand, is similar in the two programs. In both programs the predominant family form consists of one parent with one child or more, with two-parent families comprising a small fraction of the population in both programs. The mean household sizes are 2.38 and 2.61 for voucher and certificate holders, respectively. The median ages of household heads in the voucher program are 45 for men and 35 for women. For the certificate program, the median ages are 55 for men and 35 for women.

Economic and social differences also emerge. The mean adjusted family income in the voucher program is $5,160, compared to $5,676 in the certificate program. Thus, the average family adjusted income in the certificate program is 10 percent higher than the average family income in the voucher program.

The fraction of housing voucher recipients getting other forms of public assistance is larger than the corresponding share of certificate recipients. This finding is consistent with the lower mean adjusted income in the voucher program. Sixty-four percent of the housing voucher recipients receive other forms of public assistance, as compared to 54 percent in the certificate program.

ANALYSIS OF IMPACTS OF VOUCHERS AND CERTIFICATES ON BLACKS

The focus of this study is a comparison of the relative impacts of the housing voucher program and the housing certificate program on black families. This leads us to ask two central questions: 1) What types of neighborhoods do housing assistance recipients live in? and 2) How are blacks faring in terms of out-of-pocket costs in both programs?

Location

Examining the geographic location of the recipient population in both programs reveals uneven population distributions across the city. In fact, 72 percent of the certificate recipients and 78 percent of the voucher recipients live in 30 percent of the regional planning districts. The characteristics of these neighborhoods are discussed here and are used as proxies for housing quality, since the variables are assumed to be highly correlated.

This analysis examines neighborhood quality using seven indices: the mean family income of renters (INC A), the mean family income of owners (INC B), the unemployment rate of males (UN), the average rent (RENT), the percent of the population that is black (RACE), the percent of units that are owner-occupied (OCC), and the proportion of the population with no high school education that lives in the neighborhood (EDUC).[8] It is hypothesized that higher mean income, lower unemployment rate, higher rents, lower percentage black, higher fraction of owner-occupied units, and lower percentage of the population with no high school, would increase the quality of the neighborhood.[9]

In Baltimore City, mean household income of renters is $11,810.[10] For owners, the mean household income is $20,935. The male unemployment rate in the city is 18.7 percent. As noted above, the average rent is $214. Fifty-five percent of the residents are black, and forty-seven percent of the housing units are owner-occupied.

The districts with the largest number of voucher recipients are Gardenville, Waverly, Govans-Northwood (which is also called Northwood), and West Baltimore. Certificate recipients disproportionately reside in West Baltimore, East Baltimore, and Lower Park Heights. An examination of the social and economic indices for these districts shows that these areas are very different from each other.

In terms of renter household income, the three districts with the largest share of voucher recipients—Gardenville, Waverly, Govans-Northwood—all have mean income greater than the average for the city. This is not the case for certificate holders. The three districts with the largest share of certificate holders have mean incomes less than the average for the city.

A similar pattern exists for mean household income of owner-occupied units. Gardenville (the district with the largest number of voucher recipients) has a mean household income for owners of $20,856. West Baltimore (the district with the largest number of certificate recipients) has a mean household income for owners of only $16,559, over four thousand dollars less than the mean for the city.

The male unemployment rate for Baltimore City is 18.7 percent. (It is rounded to 19 percent in Table 1.) Each of the top three voucher districts has an unemployment rate slightly lower than the city's average, while each of the top three certificate districts has an unemployment rate higher than the average.

Racial differences also exist among the districts with the largest share of program recipients. Although fifty-five percent of the population in Baltimore is black, the district with the largest shares of voucher recipients (18 percent) has only a 36 percent black population. The three districts with the largest shares of certificate recipients have populations that are greater than 80 percent black.

Differences in the percent of housing units per district that are owner-

TABLE 1
Social and Economic Characteristics of Regional Planning Districts

Regional Planning Districts RPD Name	Certificates	(%)	Vouchers	(%)	INC (A)	INC (B)	UN	RENT	RACE	OCC	EDUC
113 Gardenville	161	5.35%	140	17.88%	11898	20856	16	219	0.36	0.48	0.04
111 Waverly	204	6.78%	121	15.45%	12131	19213	18	213	0.66	0.30	0.06
105 Govans-Northwook (Northwood)	201	6.68%	119	15.20%	13065	22737	18	242	0.73	0.63	0.03
117 West Baltimore	413	13.73%	91	11.62%	9216	16559	21	180	0.82	0.18	0.14
120 Highlandtown	231	7.68%	51	6.51%	11776	16383	18	210	0.07	0.62	0.10
108 Lower Park Heights	363	12.07%	44	5.62%	10992	18906	20	240	0.95	0.35	0.05
119 East Baltimore	369	12.27%	43	5.49%	9012	16557	21	177	0.91	0.21	0.11
107 Forest Park	238	7.91%	31	3.96%	13527	23520	21	228	0.91	0.49	0.04
116 Rosemont	123	4.09%	26	3.32%	12403	15980	22	232	0.89	0.48	0.06
106 Hamilton	36	1.20%	18	2.30%	10495	22840	15	232	0.11	0.68	0.05
112 Clifton	30	1.00%	18	2.30%	10801	18815	16	188	0.16	0.71	0.03
122 Morrell Park (Violetville)	30	1.00%	16	2.04%	16115	19340	17	252	0.12	0.67	0.02
109 Druid Hill	78	2.59%	14	1.79%	10601	18832	21	219	0.98	0.47	0.02
104 Chinquapin (Cedarcroft)	73	2.43%	12	1.53%	13188	22019	18	233	0.32	0.54	0.02
114 Ten Hills	38	1.26%	11	1.40%	12989	24163	17	207	0.58	0.47	0.01
118 Metrocenter	92	3.06%	6	0.77%	11427	25304	15	201	0.39	0.07	0.02
115 Irvington	58	1.93%	4	0.51%	14566	20407	20	248	0.83	0.64	0.03
125 Cherry Hill	56	1.86%	4	0.51%	10406	18414	20	171	0.74	0.30	0.02
121 Canton	33	1.10%	3	0.38%	10702	18094	18	173	0.08	0.57	0.04
103 Roland	10	0.33%	3	0.38%	19929	44529	10	318	0.04	0.49	0.01
123 Carroll Park	12	0.40%	2	0.26%	10659	14460	20	204	0.25	0.42	0.01
124 South Baltimore	20	0.67%	2	0.26%	11608	17471	17	219	0.05	0.64	0.03
110 Hampden	10	0.33%	1	0.13%	10395	18678	15	176	0.11	0.45	0.02
126 Brooklyn	39	1.30%	1	0.13%	12855	19420	18	226	0.04	0.54	0.03
101 Upper Park Heights	83	2.76%	1	0.13%	15549	28626	17	286	0.24	0.43	0.02
102 Mt. Washington	6	0.20%	1	0.13%	25179	37299	12	353	0.08	0.54	0
Baltimore City	3007	100%	783	100%	11810	20935	19	214	0.55	0.47	

Source: Voucher and Certificate data taken from A Statistical Bulletin (1988).
Note: A map of Baltimore neighborhoods is available from the Department of Housing and Community Development.

occupied also exist between the two programs. In Gardenville, 48 percent of the housing units are owner-occupied. Only 18 percent of the housing units are owner-occupied in West Baltimore. (The mean for the city is 47 percent).

There are also educational differences among the districts with the largest numbers of program recipients. Of the portion of the city's population that did not attend high school, 14 percent reside in West Baltimore, while only four percent of this population reside in Gardenville.

In general, we see voucher recipients living in more desirable neighborhoods than certificate recipients, when desirability is measured by the indices noted above—mean family income of renters, mean family income of owners, unemployment rate of males, average rent, percent of population that is black, percent of units owner-occupied, and the proportion of the population lacking a high school education. When comparing the districts with the largest shares of recipients in both programs, "voucher neighborhoods" have higher mean household incomes than "certificate neighborhoods," as well as lower unemployment rates, higher rents, lower percentages of blacks, higher owner-occupancy rates, and a lower fraction of the population with minimum educational levels.

Regression Models

Thus far, we have compared the neighborhoods with the largest number of program recipients and examined whether particular districts are more likely to have voucher or certificate recipients. A multiple regression model is used to examine which factors are highly correlated with the allocation of vouchers and certificates by locality.

Three equations are estimated: the likelihood of a district having vouchers; the likelihood of a district having certificates; and the difference between the likelihood of a district having vouchers and the likelihood of a district having certificates. The three estimating equations are:

$$(1) \quad \text{Log } V = a_0 + a_1 \text{Inc}(A) + a_2 \text{INC}(B) + a_3 \text{UN} + a_4 \text{Rent} + a_5 \text{Race} + a_6 \text{OCC} + a_7 \text{Ed} + e$$

$$(2) \quad \text{Log } C = b_0 + b_1 \text{Inc}(A) + b_2 \text{INC}(B) + b_3 \text{UN} + b_4 \text{Rent} + b_5 \text{Race} + b_6 \text{OCC} + b_7 \text{Ed} + u$$

$$(3) \quad \text{Log } V - \text{Log } C = (a_0 - b_0) + (a_1 - b_1) \text{Inc}(A) + (a_2 - b_2) \text{Inc}(B) + (a_3 - b_3) \text{UN} + (a_4 - b_4) \text{Rent} + (a_5 - b_5) \text{Race} + (a_6 - b_6) \text{OCC} + (a_7 - b_7) \text{Ed} + (e - u)$$

where

$V = P(\text{Voucher})/[1\text{-}P(\text{Voucher})]$

$C = P(\text{Certificate})/[1\text{-}P(\text{Certificate})]$

The results obtained from estimating these equations are shown in Table 2. The results for Equation (1) suggest that the likelihood of vouchers is

TABLE 2
Regression Results

Variables	Equation 1 Vouchers	T	Equation 2 Certificates	T	Equation 3 Vouchers - Certificate	T
IncA	-0.0000	-0.4639	-0.0001	-1.3887	0.0000	0.2963
IncB	-0.0001	-1.1523	0.0000	-0.0920	-0.0001	-1.3096
UN	-0.3081	-2.5452 *	-0.0075	-0.1207	-0.3006	-2.9428 **
Rent	0.0003	0.0379	0.0051	1.2708	-0.0048	-0.7293
Race	2.7136	3.9419 **	0.7143	2.0187 *	1.9992	3.4418 **
Occ	1.7568	1.7950 *	-0.1296	-0.2576	1.8864	2.2842 *
Edu	7.4666	1.6823	8.1432	3.5691 **	-0.6766	-0.1806
Constant	3.2646		-2.2854		5.5499	
R-Squared	0.5992		0.7612		0.4513	
No. Obs.	26		26		26	

*5 percent level of significance
**1 percent level of significance

explained by Unemployment, Race, and Education. The larger the fraction of blacks within the district the higher are the odds of a district having voucher recipients. As the proportion of people with less than a high school education who are living within the district increases, the higher are the odds of the district having voucher recipients. The variable most difficult to explain is Unemployment. The results suggest that as unemployment increases, the odds of the district having voucher recipients decreases.

The results for Equation (2) suggest that the likelihood of certificates is explained by Race and Education. As the percent of the population that is black increases so do the odds of the district having certificate recipients. And, as the proportion of people with less than a high school education increases so do the odds of a district having certificate holders.

Both equations suggest that black neighborhoods are more likely to have voucher and certificate recipients than white neighborhoods. Do the factors that affect the odds of vouchers within a district affect the odds of certificates within a district, differently? In other words, are the coefficients of the variables statistically significantly different for vouchers and certificates? The third equation helps to answer this question. Given certain assumptions about the structure of the error terms, the coefficients of the variables in the two programs were tested to see if they were statistically different.

The results suggest that the coefficients of unemployment, race, and owner occupancy are statistically significant. Equation (3) supports the view that voucher recipients live in areas with higher rates of owner-occupancy and experience higher employment rates than certificate recipients. The race coefficient suggests that race plays a more significant role in predicting whether a district has voucher recipients than whether a district has certificate recipients.

Average Rent

Our second area of concern is how much rent the recipients of housing vouchers pay relative to recipients of housing certificates. In the housing voucher program there is a potential for recipients to be better off than in the certificate program, if they can locate and lease units with rents less than the FMR. The voucher program has a fixed subsidy amount (FMR minus 30 percent of adjusted income) regardless of the rental price of the unit. Even if the rent on the unit is less than the FMR, recipients still obtain the guaranteed subsidy. If the rental price is less than the FMR, the recipient can use the differential on non-housing goods or use it to lower out-of-pocket housing costs. In the certificate program, the recipient has no incentive to find a unit renting below the FMR. If the rental is below the FMR, then the subsidy is reduced by that amount. Only in the voucher program can a recipient influence his/her out-of-pocket costs for housing.

One way to measure the impact of housing vouchers on black families is to calculate the average out-of-pocket cost for rent (hereinafter referred to as rent burden). This rent burden then can be compared to the rent burden in the housing certificate program. The rent burden of blacks is also compared to that of whites. This measure provides a yardstick for estimating racial differences between the voucher and certificate programs.

The rent burden is calculated as the difference between the actual unit rent and the housing assistance payment. The average rent burden (B) for all recipients is calculated as:

$$B = \frac{\sum_t (\text{Rent}_t - \text{Housing Subsidy}_t)}{t}$$

t = number of individuals in the sample.

To test whether blacks are financially better or worse off in the voucher program than in the certificate program, the average rent burden is calculated for the housing voucher and housing certificate programs by race.[11] The results show that the average rent burdens for blacks are $66 and $67 in the certificate and voucher programs, respectively. Whites, on the other hand, have average rent burdens of $89 and $68 in the certificate and voucher programs, respectively.

The results suggest that whites in Baltimore on average have a higher rent burden than blacks in both the certificate and voucher programs. In the housing voucher program, however, whites' average rent burden is not significantly different from that of blacks. Whites' average rent burden in the certificate program is 35 percent higher than that of blacks. Thus, the main racial difference in rent burden arises in the certificate program.

In terms of out-of-pocket costs, blacks are no better off in the voucher program than they are in the certificate program. Whites, however, are better off in the voucher program. Whites pay an average of 30 percent more in the certificate program than in the voucher program. In the voucher program in Baltimore City, whites have been able to decrease their rent burdens by renting units below the FMR in the voucher program. Although their rent burdens are less than those of whites, blacks, however, have not been able to decrease their rent burdens in a similar manner.

CONCLUSION

The purpose of this study was to examine the impact of the housing voucher program on black families in Baltimore City, Maryland. This impact was measured in two ways. First, the geographic locations of voucher recipients were examined. Second, the out-of-pocket costs of blacks and whites in the housing voucher and housing certificate programs were compared.

In addressing both issues, the regional planning districts where recipients in both the voucher and certificate programs live were characterized. The examination of the districts focused on neighborhood quality. Seven indices of neighborhood quality were used: mean household income of renters, mean household income of owners, male unemployment rate, gross rent, percent of the population that is black, percent of housing units that are owner-occupied, and the proportion of the population with no high school education that reside in the district. The analysis suggests that the higher the percent of the population that is black and the higher the fraction of owner-occupied housing units, the greater the odds of a district having voucher recipients than certificate recipients.

Another interesting indicator of the effect of the housing voucher program on blacks is the out-of-pocket costs or the rent burden for housing. The rent burden was measured as the difference between the rent and the housing subsidy. Our results show that while blacks in Baltimore generally have lower rent burdens than whites, they experience no differential benefits from the housing voucher program compared to the certificate program. Their rent burdens are as great in the voucher program ($66) as they are in the certificate program ($67). In contrast, white recipients can expect to pay 30 percent more in the certificate program ($89) than in the voucher program ($68). If the quality of housing occupied by the different races were the same in both programs, then the conclusion would be that housing vouchers do not improve the economic well-being of blacks.

Some troubling issues must be addressed by policymakers in light of these findings. First, if rent burdens of blacks are as great in the housing voucher program as they are in the certificate program, could this be because of discriminatory practices by landlords? Since we find the rent burden among whites to be considerably lower in the housing voucher program than it is in the certificate program, the specter of racial discrimination in low-income housing indeed arises.

Second, how do these alternatives to public housing contribute to improving the housing status of the recipient populations? At the outset of this study we mentioned the low-quality of housing often found in public housing projects. Can we unequivocally say that the poor are better off now with vouchers or certificates? These questions ought to guide continuing debate about the future of vouchers. The day when society can honestly say that the housing needs of the poor have been met seems very far off. It may be even farther off if we fail to address what appear to be racially unequal impacts of what are purported to be novel alternatives to public housing.

NOTES

This article is based on a paper entitled "The Impact of Housing Vouchers on the Black Family," which was funded by the Baltimore Urban League and presented at the National Conference of Political Scientist, March 1989.

1. U.S. Bureau of the Census, *1980 Census of Population and Housing*, Census Tracts, PHC80-2-28, (July 1983), Baltimore MD, SMSA.
2. Claire Hammond, *The Benefits of Subsidized Housing Programs, An Intertemporal Approach* (Cambridge University Press, 1987).
3. *Housing and Development Reporter*, Vol. 18, No. 12 (August 6, 1990), p. 233.
4. This opinion is expressed by Lowry:

The portability of housing allowances led some observers to speculate that a full-scale program would result in substantial spatial rearrangements of low-income households, particularly those belonging to racial minorities. Some thought that the program would help achieve a desirable pattern of residential integration, dispersing low-income and minority households among more prosperous white neighborhoods. Others worried that participants would abandon deteriorating neighborhoods. . . . Still others were skeptical that the program would much alter the residential distribution of participants. (Ira S. Lowry, *Experimenting with Housing Allowances: The Final Report of the Housing Assistance Supply Experiment* (Oelgeshclager, Gunn & Hain, Publishers, Inc., Cambridge, MA, 1983).

5. Abt Associates Inc., *Participation and Benefits in the Urban Section 8 Program: New Construction and Existing Housing*, Vols. 1 and 2, Contract H-2902, Tasks 5 and 6 (1981).

6. The data is from *Section 8 Housing Programs, A Statistical Bulletin*. Unpublished Statistics, Baltimore Public Housing Authority (August 18, 1988).

7. Participation rate is defined as the number of participants by category divided by the total number of participants in the study.

8. EDUC is defined as the ratio of all in the neighborhood without a high school education to all in the city without a high school education.

9. This hypothesis might be invalidated in a city such as Baltimore that is 55 percent black; here a high percentage of blacks in a neighborhood could be associated with a high quality neighborhood as often as it is with a low quality neighborhood.

10. The data are from the U.S. Bureau of the Census, *County and City Data Book, 1982* (A Statistical Abstract Supplement) (U.S. Government Printing Office: Washington, D.C., 1983.)

11. The data is from *Section 8 Housing Programs, A Statistical Bulletin*, Unpublished Statistics, Baltimore Public Housing Authority (August 18, 1988).

7

URBAN RENEWAL: THE CASE OF BUFFALO, NY

Alfred D. Price

Scholars of urbanism have long been critical of America's post-World War II efforts at urban renewal. What is generally less well understood is the theoretical context out of which urban renewal policy arose.

This analysis sets forth the key precepts of modernist thinking in city planning as the explanation for urban renewal's policy miscalculations. Data for Buffalo document the case, with emphasis upon the exclusion of blacks in the redevelopment process.

Following three decades of failure, 1950 to 1980, a neighborhood-based renewal project is now showing promise in meeting the housing needs of inner-city black households.

This article explores the reasons why urban renewal policy and practice did not result in neighborhood renewal in Buffalo, NY, and, by implication, in other American cities. With the possible exception of the British New Towns Act of 1946, which was intended to rebuild England after the devastation of World War II, never has so massive a program of city building been attempted; yet, urban renewal's record of accomplishment is marred by significant failures. The subject merits the attention of scholars and students of public policy, since federal funding for America's cities remains a subject of public controversy.

Complex historic, economic, and socio-cultural factors all contribute to the explanation of urban renewal's failure. In contrast, a current housing and community renewal experiment in Buffalo is presented as a practical and successful example of what, in retrospect, should have been taking place in American inner cities over two decades ago.

The first section defines what is meant here by ''modernism'' and "postmodernism," and elaborates on the pivotal role this thinking played in shaping urban policy in post-World War II America. The next section discusses urban renewal policy and practice, and enumerates five significant misunderstandings which lead ultimately to its rejection. Thereafter, a capsule history of the City of Buffalo's development is offered, in order to place the last quarter century of its inner-city housing market's changes into perspective. In the next section, attention is focused upon the impacts of urban renewal policies and practices in Buffalo's Ellicott District in the period from 1950 to 1980, to render clearer the reasons for failure of renewal efforts.

Data are presented to document Buffalo's 1950–1980 loss in population due to "white flight" and its simultaneous increase in black population. Differences in household income will illustrate central city blacks' relatively greater poverty, as well as their geographic concentration in the inner city. The critique of public housing policy then takes two forms: the inappropriateness of the physical form of replacement housing stock built under urban renewal in the 1950s and 1960s, and the lack of direct connection between housing policy and the underlying issue of structural poverty.

After charting these policy failures, the Pratt-Willert Village experiment—a publicly-sponsored, deep subsidy, single-family ownership program—is then described as the eventual local alternative to nearly three decades of market stagnation, neighborhood deterioration, and black community frustration. The concluding section attempts some guarded speculation about the applicability of such an approach to communities with similar circumstances in other cities.

MODERNISM, POST-MODERNISM, AND CITIES

An important element of the line of reasoning developed in this treatment of urban renewal concerns its historic relationship to early twentieth century thought about urban development. The "modern period" in city planning falls roughly between 1890 and 1945, and thought in this period led city planners to what William Alonzo calls "top down technical solutions."[1] Modernism, he argues quite rightly, excluded the views and opinions of those most directly affected by urban renewal in the decades following the war: the poor and increasingly black residents of inner cities.

Modernist thinking in city planning by and large embraced industrialization and the machine age, placing faith in new materials, technologies, and the then-futuristic visions of the good life that these developments held out as possible.[2] Anything old, including styles of architecture, was to be discarded in favor of the products of the scientific method of problem-solving. The significance of such thinking for housing design and city planning is captured in the fact that the "social sciences" achieved academic respectability in this same period of time. A remarkably rich range of city planning schemes and dreams were generated in the brief period from 1890 to 1945.[3] Of all these plans, those of Le Corbusier can be classified as the most radical manifesto, because of his proposal to demolish entire sections of cities, reconstructing them with modern skyscrapers.

Modernist theory was propelled into practice following World War II, and is reflected in the Housing Act of 1949 which established urban renewal. Indeed, urban renewal may be viewed as the first attempt of any modern democratic political state to advance a social reform package, albeit one cloaked in the veneer of economic development.

One of the urban renewal program's main goals was the eradication of the slums in American cities. Alonzo notes:

Slums, often likened to cancerous growths, were not just the place where "social pathology" abounded: They were themselves the source of this pathology. The idea behind urban renewal was that improving these places would improve the physical and moral caliber of their dwellers.

The problem with this was, of course, that urban renewal improved an area and reduced its poverty, health, and crime rate by razing it and rebuilding it for a "better class of people." Planners, trained to think in terms of sites and projects, judged improvement by geographical areas rather than by groups of people.

A second source of planners' intellectual deformity stemmed from what little sociology they were taught. This was a warmed-over version of the Chicago sociology of the 1920's, which had adopted many of its ideas from European sociologists of the previous generation. Planners had been taught that people in slums suffered from anomie and disorientation: that what values they had differed from those of society in general; that the slums had no "social organization." Therefore, top-down technical solutions seemed natural to urban planners, and consultation with the residents was viewed as unnecessary."[4]

In this regard, more recent developments may be properly referred to as "post-modern" to the extent that they embrace the interests and circumstances of the people being served. Historian Charles A. Jencks has argued that modernism ends, and the post-modern period officially begins, in 1972, at the precise instant when the wrecker's first dynamite charge was detonated to level the Pruitt-Igoe public housing project in St. Louis.[5] The inner-city riots of the late 1960s might well be seen as the first mass action against modernism. The point to be stressed here is that modernist city plans of an extraordinary scale were being envisioned, and in the case of urban renewal carried out, without so much as comment on, much less participation in, their formulation by those persons most directly affected by them. The contrast between pre-World War II and postwar public housing efforts highlights the postmodern critique of urban renewal.

The construction of pre-World War II housing constituted social and economic policy, as much as it did housing policy. The poor, economically displaced by the Depression, were hired to build units in which they could then afford to live. Physical design of these projects reflected the assumption that as the American economy improved, families in public housing would reenter the mainstream. The public role was to subsidize the cost of building what would today be called "garden apartments" for what was then a largely poor white inner-city population. For them, public policy on jobs and employment, income maintenance, and housing all came together.

In contrast, public housing in postwar America can be demonstrated to bear little relationship to the needs and interests of those being housed. Under urban renewal, there was no concerted effort to coordinate public works jobs for inner-city residents being displaced by slum clearance. While the sanitization of the slums may arguably be reckoned to have been in the best interests of all social classes, the type and style of replacement stock built under urban renewal made no reference to the life styles or preferences of poor and increasingly black inner-city housing consumers. Uncoordinated with other forms of social policy, the housing built under urban renewal was not only physically unsuitable, it left the poor locked in a continuing cycle of poverty and public dependency.

The popular voice was not recognized formally via mandatory community participation in federally-sponsored projects until nearly two full decades of disastrous public housing efforts following World War II. Insofar as American society is predicated upon and espouses the ideal of social equality, policies aimed at promoting public well-being must ultimately address the economic enfranchisement of the poor. In housing policy, as John F. Bauman has noted in his recent book on urban renewal in Philadelphia, this must mean more than simply "warehousing" people;[6] yet that, in large measure, is what urban renewal did.

URBAN RENEWAL'S FIVE MISUNDERSTANDINGS

Urban renewal is not a topic that receives much praise from a minority perspective. As a characterization of the slum clearance practices carried out pursuant to the federal Housing Acts of 1949 and 1954, urban renewal has been dubbed "Negro removal" by authors whose work has appeared in this journal,[7] among other places. Certainly, there is evidence to support this interpretation of the historical facts. But as seasoned housing practitioners such as Edward J. Logue are quick to point out, American urban renewal legislation represented potentially the most powerful kit of public policy tools for city-building anywhere in the country in this century. What was done with those tools is another matter. Demolition, though painful, was efficient. Renewal, it will be argued here, was both economically wasteful and politically excruciating, in that it excluded the interests of black community residents in the name of modernization.

Five important misunderstandings within the modernist ethos of urban renewal doomed the policy and practice to failure in city after city in America. First, as Barnett pointed out in *The Elusive City*,[8] public officials misunderstood or miscalculated the impact of the automobile on the urban formation. He also argued, quite rightly, that zoning—the major means of controlling development in the public's interest—was ill-equipped to handle the very tall buildings that modern technology had made possible.

Second, paralleling these misunderstandings, policy-makers tended to over-value centrally located urban land. A key notion in both Burgess'[9] and Hoyt's[10] work on urban land value structure was that prime development land was centrally located, i.e., in or proximate to downtown central business districts. Just four years prior to the passage of the Housing Act of 1949, Harris and Ullman[11] were calling attention to the centrifugal, outward development pressures that would transform metropolitan land value structure; but their work was still too new to inform policy choices. As an example, the City of Buffalo was re-zoned for higher central city density at the start of the urban renewal era in 1953,[12] based upon an assumption of continued population growth in the city which, of course, later proved to be erroneous.

A third misunderstanding was the unforeseen impact of the virtual revolution in electronic telecommunications technology beginning at mid-century. This transformed both the ways and the places in which America did business, and correspondingly influenced where people chose to live. Policy-makers of the 1950s, looking backwards at the preceding five decades, bet their money on continued growth in city population, while technical innovations such as radio, telephone, television, and computers were supporting development outwards on cheaper suburban land, rather than upwards on mistakenly overvalued city sites.

The fourth misunderstanding that misguided urban renewal policy stemmed from the vast revisions to the system of providing home mortgages that had been implemented as a result of the National Housing Act of 1934, which created the FHA. As urban historian Robert Fishman points out in *Bourgeois Utopia: The Rise and Fall of Suburbia*, ". . . insured mortgages of up to 90 percent of [home] value . . . rationalized the crazy quilt structure of mortgage financing left over from the 1920's."[13] That cities (whose dense neighborhoods would have to be demolished before they could be rebuilt) thought they could compete with suburbs (where demolition was unnecessary) for development investment and mortgage financing was a serious miscalculation of market perceptions and development timing, if not of actual cost.[14] Of the rapid emergence of post-World War II automobile suburbs, Fishman writes, "For a brief moment modernist architecture, populist aspirations, and the requirements of the market came together."[15]

But fifth, and most significant for the purposes of this analysis, the persistent and increasingly vitriolic strain of racism in the American character was ignored. Then, as now, Americans were uncomfortable acknowledging the existence of racism, because such ugliness runs contrary to the mythology of the pluralist, egalitarian ethic upon which the nation was founded. As Bauman documented so persuasively in *Housing, Race and Renewal*,[16] the importance of race as a determining factor in the failure of America's attempts at a housing and community renewal policy must not be underestimated. Racism was the crucial variable in the equation of urban renewal, and misunderstanding it cemented the program's fate.

Moreover, little recognition was accorded to the wholesale destruction of the neighborhood markets upon which existing commercial development depended. As residents relocated, so did the commercial, institutional and other developments that had served them. By the time replacement housing was built, these supports for residential life had followed their markets out of central neighborhoods such as Buffalo's Ellicott District to other city neighborhoods. The dense concentrations of the poor in high-rise urban renewal public housing projects built as replacement stock did little to attract commercial development back to the inner-city.

Simultaneous with the changes wrought by urban renewal inside the city were several other key developments that fostered metropolitan decentralization. Passage of the Highway Trust Fund Act in 1946, initially intended to create the federal interstate highway system, led very quickly to inner-city expressways and loop roads to facilitate intra-metropolitan automobile commuter traffic. In addition, the 1948 amendment to the Internal Revenue Service Code permitting the deductibility of interest on home mortgage loans created the largest housing subsidy program in America's history[17] (although the middle and upper classes who most benefit from it choose not to view it as a public subsidy).

The first four policy miscalculations noted above, taken together with federal highway and tax policies, would seem a sufficient set of preconditions to cause any housing consumer to leave the inner city. But the key ingredient in white flight to the suburbs in response to urban renewal was the attempt to escape from the perceived evils of city life so convincingly documented by Fishman in *Bourgeois Utopia*. Central to this analysis of the urban renewal era is that one of the perceived evils of city life was the ever more pressing prospect for whites in the 1950s and 1960s of living next door to "them," i.e. the black inner-city families displaced by slum clearance.

BUFFALO: FROM INDUSTRIAL PROMINENCE TO ECONOMIC DEPENDENCE

Buffalo should not escape close investigation as an object of scholarly inquiry by those interested in rebuilding American cities. It has been labeled both a rustbelt and a frostbelt city, and data in this analysis on industrial decline and regional outmigration certainly support the former characterization. Popular impression and geographic location support the latter.

Buffalo's housing market characteristics show evidence of the area's industrial and working class heritage. Its decline from a place of national economic pre-eminence to its present position of relative regional dependency within the national and international economy has been well-documented by others.[18]

Population

When Buffalo was incorporated as a city in 1832, its recorded population was about 10,000 persons, almost exclusively of European descent, who had migrated along the route of the Erie Canal (authorized in 1817; opened for operations in 1825). Its late nineteenth century industrial prominence was led by grain milling, situated as it was between the agricultural heartland of the midwest and major market centers in the east. Industrial growth swelled the city's population to 352,000 by the year 1900, the same year that the population of Los Angeles reached only the 10,000 mark. Most of this increase was the result of the two waves of European immigration in the nineteenth century. Continued industrial growth as a processing center for bulk commodities, including ore refining, milling and metal fabrication, fueled population increases through the mid-twentieth century. City population climbed to a high of 580,000 by 1950, in a metropolitan region of about a million people.

Population statistics for the City of Buffalo chart its growth and eventual decline. (See Table 1.) From 1900 to 1950, total population and total households increased, and thereafter show evidence of the process of decentralization. Comparing population data for the city to the urbanized county in which it is located shows evidence between 1950 and 1970 of city out-migration to surrounding suburbs, which was in part the direct result of urban renewal policies and practices of the 1950s and 1960s. After 1970, population loss is evident both in the city and county, and is better explained by interregional population shifts throughout the United States as a whole, as a response to the Buffalo area's lagging regional economy.

Because it represents historically the heart of Buffalo's black community, the Ellicott Councilmanic District is used throughout as a means of comparing data for blacks and whites on population change, housing, and income characteristics of the population. Ellicott District data also help to clarify the arguments advanced herein concerning urban renewal policies, as this district was the primary target of local urban slum clearance and renewal efforts in the 1950s and 1960s. Data from selected census tracts representing the core of Ellicott are presented for comparison with city-wide data, and data for Erie County (which represents the bulk of the urbanized region).

TABLE 1
Population by Race

	1950		1960		1970		1980	
	Number	Percent[1]	Number	Percent[1]	Number	Percent[1]	Number	Percent[1]
Erie Co. (incl. city)	899,238	100.0	1,064,688	100.0	1,113,843	100.0	1,015,472	100.0
White	856,212	95.2	985,443	92.5	1,006,843	90.4	893,195	87.9
Black (inside city)	36,635	4.1	70,904	6.7	94,329	8.5	95,116	9.4
Black (outside city)	3,707	0.4	3,976	0.4	4,909	0.4	7,831	0.7
Buffalo City	580,132	100.0	532,759	100.0	462,768	100.0	357,870	100.0
White	542,432	93.5	459,371	86.2	364,367	78.7	252,365	70.5
Black	36,645	6.3	70,904	13.3	94,329	20.4	95,116	26.6
Ellicott District	73,341	100.0	53,272	100.0	36,691	100.0	19,025	100.0
White	43,978	59.9	21,095	39.6	7,807	21.3	3,257	17.1
Black	28,945[2]	39.5	31,867	59.8	28,597	77.9	15,104	79.4

[1] Percentage figures will not total 100.0 because minorities other than blacks are not presented in this analysis. Such minorities comprise so small a fraction of total population (only 2% of the county and less than 3% of the city in 1980) that they need not be considered in this analysis of Buffalo.

[2] Blacks in Ellicott in 1950 accounted for 78.9% of Buffalo's total blacks and 71.7% of Erie County's black population; in 1960, 44.9% and 42.6% respectively; in 1970; 30.3% and 28.8%; and in 1980, 15.9% and 14.7%.

Source: U.S. Department of Commerce, Bureau of the Census, United States Census of Housing: 1950, Volume V, Part 24, ''Buffalo, New York Block Statistics.'' For 1960–1980, ''Census of Population and Housing,'' unless otherwise indicated.

Employment and Income

The Western New York region did not fare well in what would later come to be known as the post-industrial era following World War II. Automation of basic industrial processes eliminated jobs; and the lack of true economic base diversification, coupled with out-of-town ownership and control, left the resident population at the mercy of the long-term shifts in the national economy as a whole.

Taking the flour-milling industry as but one of several key local industrial sectors, statistics on milled grain output in Buffalo from 1935 to 1975 show little more than minor cyclical variation, with the exception of temporary World War II-era increases. However, employment in that industry in the same period dropped from over 2,000 to about 200. In more recent years, 1974 to 1984, analysis of the local steel milling sector illustrates further the pattern of job loss in basic industries. In that sector during those years, a total of 19,914 permanent jobs were lost, a decade-long reduction of over three-quarters of that sector's labor force.[19]

The black community's growth and development, and decline and change, track closely the city's economic patterns. Following nineteenth century "Emancipation" and Reconstruction, Buffalo, like other northern cities, came to represent a desirable destination for black migration from the rural south,[20] well into the middle of the twentieth century. However, opportunities for industrial employment for blacks (largely unskilled or semiskilled workers) slowed appreciably in the post-World War II period, markedly reducing their income-earning options. (See Table 2.)

Blacks' settlement in Buffalo in significant numbers followed World War II, and the mid-twentieth century declines in industrial employment opportunity. In comparison to other ethnic groups, this meant that they faced tougher circumstances in housing markets. Locational choices were constrained—both by income levels and by historic racial discrimination—to the oldest residential areas of the city, primarily the Ellicott Councilmanic District, in neighborhoods immediately east of the downtown central business district. It was here that some of the oldest housing stock in the city existed, and its age was a good surrogate for condition. The map below illustrates that Buffalo's ethnic neighborhoods were clearly identifiable from one another. The Ellicott District's location can be identified in the same illustration. (See Figures 1A and 1B.)

TABLE 2
Median Household Income by Race

	1950	1960	% Change '50-'60	1970	% Change '60-'70	1980	% Change '70-'80
Erie Co.	$3,206	$5,649	76.2	$8,769	55.2	$17,119	95.2
Black	N.A.	$3,368	----	$5,375	59.5	$ 8,573	59.4
Black/All	----	0.59		0.61		0.50	
Buffalo, City	$3,079	$4,817	56.4	$6,568	36.3	$11,593	76.5
Black	N.A.	$3,351	----	$5,307	58.3	$ 8,992	69.4
Black/All	----	0.69		0.80		0.70	
Ellicott	$2,253	$2,871	27.4	$3,383	17.8	$ 5,843	72.7
Black	$1,927	$2,775	44.0	$3,428	23.5	$ 5,725	67.0
Black/All	0.85[1]	0.96[2]		1.01[2]		0.97[2]	

[1] The relative parity in household incomes for blacks and whites in Ellicott in 1950 is explained by the black community being more racially concentrated despite income and social class distinctions, a function of both historic discrimination, household location preference, and the fact that urban renewal and slum clearance had not yet begun (See Figures 2a, 2b, 2c).

[2] Improvements in income parity are explained by a black middle class dispersal that occurs after and is slower than white flight, and by the very low incomes of whites remaining in Ellicott as it is subjected to slum clearance and urban renewal.

Source: U.S. Census Bureau

FIGURE 1A
Buffalo's Ethnic Heritage, 1920

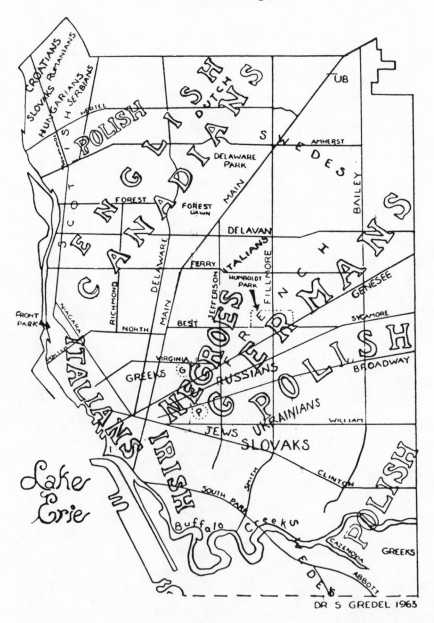

Source: S. Gredel, *Pioneers of Buffalo* (Buffalo Council of Human Relations, 1963).

FIGURE 1B
Buffalo's Minor Civil Jurisdictions

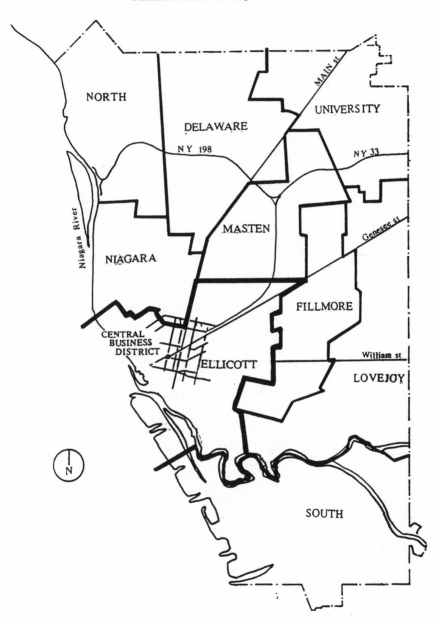

Source: Office of the President, Buffalo Common Council

Buffalo's Inner-City Black Community

The statistics on Buffalo's black population in the urban renewal era, 1950–1980, are noteworthy. Beginning in 1960, blacks show large increases when expressed as a percentage of total, but relatively small absolute increases. These data support the observation that black in-migration slowed in the post-World War II period, as economic opportunities declined. The percentage increases in the black population of the city between 1960 and 1980 are more a function of decreases in white population than of black growth.

Data on population by household groupings show similar trends, with some variation. Between 1970 and 1980, the city's loss in total population accompanied by an increase in households for Erie County is explained by a larger number of single-person households at several age levels: younger persons deferring marriage, married couple households subdividing as a result of the increased divorce rate, and an aging populace. Comparing the loss of white households to that of blacks in Ellicott is certainly indicative of "white flight," since white households continue to decline in the city while increasing in the county after 1960. What is also interesting is that black households increase from 1950 to 1970, but decline from 1970 to 1980. As noted in the following section on Ellicott, this is evidence of the continued overall devaluation of Ellicott's neighborhoods in response to urban renewal policies. (See Table 3.)

The relatively greater parity of black to white household incomes in the City of Buffalo as compared to Erie County is explained by "white flight" to suburban jurisdictions beginning in the mid-1950s. County-wide income data lead the city's figures since they include all suburban jurisdictions. Data for Ellicott, the historic heart of Buffalo's black community, are interesting for several reasons. First, household income figures document both the neighborhood's true poverty in relation to the rest of the region; and second, they illustrate the greater poverty of blacks there than in the rest of the city.

More interesting, when black household income is expressed as a ratio of all households' incomes, the Ellicott data show incomes of blacks approaching and then exceeding incomes for all households by 1970 and declining thereafter. This is explained by two facts: (1) the whites remaining in Ellicott were the poorest of poor whites who lacked the resources to relocate, and (2) vestiges of a proud and committed middle-income black community of business owners and residents who chose to stay and fight for their neighborhood's future (see notes to Table 2).

TABLE 3
Households by Race

	1950		1960		1970		1980	
	Number	Percent[1]	Number	Percent[1]	Number	Percent[1]	Number	Percent[1]
Erie Co.	252,247	100.0	316,460	100.0	346,374	100.0	365,217	100.0
White	242,794	96.2	294,137	92.6	313,122	90.4	323,038	88.4
Black	9,453	3.7	21,058	6.6	29,308	8.5	36,424	9.9
Buffalo City	164,685	100.0	169,086	100.0	157,951	100.0	140,954	100.0
White	156,292	94.9	148,772	87.9	128,256	81.2	103,654	73.5
Black	8,393	5.0	19,717	11.6	27,961	17.7	34,049	24.5
Ellicott	18,445	100.0	16,422	100.0	12,229	100.0	7,710	100.0
White	11,865	64.3	7,364	44.8	3,118	25.4	1,006	13.0
Black	6,580	35.6	8,976	54.6	9,018	73.7	6,086	78.9

[1] Percentage figures will not total exactly 100.0 due to rounding, as well as the presence of a small number of nonwhite households other than black.
Source: U.S. Census Bureau

BUFFALO'S ELLICOTT DISTRICT

In 1950, blacks in the Ellicott core accounted for over three-quarters of Buffalo's black population. A decade later in 1960, Ellicott still was home to nearly half of the city's black population (44.9%); and as recently as two decades ago, close to one-third of all blacks in Buffalo lived in the same core neighborhoods. But during the same period, while Erie County experienced net growth of 12 percent, overall City of Buffalo population losses were extraordinary. Still, the 74 percent population loss in Ellicott over the thirty-year study interval is almost exactly double the city's 38 percent loss rate.

The maps illustrating the changes in the geographic distribution of Buffalo's black households between 1960 and 1980 document the foregoing arguments (see Figures 2A, 2B, and 2C). As the demolition of inner-city neighborhoods proceeded in Ellicott, blacks relocated first north and then eastward. Certainly this represented an expansion of housing location opportunities for blacks within the city, albeit fueled by the prior relocation of white households outside the city's boundaries. With the exception of public housing projects, Ellicott remained undeveloped for the better part of two decades, its vacant blocks in some cases not more than five minutes' walk from the heart of the downtown central business district.

Table 4 documents both the low density pattern on which the Buffalo region is developed as well as the city's housing stock loss over the period under analysis. Although prior to 1960, the United States Census distinguished only single-family homes from multiple dwellings, Buffalo can be seen as a city of essentially one-family homes and two-flat dwellings. Note that while Erie County shows nearly a doubling of its single family stock from 1950 to 1980, within the city, losses in stock are registered in every dwelling size category. This is de facto evidence of both extensive slum clearance in older inner city neighborhoods in Ellicott, as well as extensive "spot demolitions" in adjacent areas.

The impact of slum clearance and urban renewal in Buffalo was a mixed blessing at best for the black community. As the data in Tables 5 and 6 illustrate, home ownership among blacks certainly increased between 1950 and 1970. To the extent that ownership represents increased economic enfranchisement, it might be viewed as a positive sign from the black perspective. But one is compelled to ask, "Ownership of what?" In that connection, data in Table 6 document for black owners in Ellicott that while their incomes increase over time, the rate of income growth

FIGURE 2A
Distribution of Black Population, 1960

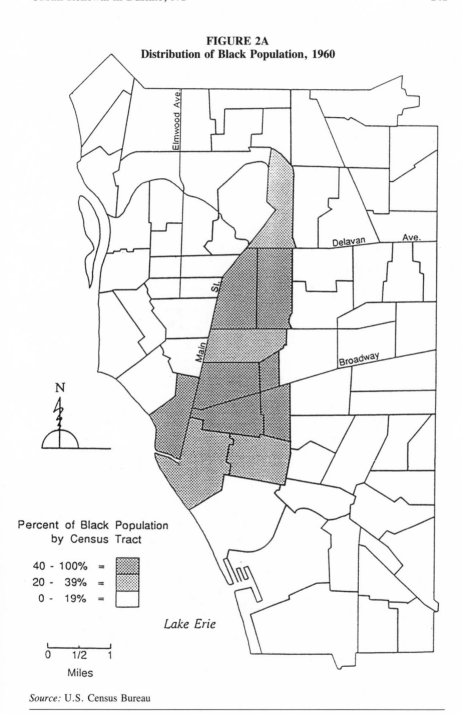

Percent of Black Population
by Census Tract

40 - 100% =
20 - 39% =
0 - 19% =

Lake Erie

0   1/2   1
Miles

Source: U.S. Census Bureau

FIGURE 2B
Distribution of Black Population, 1970

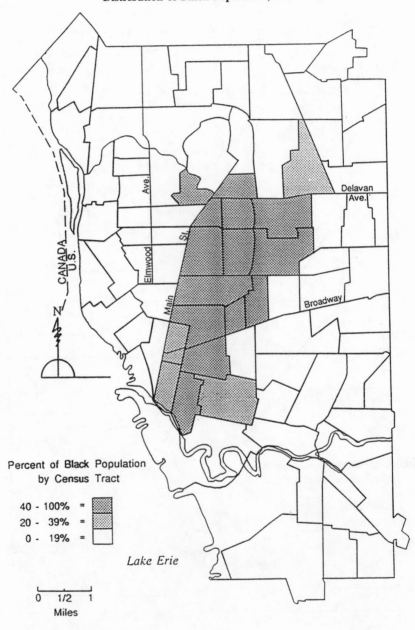

Source: U.S. Census Bureau

FIGURE 2C
Distribution of Black Population, 1980

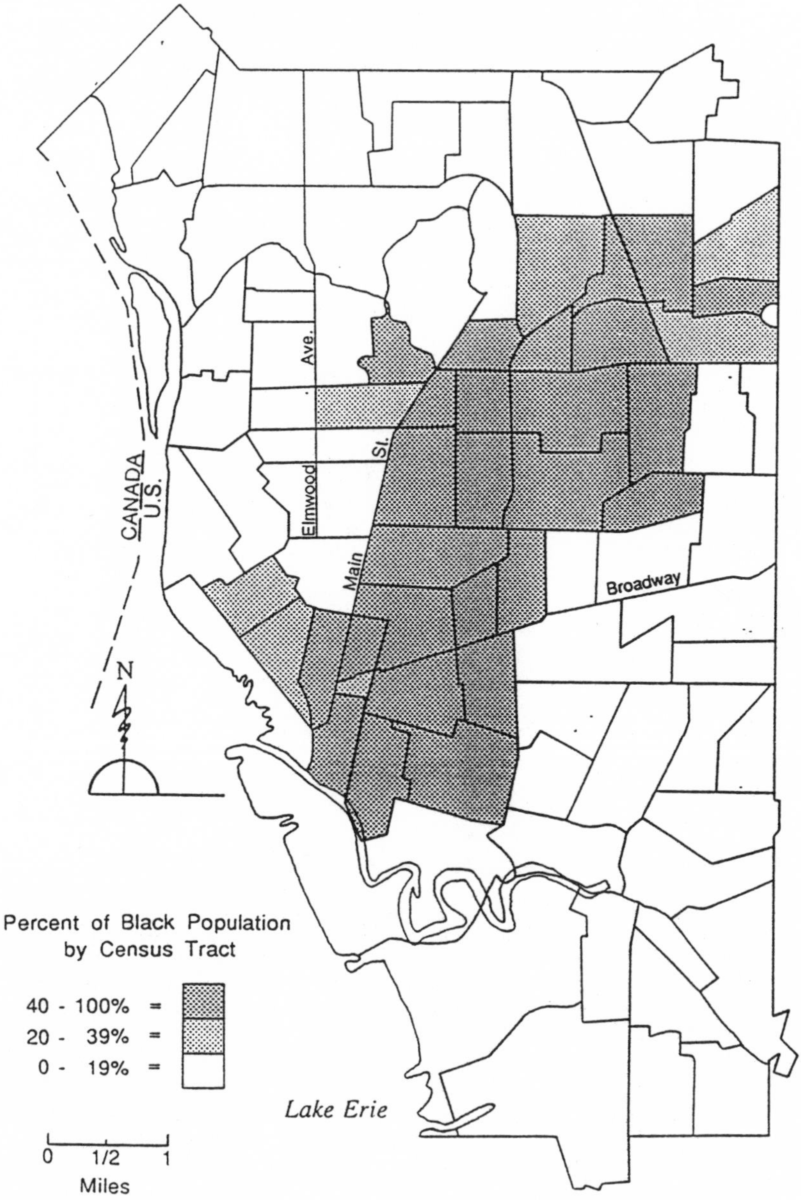

Percent of Black Population
by Census Tract

40 - 100% =
20 - 39% =
0 - 19% =

0   1/2   1
Miles

Lake Erie

Ave.

St.

Elmwood

Main

Broadway

CANADA
U.S.

N

Source: U.S. Census Bureau

TABLE 4
Dominant Type Housing Stock

	1950[1]	1960	1970	1980
Erie Co.				
Single Family	108,194	177,858	188,695	206,845
Two-Family		96,685	105,661	101,148
3-4 Unit	152,963	32,606	33,551	32,364
5+ Unit		27,743	31,477	44,012
Total Dwellings	261,157	334,892	359,384	384,369
Buffalo City				
Single Family	45,252	50,189	45,103	44,376
Two-Family		79,554	76,937	70,745
3-4 Unit	121,491	23,277	21,919	18,780
5+ Unit		24,190	22,147	22,471
Total Dwellings	166,743	177,210	166,106	156,372
Ellicott				
Single Family	12,689	3,601	2,463	2,281
Two-Family		5,880	4,806	3,105
3-4 Unit	5,975	3,426	2,620	1,339[2]
5+ Unit		5,184	3,961	3,532
Total Dwellings	18,664	18,091	13,850	10,257

[1] In 1950, the only distinction made by the Census Bureau was between single family units and "Multiple Dwellings."
[2] Greatest losses in stock were in larger three-and four-unit structures that had in earlier years been subdivided or built onto, in order to provide supplemental rental income. Three- and four-unit structures declined 61% in the two-decade period from 1960 to 1980, with two-unit structures declining 47%. The loss in number of units in structures with five or more apartments is only 31%, surprisingly below the single family loss rate of 36%. This is due in large measure to construction of new public housing units in high-rise, high density projects.
Source: U.S. Census Bureau

among whites in the city and suburbs is far higher. By 1980, the value of ownership housing in Ellicott was only half that of the city as a whole, and only one quarter of median value county-wide.

The data in Table 6 on home value show Ellicott consistently below city and county figures, evidence that what blacks own is worth substan-

TABLE 5
City Home Ownership Rate by Race

	1950	1960	1970	1980
Buffalo City				
No. Renters	92,964	4,241	88,498	78,240
No. Owners	71,721	74,845	69,453	62,714
Ownership Rate	43.55%	44.26%	43.9%	44.5%
Buffalo City White Households				
No. Renters	86,472	79,534	67,683	53,098
No. Owners	69,820	69,835	61,104	50,556
White Ownership Rate	44.7%	44.6%	47.4%	48.8%
Buffalo City Black Households				
No. Renters	6,492	14,707[1]	19,794	22,583
No. Owners	1,901	5,010[1]	8,169	11,466
Black Ownership Rate	22.6%	25.4%	29.2%	33.7%
Black Households As Percent of Total				
Renters	6.98%	15.6%	22.4%	28.9%
Owners	2.65%	6.7%	11.8%	18.3%
Black Households in Ellicott				
No. of Renters	5,344	7,494	7,583	5,019
No. of Owners	1,147	1,482	1,510	1,125
Black Renters as % of				
All Renters	38.1%	58.1%	77.7%	83.7%
Black Owners as % of				
All Owners	25.9%	42.0%	61.1%	65.5%

[1] This statistic is recorded as "Non-white" for 1960 and earlier. Non-black minorities constitute a negligible fraction of total for Buffalo.
Source: U.S. Census Bureau

tially less than is true for other groups. Value-to-income ratio data illustrate the generally depressed housing market in the City of Buffalo compared to suburban Erie County. This is the result of de-industrialization and accompanying regional out-migration of population. For Ellicott, the value-to-income ratio data indicate the virtual "rock bottom" market

TABLE 6
Home Ownership Burden:
Ratio of Median Value Owner-Occupied Housing to Median Income

	1950	1960	1970	1980
Median Value Own-Occ. Housing				
Erie Co.	$9,835	$15,000	$18,500	$40,100
Buffalo, City	$8,816	$11,700	$12,800	$22,300
Ellicott	$4,454	$ 7,100	$ 6,500	$11,100[1]
Median Household Income (Fam & Unrel)				
Erie Co.	$3,206	$5,649	$8,769	$17,119
Buffalo, City	$3,079	$4,817	$6,568	$11,593
Ellicott	$2,253	$2,871	$3,383	$ 5,843
Value/Income Ratio				
Erie Co.	3.06	2.65	2.10	2.34
Buffalo, City	2.86	2.42	1.94	1.92
Ellicott	1.97	2.47	1.92	1.89

[1] N.B. While between 1960 and 1970, Buffalo area prices lagged behind national norms, they show signs of starting to catch up by 1970 and 1980. But in Ellicott they drop between 1960 and 1970, and then jump sharply in 1980. An apparent "dummy" variable of $10,000 appears for all tracts in Ellicott except 25.01, where the median value of homes is listed as $18,800—a whopping 88% higher than ownership housing in all other tracts in Ellicott. This extraordinary threefold increase in ownership home values in 1980 in one small part of Ellicott is attributable to public property takings in anticipation of the Elm-Oak "Hi-Tech" commercial corridor redevelopment.
Source: U.S. Census Bureau

position of ownership housing in the district. With the exception of 1960, the data for Ellicott indicate that home values had little room to fall. In nominal dollars, home values in Ellicott failed to appreciate at the same rates as city- and county-wide medians.

Data in Table 7 comparing rent burdens for Ellicott residents to the rest of the city and county from 1950 to 1980 show similar patterns. Although rents increase for everyone throughout the period under study, higher incomes of suburban whites in Erie County indicate that in 1980 they paid smaller fractions of income for rent than in 1950. City-wide percentages are comparatively stable over time. But in Ellicott, as rents increase without incomes keeping pace, rent burdens increase significantly.

Urban renewal in Buffalo, thus, meant several things, all of them interrelated. First, middle-income whites left the city to relocate in sur-

TABLE 7
Rent Burden:
Ratio of Annualized Median Contract Rent to Median Income

	1950	1960	1970[1]	1980
Median Rents				
Erie Co.	$ 396	$ 696	$ 912	$ 1,860
Buffalo, City	$ 384	$ 660	$ 840	$ 1,608
Ellicott	$ 293	$ 552	$ 756	$ 1,308
Median Income				
Erie Co.	$3,206	$5,649	$8,769	$17,119
Buffalo, City	$3,079	$4,817	$6,568	$11,593
Ellicott	$2,253	$2,871	$3,383	$ 5,843
Rent/Income				
Erie Co.	0.1235	0.1232	0.1040	0.1086
Buffalo, City	0.1247	0.1370	0.1278	0.1387
Ellicott	0.1300	0.1923	0.2234	0.2238

[1] Prior to 1970, Median Income was reported only as "Families and Unrelated Individuals." This category was split beginning in 1970 into "Families," and "Families and Unrelated Individuals," with income of intact families not surprisingly exceeding that of "Families and Unrelated Individuals." To maintain integrity of comparisons, figures for "Families and Unrelated Individuals" for 1970 and 1980 are used here.
Source: U.S. Census Bureau

rounding suburban jurisdictions, leaving behind less affluent blacks as greater percentage contributors to, or dependents upon, the city's declining tax base. Second, while white flight opened up other city neighborhoods as choices of residential location for blacks (and indeed, they did relocate between 1950 and 1970), the housing circumstances of blacks compared to whites showed little improvement.

In summary, the outcome of urban renewal in Buffalo's Ellicott community was that blacks gained an increased economic share in neighborhoods of rapidly declining value.

A CRITIQUE OF SOCIAL HOUSING DESIGN IN BUFFALO

To better understand the dynamics of Buffalo's housing market and the place of public housing within it, it is important to point to three features of the local housing market which mark Buffalo as a crossroads city

between the east coast and the midwest: (1) the preponderance of single
and two-family detached dwellings which have always dominated its
market; (2) the absence of the rowhouse or townhouse physical form that
is so common to northeastern American cities with similar social and
economic histories; and (3) the "softness"[21] of the local market, as
reflected in sales prices well below national and northeast regional norms.[22]

Data on loss of housing stock are particularly revealing for Ellicott (see
Table 4, above). The city's 6.2 percent overall reduction in stock pales in
comparison to Ellicott's 45 percent loss. While nearly 5,000 units of
single family housing were added to Buffalo's total stock between 1950
and 1960, single family units in Ellicott dropped from 12,689 to only
3,601. This precipitous decline in single family units in a single decade
documents how massively Buffalo's slum clearance program was concentrated in the black community. The increasing fraction of Ellicott's
housing stock accounted for by structures containing five or more dwelling units is explained by the fact that more new public housing units were
built in Ellicott than in any other district of the city.

The construction of the ill-fated Dante Place, the Commodore Perry
Extension, the Ellicott Mall, and the Talbert Mall (now Frederick Douglas Towers) provided over 3,500 units of new public housing in the
period 1950–1970. For years after their completions, these eight-story
structures stood naked in the blocks leveled by urban renewal. Their
particular physical form is adapted directly from the modernist concep-
tions of Le Corbusier, as was the notion of broad-scale demolitions which
made way for them. The poor, of course, had not been asked if high-rise
was their preferred choice of housing accommodation; and many of the
poor in-migrants from the rural South who became public housing tenants
were altogether unaccustomed to dwellings removed from the true ground
plane.

Unlike the public housing projects built pursuant to the Housing Act of
1937, these postwar urban renewal projects were not designed for a
temporarily indigent white working and middle class. Gone was any
semblance of a front door or street address that was the resident's own,
as was any "sense of the street" across which one greeted neighbors.
Gone were the laundry drying yards, the easily supervisable tot lots and
playgrounds. Gone, too, was any connection to semiprivate open space,
what Oscar Newman later called "defensible space."[23] The high-rises
became a management nightmare almost as soon as they were constructed. Some in Buffalo, mirroring Pruitt-Igoe in St. Louis, were never

more than 54 percent occupied, since even the poor refused to live in them. But unlike the St. Louis case, in Buffalo's Ellicott District they were not demolished. Today, most are vacant and boarded up and are being maintained at an annual aggregate cost to the city in excess of $2.5 million.

As the regional economy of Western New York declined between 1960 and 1980, Buffalo became a "soft" real estate market. As an illustration of how soft inner-city urban renewal neighborhoods became, a comprehensive 1973 study conducted by the Greater Buffalo Development Foundation[24] found local land values peaking at $75.00 per square foot in the downtown Central Business District, while falling to zero in Ellicott's residential neighborhoods only a few blocks east. The same study noted that residential land values in the wealthiest Buffalo neighborhoods reached $5.00 per foot, averaging $0.65–$0.99 for all residential areas in the city. However, in Ellicott residential land values ranged only from $0.00– $0.29.

Local housing officials tried experiment after experiment in Ellicott to stimulate housing construction, mostly low-rise walk-up rentals such as Town Gardens. Each such attempt failed to trigger the hoped-for wider market response needed for community renewal. This was due largely to the huge negative economic externalities imposed on development sites by the surrounding vacant blocks, coupled with the stigma of dense concentrations of public housing projects.

With the passage of the Housing and Community Development Act of 1974, in the then vastly decimated and depopulated Ellicott District of Buffalo, greater local autonomy over development policy translated into a local non-black political majority voting to allocate federal block grant funds to job-creating downtown commercial revitalization projects and away from neighborhood housing. The fact that the Ellicott District encompassed both the city's most abandoned residential neighborhoods and the central business district eventually worked against neighborhood renewal interests, since formula-based funds were too easily diverted from neighborhood housing to downtown commercial projects.

During the period from 1970 to 1980, persistent efforts by the city to negotiate a federal or state takeover of the vacant high-rise, high-density public housing projects in Ellicott met with continued rejection. Round after round of talks, reported in the local press, deteriorated into finger-pointing and blame-laying exercises, with all public parties to such discussions seeking to minimize their own culpability. In the meantime, the neighborhood organizations that had been created by Model Cities program legislation of the 1960s were whip-sawed between the polarities of several no-win situations.

Along one axis of the debate over neighborhood renewal, the black community saw the federal authorities as the perpetrators of the cruel destruction of their community, but their only likely salvation from the perceived narrow-minded racism of local officials. Along a cross-axis to this debate, the black community saw its aspirations out of poverty being dependent upon public largesse (meaning, in pertinent part, some form of social housing), yet the community residents rejected the dreaded housing projects as a solution.

Eventually, by the early 1980s the neighborhood organizations of the 1960s were galvanized into a single voice. This occurred in part because, as block grant formula funds dwindled under the Reagan administration, the city was no longer willing to pay for the duplicative administrative overhead associated with keeping so many of them going simultaneously. The Pratt-Willert Village plan emerged as a "cause celebre" for the Ellicott District. With community pressure, Buffalo's only black architect was commissioned to prepare at public expense a housing and community renewal plan for the Pratt-Willert neighborhood. After several months of lengthy community meetings, the architect presented a scheme calling for blocks of attached two-story brick rental apartments, quite similar in appearance to prewar public housing.

Community representatives were shocked and incensed at what they correctly saw as a low-rise version of the high-rise public housing projects that had proven so disastrous. At the meeting in City Hall to review the proposal, a recognized community leader rose to respond to the plan. Summoning all his ire into a single observation, he pounded his fist on the table, and shouted, "Damn it! We're talking about HOMES! HOUSES! Not housing!"[25]

Thus, the stage was set for what may prove to be a most significant experiment in American social housing policy and neighborhood renewal.

TOWARD THE "CITY EGALITARIAN": BUFFALO'S PRATT-WILLERT VILLAGE

The physical distinctions between prewar and postwar public housing designs have already been established, as has the distinctly modernist ethic which governed postwar efforts at urban renewal. What is decidedly postmodernist about the present Pratt-Willert Village housing and community renewal experiment in Buffalo's Ellicott District is that it addresses the issue of structural poverty in the black community.

For the postmodern era, the major housing policy planning issue has become how to provide homes and to increase ownership among inner-city blacks whose incomes are limited by a historically documented unequal access to education and jobs. Related to this is the question of whether or not "filtering"[26] in market-rate housing can be accelerated, so that a superior level of low-cost rental housing can reach the income levels of the poor sooner, thus potentially reducing their public dependency.

In addition to being associated with neighborhood stability in the thinking of planners and government officials, home ownership is also a key ingredient of wealth formation, as William Bradford has documented in a recent study.[27] Indeed, with less chance of inheriting wealth, achieving home ownership status is even more important for the working poor and middle classes than for upper-income households. In reaction against the massive cost of urban renewal-era public housing in the 1950s and its rejection (involving, in many cases, physical destruction) by housing project tenants in the 1960s, the increasingly politically conservative American electorate of the 1970s began to support a dismantling of national housing and social policy apparatus.

The black community voices from Buffalo's Ellicott District were finally heard. In the Fall of 1985, construction was started on the first of what has now become three phases of neighborhood renewal. To date, 250 units of new single-family ownership housing have been completed and are occupied, and the 59 units in the recently approved phase three will bring the total to 309 homes by 1991.

House lot sizes have been doubled from the 25' x 100' which was characteristic of the Ellicott district's nineteenth century development period, making room for off-street garage parking and yard space. Units are designed with three bedrooms and one and one-half baths, ranging in size from 1,200 to 1,400 square feet of living space. Land is assembled by the City of Buffalo, and passed through to the builder-developer written down to an average cost per lot ranging from $500 to $1,000.

Total development cost per unit is $75,000 in 1988 dollars.[28] In order to make this housing affordable to working class households, a $25,000 per unit subsidy is provided to eligible households from federal and state sources. To be eligible, households must be capable of making a minimum 5 percent equity commitment, and have a minimum income of

$18,000. (The income eligibility ceiling for the program is capped at $33,500, making middle income buyers eligible). Equity commitments can slide upwards to a more normal 10 percent downpayment, if applicant households meet guidelines of the New York State Affordable Housing Trust Fund, with Trust Fund grants allocable to meet the downpayment commitment.

This form of packaging has become known locally as a "deep subsidy" program, and as one might imagine it has been met with remarkably positive community response. Middle-income black buyers are returning to a central city neighborhood that most people had written off as unsalvageable. Since population is not growing, as they vacate lower value ownership units or higher value rental accommodations, market filtering presumably is accelerated to the benefit of lower income households. Formerly vacant residential land is back on the tax rolls of the city, and the concentration of community renewal efforts in a single vicinity is allowing strength to build upon strength. The Pratt-Willert Village project received the 1989 Award for Excellence in Inner-City Housing from the Urban Land Institute. (See Figures 3A and 3B for "before" and "after" photos of Pratt-Willert.)

CONCLUSION

The postmodern critique of urban renewal's history presented here, using Buffalo as a typical case, demonstrates two sad facts: first, that we did the wrong things with urban renewal legislation when we had its tools; and ironically, now that we have learned better, we no longer have the federal support and public policy apparatus to accomplish the rebuilding process on the scale required.

The most significant conclusion of this analysis is the suggestion that in "soft" development markets (of which Buffalo is typical), central city areas once scarred in the 1950s by what Anderson dubbed "the federal bulldozer"[29] may be witnessing renewal, thirty years after they were leveled completely. What is noteworthy about this redevelopment process is that, thankfully, it is not repeating the failed processes led by high-rise, high-density public housing, of which Pruitt-Igoe in St. Louis is perhaps the most notorious example. And curiously, it is not attributable to the process of gentrification so common in "hot" demand markets such as Boston, Washington, DC or San Francisco. (In those areas, poor minority residents were displaced by upwardly mobile whites in search of metro-

FIGURE 3A
Pratt-Willert Village: The Legacy of Urban Renewal

Source: June 1989, by the author.

FIGURE 3B
Pratt-Willert Village Today: Postmodernist Urban Renewal

Source: June 1989, by the author.

politan housing bargains in rapidly inflating markets.[30]) Something different is now afoot in Buffalo, an after-the-fact, homegrown version of urban renewal, which refutes the basic tenets of early twentieth century modernist thinking; and this experiment merits the close scrutiny of housing analysts.

No locality, and probably no state in the United States has the income redistribution capacity to address wholly the question of equity in housing markets for blacks. Even the modest-sized Pratt-Willert Village experiment in Buffalo required federal resources; and as most housing analysts know all too well, the federal role in housing in recent years has been vastly diminished. In that light, the Buffalo case may seem a drop not just in the bucket, but in the ocean.

What commends the Pratt-Willert Village experiment to those interested in the political economy of urban America is its sound base in social equity and social justice. For, however few black households it serves, Pratt-Willert serves them well. Similarly conceived small-scale equity experiments in other cities such as Cleveland, Pittsburgh, and St. Louis may have a slow but steady impact on improving blacks' equity stake in the American dream.[31]

After three decades of public policy failure—first of slum clearance and neighborhood destruction, then of modernist-influenced public housing design, and finally of market guesswork and civic administrative exasperation—the Pratt-Willert development is emerging as a prospectively viable redevelopment alternative in Buffalo's inner city. In it may lie a key to not only Buffalo's urban renewal hopes, but to those of similarly situated cities.

NOTES

1. William Alonzo, "The Unplanned Paths of Planning Schools," *The Public Interest* 82 (Winter 1986): 64.

2. For a thorough exposition of industrialization, see Reyner Banham, *Theory and Design in the First Machine Age* 2d ed. (New York: Praeger, 1967). Among the most widely cited sources on scientific rationalism and the paradigm shift that was occasioned by "modern" science is Thomas S. Kuhn, *The Structure of Scientific Revolutions* (Chicago: University of Chicago Press, 1962), although a more straightforward version may be found in Part I on "World Views" in Jeremy Rifkin, *Entropy: Into the Greenhouse World* (New York: Bantam Books, 1989). For a thorough description of the impact of modernist thinking on early twentieth century city planning, see Robert Fishman *Urban Utopias in the Twentieth Century: Ebenezer Howard, Frank Lloyd Wright, Le Corbusier* (Cambridge: MIT Press, 1982).

Modernism in city planning is discussed in Jonathan Barnett, *The Elusive City: Five Centuries of Design, Ambition and Miscalculation* (New York: Harper & Row, 1986), and briefly in Charles A. Jencks, *The Language of Post-Modern Architecture* (New York:

Rizzoli International, 1977). Robert Fishman devotes an entire section to Le Corbusier's theories on modern city form in *Urban Utopias*.

Le Corbusier's proposal to build the modern city rested on the proposition that population density could be increased, vehicular traffic congestion reduced, and "sun, space and greenery" preserved simultaneously. This was to be accomplished by demolishing the low-rise commercial and residential buildings of the historic city, replacing them with massive steel and glass structures made possible by new technology.

Following the stock market crash of 1929, the Great Depression, and World War II, as Europe turned its attention to rebuilding its cities with the help of the Marshall Plan, America embarked upon an era in which it would attempt to renew the deteriorated and crowded slums in its own cities. There being no domestic model for this extensive rebuilding process, it is not surprising that America turned once again to a European model; and even less surprising that that model should have been Parisian in origin. Washington, DC, the nation's capital, had been designed in 1789–91 by a Frenchman, Maj. Pierre L'Enfant. A free black man, Benjamin Banneker, self-taught mathematician, astronomer, and later widely regarded publicist, was one of four chief assistants to L'Enfant in this task; but the distinct similarity of Washington to the plan of Paris is undeniable.

Le Corbusier's 1920s and 1930s ideas on urbanism held a special appeal for the American mentality. The proposal for gigantic towers gracing a pastoral landscape interlaced with high-speed highways was distinctly new and forward-looking, both characteristics which struck a resonant chord in the American heart. Bigger had always been synonymous with better in America, a debatable but widely held viewpoint associated with the alleged social benefits that attended economic growth and expansion. Statistics on growth of America cities up to and including 1950 appeared to support planning for even higher urban densities, while at the same time the need for increasing automobile movement efficiency was recognized.

3. As evidence of the infancy of the base of knowledge upon which modernist thinking in city planning rested, the emergence of sociology as a scientific discipline, associated with the University of Chicago in the 1920s, is an indication of how very immature the social sciences were at the height of the modern period. Indeed, the appearance of Ernest W. Burgess's work in 1925 in a book entitled *The City* was the first attempt at a theory of urban spatial ecology. His "concentric zone" model was modified by empirical findings published in 1939 by the real estate economist Homer Hoyt, who worked for the Federal Housing Administration during the 1930s. Hoyt's "sectoral theory" advanced what was still rudimentary knowledge of urban development with the observation that otherwise uniform patterns of urban land use tended to be influenced heavily by the location of transportation arterials, thus carving the concentric pie into slices.

Despite the eruption of the Second World War, by 1945 the theorizing of the early modernists was modified yet again by geographers Chauncy Harris and Edward L. Ullman, who developed a substantial revision to the earlier work by Burgess and Hoyt. Their theory that urban regions possessed "multiple nuclei" of concentrated economic activity, i.e., more than one business district, quite radically altered what modern science knew of the urban social formation. Presaging what would come to be known in the 1950s as regional science, with the work of Harris and Ullman what had been known at the turn of the century as "city" planning became known after World War II as "urban" planning.

The bracket of years referred to as the "modern period" represents a virtual explosion in city planning thought. Louis Sullivan's plan for the 1893 Chicago World's Fair was followed quickly by Daniel Burnham's 1909 Plan for Chicago.

In England, Ebenezer Howard's 1898 Garden City proposal, was begun in Letchworth in 1901. See Ebenezer Howard, *To-Morrow: A Peaceful Path to Real Reform* (London:

Swan Sonnenschein and Co. Ltd., 1898), reprinted in 1901 under the title by which it is now commonly known, *Garden Cities of Tomorrow*. The Garden City idea was transplanted to the United States in 1926 by Clarence Stein and Henry Wright at Radburn, NJ. See Clarence S. Stein, *Toward New Towns for America* (Cambridge: MIT Press, 1957). In France, Tony Garnier's generic proposal for a completely new, industrial age city was published in 1917, its implementation at Lyons, France forestalled only by World War I. See Tony Garnier, *Une Cite Industrielle: Etude Pour La Construction Des Villes* (An Industrial City: A Study in the Building of Cities), New York: Princeton Architectural Press, 1989), trans. Marguerite E. McGoldrick. LeCorbusier's visionary scheme of 1922–25 for "The Contemporary City" was supplemented by his more ambitious version of the concept entitled "The Radiant City" in 1932–35. For a description, see Robert Fishman, *Urban Utopias in the Twentieth Century: Ebenezer Howard, Frank Lloyd Wright, Le Corbusier* (Cambridge: MIT Press, 1982) at pp. 163–263. Celebrated American architect Frank Lloyd Wright's controversial proposal for "Broadacre City," published in 1935, is also described by Fishman at pp. 91–160.

All this modernist theorizing had its effect on city planning practice in the same historic interval. New York City adopted the first major zoning ordinance of any American city in 1916, and the Supreme Court of the United States upheld the validity of zoning in the 1926 landmark case of Village of Euclid v. Ambler Realty. See Richard F. Babcock, *The Zoning Game: Municipal Practices and Policies* 2d ed. (Madison: The University of Wisconsin Press, 1969) at p. 4. The Regional Plan Association was formed in the late 1920s. For a description see Lewis Mumford, *The Culture of Cities* 3d ed. (New York: Harcourt, Brace, Jovanovich Inc., 1970) at pp. 306–315. Through the RPA's efforts and the publicity they generated, what had been theoretical vision informed by modern science came increasingly to be viewed as possible, plausible, and desirable.

4. Alonzo, "Unplanned Paths," 63-64.

5. Charles A. Jencks, *The Language of Post-Modern Architecture* (New York: Rizzoli International, 1977), 9. Jencks is partly facetious and partly serious in this observation. Other historians have quibbled over distinctions between "early modern" vs. "late modern." For purposes of this article, the year 1945 is used to mark the end of the period because the generation of city planning ideas in a modernist manner stops here, and because design of prewar and postwar public housing is so stark. However, as Jencks notes, the impact of modernist thinking is attenuated over several decades following World War II.

6. John F. Bauman, *Public Housing, Race, and Renewal: Urban Planning in Philadelphia, 1920–1974* (Philadelphia: Temple University Press, 1987), xii.

7. Patricia Thompson, "Public Housing and Displacement: A Response to the Leigh-Mitchell Paper, *The Review of Black Political Economy* Vol. 11, No. 1 (Fall 1980): 79.

8. Jonathan Barnett, *The Elusive City: Five Centuries of Design, Ambition and Miscalculation* (New York: Harper & Row, 1986), 87–135.

9. Ernest W. Burgess, "The Growth of the City," in *The City*, ed. R.E. Park, E.W. Burgess, and R.D. MacKenzie (Chicago: University of Chicago Press, 1925), 47–62.

10. Homer Hoyt, *The Structure and Growth of Residential Neighborhoods in American Cities* (Washington, DC: Federal Housing Administration, 1939).

11. Chauncy Harris and Edward L. Ullman, "The Nature of Cities," *Annals of the American Academy of Political and Social Science* 242: 7–17.

12. A.D. Price et al., *Masten Community Renewal Project* Vol. III, prepared for the City of Buffalo, Department of Community Development, January 1984, 26.

13. Robert Fishman, *Bourgeois Utopia: The Rise and Fall of Suburbia* (New York: Basic Books, 1987), 175.

14. The Housing Act of 1954 provided that localities could use federal urban renewal funds for property acquisition, relocation expenses of displaced residents, slum housing demolition, and land cost "write-downs," i.e., offering of land for sale to developers at prices not designed to recoup the aforementioned costs. For a discussion, see Chapter 7 in Henry J. Aaron, *Shelter and Subsidies: Who Benefits from Federal Housing Policies* (Washington, DC: The Brookings Institution, 1972).

However, to speculative developers, a significant out-of-pocket expense is the cost of borrowed capital during the construction period. For a discussion, see Stephen A. Pyhrr and James R. Cooper, *Real Estate Investment: Strategy, Analysis, Decisions* (New York: John Wiley & Sons, 1982). Consequently, suburban sites for home-building were differentially attractive over inner-city urban renewal sites for development. Land economy was largely a function of relative bureaucratic efficiency: in the suburbs there was no waiting period required for public acquisition, relocation, demolition, or site preparation. Moreover, as Mumford notes in *The City in History* (New York: Harcourt, Brace & World, 1961), suburbs offered "a parklike setting for the family dwelling house." No doubt, this was a definite advantage over inner-city neighborhoods whose images of decay and overcrowding lingered in the popular mind.

15. Fishman, *Bourgeois Utopia*, 177.

16. Bauman, *Public Housing, Race, and Renewal*, 201–202.

17. Henry J. Aaron, *Shelter and Subsidies: Who Benefits from Federal Housing Policies* (Washington, DC: The Brookings Institution, 1972), 53–73.

18. David C. Perry, "The Politics of De-industrialization in America: The Case of Buffalo, New York," in *The Capitalist City: Global Restructuring and Community Politics* ed. Michael Peter Smith and Joe R. Feagins (London: Basil Blackwell, 1987).

19. U.S. Department of Commerce, Bureau of the Census, Census of Manufacturing, "County Business Patterns" Erie County, NY 1974, 1977, 1980, 1983, and 1984. Analysis courtesy of Center for Regional Studies, State University of New York at Buffalo.

20. This national phenomenon is well documented in James Grossman, *Land of Hope: Chicago, Black Southerners, and the Great Migration* (Chicago: University of Chicago Press, 1989). For an informative discussion of Buffalo's experience with black in-migration from the South in the early and mid-twentieth century, see the monograph by William L. Evans, "Housing and Race Fear" (Buffalo: Buffalo Urban League, 1946).

21. In the parlance of real estate development, markets are referred to as "soft" when effective demand for space is well below supply, usually associated with lagging income growth rate or overall urban or regional economic decline. Need for space may still exist, but the income to afford is generally not readily available. The opposite market condition, where effective market demand exceeds supply (usually only for periods of a few years, as the supply side adjusts), is commonly referred to as "hot," to denote excitement over numerous opportunities for profit. Academic usages of the terms are not common, but these adjectives are frequently used in journalistic and trade publications.

22. John Oliver and Alfred D. Price, "Housing New York's Black Population: Affordability and Adequacy," Institute Document #88-1 (Albany: New York African-American Institute, State University of New York, January, 1988), 41.

Average resale housing prices for the northeast region compared to United States averages and other regions are skewed by the extraordinary price levels in a few northeastern cities. In 1987, New York City prices led the nation at $183,000, with Boston ranked second at $181,600, Hartford ranked fifth at $165,000, and Providence eighth at $126,000. In the same year, average sales prices in Buffalo were $55,900, placing it well below national and regional average price levels.

23. Oscar Newman, *Defensible Space: Crime Prevention through Urban Design* (New York: Macmillan, 1973).

24. Greater Buffalo Development Foundation, "Generalized Market Value of Land, Buffalo, New York," prepared by D. Garrecht and R.W. Waxmonsky (Buffalo: 1973).

25. The author was a member of the Citizens' Advisory Committee for the Pratt-Willert Village Project, and was present at the review meeting where the Rev. James Hemphill made these remarks.

26. "Filtering' is an indirect process for meeting the housing demand of a lower-income group. When new quality housing is produced for higher-income households, houses given up by these households become available to the lower income group. Though it is a 'well-recognized' phenomenon, filtering provides an issue of public policy that has long commanded the attention of housing economists—whether or not it is fundamentally desirable that low-income housing needs be met in this way." See Wallace F. Smith, "Filtering and Neighborhood Change," in *Internal Structure of the City*, ed. Larry S. Bourne (New York: Oxford University Press, 1971), 170–179.

Traditionally, the debate over whether filtering in housing markets serves the needs of low-income households is linked to the stock's deteriorating physical condition over time. Without public intervention, the market could be expected to allocate the most aged and deteriorated stock to the poor; thus, the justification for public housing.

Only in recent years in the debates over "privatization" have analysts begun to examine whether it is plausible to expect that the normal filtering process might be accelerated, presumably allocating more desirable housing sooner to lower-income households at a reasonable price. See Thomas Bier, "The Prospect of Accelerated Housing Filtering in the 1990's: Opportunity for Planning" (unpublished paper: Cleveland State University, October 1988).

27. William D. Bradford, "Wealth, Assets and Income of Black Households" (unpublished paper, College of Business and Management, University of Maryland, June, 1989).

28. "Report of the Commissioner of Inspections and Licenses," Division of Neighborhood Renewal, Department of Community Development (Buffalo: February, 1990).

29. Martin Anderson, *The Federal Bulldozer: A Critical Analysis of Urban Renewal, 1949–1962* (Cambridge: MIT Press, 1964).

30. Chester Hartman, Dennis Keating and Richard LeGates, *Displacement: How to Fight It* (Berkeley: National Housing Law Project, 1982).

31. It is not clear what relationship Buffalo's Pratt-Willert Village bears to New York City's "Nehemiah" program, or to the federal version of it. Both were developed in the late 1980s, and both "package" multiple forms of subsidy in order to place new single-family detached homes within the economic reach of low- and moderate-income households.

8

PUBLIC HOUSING IN CHARLOTTESVILLE: THE BLACK EXPERIENCE IN A SMALL SOUTHERN CITY

William M. Harris, Sr. and Nancy Olmsted

The history and public policies related to the public housing program are presented within the context of a small southern city, Charlottesville, Virginia. Consistent with the stormy beginnings of public housing nationally, the article reveals that the early days of the program in Charlottesville also were troubled. City policies to affect the residential mix of housing are shown to have limited the quality of affordable housing available to the poor and especially to low-income blacks. Programs designed by the city to overcome some of these disadvantages through both home ownership and renting also are discussed.

This article reviews the publicly assisted housing programs in Charlottesville, Virginia and describes the factors of race, income and public policy that are determinants of housing opportunities for the poor in this southern city. Of special concern are the impacts of public housing on the black community and, to ascertain these impacts, the study focuses on the actions of the Charlottesville Redevelopment and Housing Authority (CRHA). The article concludes with a summary of recommendations for the improvement of current policies related to public housing in the city.

HISTORY OF CHARLOTTESVILLE AND CHARACTERISTICS OF ITS RESIDENTS

Charlottesville is located in Albemarle County in central Virginia, amid the foothills of the Blue Ridge Mountains. Its picturesque beauty and social history have helped to create a city of diverse neighborhoods and southern culture.

A major influence on Charlottesville has been the University of Virginia. Thomas Jefferson located his "academical village," which opened in 1825, one mile west of Charlottesville. Today, with the city nearly surrounding the university, the institution is more than ever a major part of the city's economy, history, and culture.

In 1870 blacks comprised slightly more than the majority of the population of the city. Currently they make up nearly twenty percent of the city's approximately 40,000 residents, but include nearly one half of all families living below the poverty level. The incidence of female-headed families is nearly three times as great (44% v. 15%) among blacks as among whites. Similar to the national average, blacks are twice as likely to be unemployed as whites. Most employed blacks are concentrated in service occupations (38%) and are underrepresented in professional (7%) and administrative (8%) positions. In 1980 one quarter of all employed blacks earned less than $5,000; only 3 percent reported income of $35,000 to $50,000. While only 9 percent of blacks have completed four years or more of college, whites have a completion rate of 35 percent.

HOUSING POLICY IN CHARLOTTESVILLE SINCE 1950

In 1950, the Joint Board of Health conducted a housing survey which, along with a follow-up survey in 1957, identified housing in critical need of protection and rehabilitation. In order to respond to the housing needs, the Charlottesville Redevelopment and Housing Authority (CRHA) was established in 1954 by referendum. The objectives of the CRHA were to clear slum and blighted areas and to operate public housing programs. The Authority consisted of five citizen commissioners appointed by the city council. This was changed in 1978, when the city council appointed itself as commissioners of the Authority. At that time, the city manager was appointed executive director, with the daily operations of the Authority managed by a deputy executive director hired by the commissioners.

On March 11, 1960, the city council received an application by the CRHA under amendment 14A: Title 36 VA Code 1950.[1] (This section, referred to as the McCue amendment, required a referendum vote on public housing projects; it was overturned in 1971.) The application called for the redevelopment of the Vinegar Hill area and the construction of public housing on Ridge Street and Hartman's Mill Road. The purpose of the project was to clear a substandard area for several reasons—to facilitate the expansion of the downtown business district, to improve traffic flow, and to provide housing for many of the families who would be displaced as a result of the redevelopment.

Although the redevelopment of Vinegar Hill was viewed by many as beneficial to the city, the proposed Ridge Street and Hartman's Mill Road locations for public housing met with strenuous opposition. Three other sites were then considered, with the Westhaven site ultimately being selected. In March of 1963, CRHA received authorization from the U.S. Department of Housing and Urban Development to award a contract for the first public housing development in the city of Charlottesville. The 126 units in Westhaven were completed in 1964.

In June of 1965, CRHA petitioned the city council to hold a referendum on a second public housing project. The referendum was rejected by the voters in November of 1965. In August of 1966, the Authority made another request for a second project, but withdrew the request a month later "because of growing public opposition to the proposal and the lack of unified support among civic leaders.[2]

A third referendum vote in 1967 considered three smaller scattered sites, and all three sites were approved for public housing. Opposition to these projects came from the NAACP, which believed the projects would perpetuate racial segregation in Charlottesville because the sites were all within predominantly black areas of the city. "We realize and know that people need homes; we are for public housing, but not housing projects."[3] The NAACP continued to push for scattered site housing.

In April of 1968, the Charlottesville Housing Foundation was formed as a private, non-profit organization to:

expedite the construction of new living units in locations outside ghetto areas or areas which are generally in a deteriorating condition for low-income families who are unable to obtain adequate housing on their own.[4]

In March of 1969, the city council issued the following formal housing statement:

We realize that our problems cannot be resolved without a positive effort on the part of every individual, group and entity, both private and public, within and without the community, to make every effort to increase the availability of housing and to upgrade the quality of such housing.[5]

Charlottesville's last public housing project was privately built and named Garrett Square. While the development is privately owned, it has been managed by CRHA since its construction in 1979. This privately owned, publicly managed, category includes 480 dwelling units.

Since the 1970s, housing programs for low-income families have placed less emphasis on redevelopment, public housing, and the clearing of blight; instead, they have focused on scattered site development, rehabilitation of existing units, and affordability of home ownership. These programs involve both public and private financing. In the 1980s, more emphasis was placed on the following: providing housing for "special groups," such as the elderly and the handicapped; racially integrating and modernizing existing public housing; privately developing low- and moderate-income housing; and increasing the revenues from public housing as subsidies from the federal government declined.

Today the CRHA owns 266 nonelderly-occupied LRPH units in six locations within the city (See Figure 1). These units provide low-income persons with housing at below-market rents. The apartments, constructed with federal funds, operate with revenues from tenant receipts and HUD subsidies. The high-rise accommodation for the elderly operated by CRHA contains 105 apartment units. Qualifying persons pay 30 percent of adjusted family income for CRHA units.

BLACK AMERICAN HOUSING DEMOGRAPHICS

The 1980 Census revealed 80.4 percent of Charlottesville's population to be white and 19.6 percent nonwhite (nonwhites consist of blacks, Asians, Hispanics, and native Americans). The percentage of nonwhites in the population had increased from the 15.5 percent reported in the 1970 Census. However, in 1980 only 12.7 percent of owner-occupied housing units in Charlottesville belonged to nonwhites, although this represented an increase over the 10.6 percent reported in 1970.

Although Charlottesville is predominantly white, Charlottesville's public housing has been predominantly black since its inception, and continues to be so. In 1989, 70.1 percent of public housing heads of households were black (Table 1). This increases to 82 percent when the high-rise accommodation for the elderly is not included. Currently, 84 percent of the children living in Charlottesville's public housing are black.

The 1989 demographics of Charlottesville's public housing (Table 1) also indicate that among all residents (both black and white) heads of

FIGURE 1
Federally Subsidized Rental Housing in Charlottesville

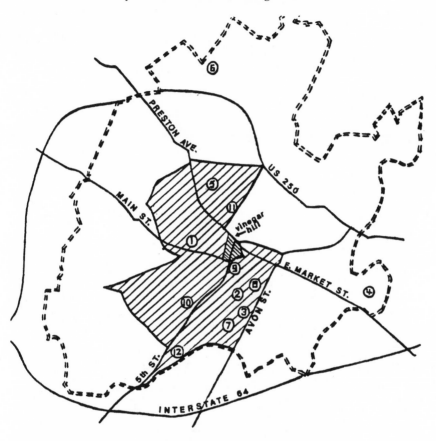

City Owned Public Housing Units Name	# of Units	Privately Owned Subsidized Housing Name	# of Units
1. Westhaven Public Housing	126	8. Garrett Square Apartments	150
2. High Rise for the Elderly	105	9. Midway Manor	98
3. Sixth Street Public Housing	25	10. Oakridge Garden	202
4. Riverside Dr. Public Housing	16	11. St. Margaret-Mary Apts.	16
5. Madison Ave. Public Housing	18	12. Ephphatha Village	14
6. Michie Dr. Public Housing	23		480
7. S. First St. Public Housing	58		
	371		

Scattered Privately Owned Housing Name	# of Units
Dogwood Housing, Ltd.	62
Section 8 (Existing & Vouchers) CRHA	154
Section 8 (Existing-Mentally Handicapped)	64
	280

Total Federally Assisted Rental Units in Charlottesville 1,131

▨ Census tracts over 30% Non-White

Source: Department of Community Development, December, 1987.

TABLE 1
Demographics of Public Housing Residents
Charlottesville, Virginia

Dec. 1989

Resident Demographics	Housing Site				
	Westhaven	Highrise+	Scattered	South 1st St.	Total
Population	126 units	105 units	82 units	58 units	371 units
Head of Household	122	98	72	49	341
Children	253	*	164	136	553
Total	375	98	236	185	894
Head of Household					
Race					
Black	82% (100)	42% (41)	85% (61)	76% (37)	70.1% (239)
White	18% (22)	57% (56)	15% (11)	24% (12)	29.6% (101)
Other	-- --	1% (1)	-- --	-- -	.3% (1)
Total	100% (122)	100% (98)	100% (72)	100% (49)	100% (341)
Gender					
Male	16% (19)	37% (36)	21% (15)	14% (7)	23% (77)
Female	84% (103)	63% (62)	79% (57)	86% (42)	77% (264)
Total	100% (122)	100% (98)	100% (72)	100% (49)	100% (341)
Age					
18-25	11% (13)	-- --	11% (8)	8% (4)	7.3% (25)
26-35	37% (45)	-- --	47% (34)	43% (21)	29.3% (100)
36-50	24% (29)	4% (4)	31% (22)	37% (18)	21.4% (73)
51-61	7% (9)	11% (11)	4% (3)	12% (6)	8.5% (29)
62+	21% (26)	85% (83)	7% (5)	-- --	33.4% (114)
Total	100% (122)	100% (98)	100% (72)	100% (49)	100% (341)

+ Highrise houses elderly, handicapped and/or disabled persons
* No children at this site
Source: Charlottesville Redevelopment and Housing Authority-Dec. 1989

TABLE 1 (continued)

	Westhaven	Highrise+	Scattered	South 1st St.	Total
Marital Status					
Single	89% (108)	93% (91)	78% (56)	88% (43)	87% (298)
Married	11% (14)	7% (7)	22% (16)	12% (6)	13% (43)
Total	100% (122)	100% (98)	100% (72)	100% (49)	100% (341)
Children					
Race					
Black	85% (215)	– –	87% (142)	79% (107)	84% (464)
White	15% (38)	– –	13% (22)	21% (29)	16% (89)
Total	100% (253)	*	100% (164)	100% (136)	100% (553)
Gender					
Male	44% (111)	– –	52% (85)	54% (74)	49% (270)
Female	56% (142)	– –	48% (79)	46% (62)	51% (283)
Total	100% (253)	*	100% (164)	100% (136)	100% (553)
Age					
0-5	28% (72)	– –	27% (45)	21.3% (29)	26% (146)
6-12	36% (90)	– –	43% (70)	40.4% (55)	39% (215)
13-17	11% (28)	– –	17% (27)	22.8% (31)	16% (86)
18+	28% (63)	– –	13% (22)	15.4% (21)	19% (106)
Total	100% (253)	*	100% (164)	100% (136)	100% (553)

households most commonly are female (77%), those 62+ years of age (33.4%), and single (87%). There is an average of nearly 2.3 children per head of household in the units having children present. The only project that meets Charlottesville's desired goal of the 65 percent / 35 percent black/white racial mixture is the aforementioned high-rise building with the elderly and disabled as tenants.

As of October 1989, 69 percent of residents paid $200 or less per month rent, with the largest share of these (41%) paying $101–$200 per month. Nearly equal shares of the tenant population (28% and 31%, respectively) paid "$0-$100" and "$201 and over" in rent.

CURRENT PROGRAMS IN CHARLOTTESVILLE

Charlottesville offers a number of housing programs that are designed to achieve several goals: meet the housing needs of the poor; provide subsidies that will enable those with low incomes to afford rents; and create opportunities for low- and moderate-income people to purchase their own homes (Table 2). These programs involve a combination of federal, state and local funds generally administered through the CRHA.

Community Development Rehabilitation Program: The Community Development Rehabilitation Program (CDRP) provides funds for rehabilitation of substandard owner and rental housing.

Homeowner Rehabilitation: Federal, state and local funds are provided to enable qualifying homeowners to make the repairs necessary to rehabilitate their homes. Two hundred and seventy-one units were funded through the program between 1975 and 1989.

Rental Rehabilitation: Owners of substandard rental units are provided federal, state and local funds to make necessary repairs. Once rehabilitated, units initially must be occupied by low- or moderate-income households. As of December 1988, eleven rental units had been renovated.

CDRP provides homeowners with both technical assistance (in determining necessary repairs and estimating cost) and material assistance (in paying for these repairs). The Charlottesville Housing Improvement Program, Inc. (CHIP) supplies much of the maintenance and repair work.

Funding is available in the form of deferred loans or grants which provide 40 percent–80 percent of the costs. No interest accumulates, and the loan is repaid when the house changes owners. Loans tailored to meet specific needs of the applicant also may be obtained. Financing for the program is provided by Community Development Block Grant (CDBG) funds, Virginia Housing Partnership funds, and by city funds through their Homeowner and Rental Rehabilitation Programs.

Section 8 Rental Assistance Programs: This program enables low-income persons to live in standard housing by subsidizing the difference between 30 percent of tenant income and the market rent of the unit.

In June 1989, CRHA (acting as an agent for the Virginia Housing and Development Authority) was provided funds by the U.S. Department of Housing and Urban Development (HUD) to assist an additional 25 existing units and 62 moderately rehabilitated units. CRHA was already

TABLE 2
Housing Assistance in Charlottesville to Date

Program	Units to Date	Lifetime Cost	1989/90 Budget
Community Dev'l Rehab.			
Homeowner Rehab	271		$165,640
Low Int. Renovation Loans	29	$150,000	
Section 8			
HUD Existing Cert.	78		
Vouchers	122		556,800
VHDA Existing Cert.	25		4,290
Mod. Rehab.	62		11,401
Public Housing			
Family	266	317,279	
Elderly	105	68,672	
	--------	(in lieu of taxes)	
	371		
House Bank Prog.	19	ave. $12,000/unit cost to city	185,000
Downpayment/	65	94,854 CDBG	33,000
Closing Cost	5 pending		
Urban Renewal			
Vinegar Hill		3,335,000	
Garrett Square		4,634,000 npc*	
Comprehensive Imp.			
Asst. Program (CIAP)			988,680

*NPC = net project cost

BUDGET REVENUE 1989/90

HUD	Subsidies/Grants	$2,468,490
VHDA	Section 8 Admin. Fees	19,980
CDGB	Admin.	39,200
CDBG	Program	383,640
City Subsidies/Grants		405,450

Sources: Personnel and Projects of the Charlottesville Redevelopment and Housing Authority, July 31, 1989
Charlottesville Redevelopment and Housing Authority Proposed Budget, 1989/90

administering 78 existing units and 122 vouchers through contracts funded by HUD in previous years.

House Bank Program: CRHA purchases vacant and deteriorating homes in targeted neighborhoods and rehabilitates them with CDBG funds. The renovated homes are then sold to qualifying low- and moderate-income persons for not more than $37,000. Proceeds from the sales are reinvested in the program. In order to provide housing for low- and moderate-income persons throughout the city, CRHA has purchased 19 existing units, 11 of which will be renovated. The others will be sold or demolished, with new units being constructed on the sites.

Downpayment/Closing Cost Assistance Program: This program was begun in 1986 with $85,000 in CDBG funds that are used to provide deferred loans for downpayments and closing costs. To qualify, the prospective buyer must meet the Virginia Housing Development Authority (VHDA) income guidelines for low or moderate income, be a first-time home buyer, agree to occupy the home after purchase, and have at least $500 with which to buy the home. Loans at 4 percent must be repaid if the home is rented or sold within five years of the purchase. If the home purchaser resides in the home for a period of five years, the interest on the loan is forgiven and the amount borrowed becomes due when the home changes ownership. Table 2 shows the city's achievements to date.

MANAGEMENT OF HOUSING PROGRAMS

Today, there are still not enough units of housing for the low-income; there is increasing homelessness as the very poor are excluded from subsidized housing. Moreover, the current policies have not desegregated existing housing projects.

The Charlottesville Redevelopment and Housing Authority currently has 21 employees overseeing its programs and maintaining its public housing units. The Authority receives federal funding through the HUD Section 8 and CDBG programs (currently channeled through the Charlottesville Department of Community Development), and state funding through VHDA.

The management of the CRHA has been criticized virtually from the organization's inception for its lack of ability to make headway in meeting the need for public housing in Charlottesville. Sites recommended by the CRHA were opposed consistently by voters. In regard to chosen sites, CRHA did not have the support of the surrounding residents or the community as a whole before the construction proposals were put to a vote. The previously mentioned objections of the local NAACP to what was perceived as CRHA's perpetuation of a segregated system through the sites selected for public housing projects caused such projects to be viewed as "black" housing, making the siting of projects even more difficult.

As did many other communities, Charlottesville maintained segregated housing in the 1960s. CRHA's first application to HUD was for "Negro" development. Westhaven, Charlottesville's first public housing project, was built in a black neighborhood, and the project remained virtually all-black until 1980.

Frustrated with the City Council's lack of commitment to public housing, the chairman of the CRHA commission suggested in 1978 that the Council *become* the CRHA commission, thereby putting the responsibility for public housing back onto the City Council. Even after this occurred, public housing has been only half-heartedly supported by the city of Charlottesville. While there seems to be support for providing public housing for city residents, there is a fear that public housing will attract too many non-city residents.

In 1980, CRHA put into effect a new tenant selection policy designed to achieve a 50/50 racial mix in public housing. The policy was later revised to state that "whenever more than 65 percent of the residents in any public housing development are black, white applicants are given preference for admission."[6] As a result, black applicants had to wait longer for available units than did white applicants.

In 1980, CRHA made economic diversity the first priority on its list of tenant selection criteria. Under the policy, the Authority favors families that can pay "top dollar".[7] The deputy director of CRHA stated, "In order to survive, we've got to turn down some of the poor."[8] The city manager of Charlottesville exemplified the concern with attracting non-city residents to CRHA when he said, "We don't think it would be wise to become a magnet for the poor from the rural counties."[9]

In 1981, the Richmond-area HUD office commended CRHA for its attempt to desegregate; however, its selection policy was suspended by the national headquarters of HUD after further review. Eventually, HUD brought suit against CRHA, claiming the policy violated 42 U.S.C. Sec. 3604(a)-(c). On July 21, 1989, the court ruled the policy was indeed a violation (*United States v. Charlottesville Redevelopment and Housing Authority*) (718 F. Supp. 461 [1989]). CRHA has since suspended use of a tenant selection policy based on racial quotas.

While historically it appears there have been acceptable technical results by the CRHA staff, the failures have equally been visible in the political arena. The housing authority has not been able to move the public to accept low-income housing in white residential neighborhoods. Similarly, there has been only a very modest production of homes for purchase by low-income people; none of these was placed in white residential areas. It is evident that all levels of the city's management and the housing authority need to more effectively commit to, acquire resources for, and produce housing for ownership [and rental] by blacks and others in lower-income brackets.

CONCLUSION

The medium-sized southern city of Charlottesville, Virginia, founded in the mid-eighteenth century, is a classic paradigm of race regulations for the area. Experiencing increasing growth for more than two centuries, the city's current population of nearly forty thousand is slightly less than 20 percent black. Over time, race-specific decisions in the city have resulted in segregated public housing.[10]

In the 1960s, the city built its first public housing units on a segregated basis. The city has expanded publicly assisted housing programs to include both rental and owner-occupied units for low- and moderate-income citizens. These programs continue to encounter a legacy of criticism by the black community that policy and program activities have not sufficiently addressed the need for housing on a fair access basis.

The article suggests that discrimination related to race is a reality in Charlottesville's public housing. First, racial discrimination is evidenced by public policy that has limited the opportunity for fair housing. Second, racial discrimination is clearly present when considered on a spatial or site-specific basis.

The article makes several recommendations that are designed to correct racial discrimination in public housing in the city of Charlottesville. In summary, the following proposals are offered:

> The city should initiate housing policies that will abate segregation patterns through the establishment of a Human Relations Commission empowered to monitor and enforce discrimination related to housing. A Human Relations Commission should be empowered by the city to do the following: advocate fair housing policies and practices, test for housing discrimination,[11] and educate the "house poor" and the larger community about matters related affordability.

> The city should try to increase the private sector's interests in building low-cost housing by: streamlining regulations related to site plan approval, exploiting slow work seasons (usually winter) for builders, and affirmatively discouraging redlining[12] by lending institutions.

The black community should act in self-advocacy to acquire funds to purchase property and homes to increase home ownership. Local black fraternal, religious, and civic organizations may form housing cooperatives, sweat equity[13] organizations, and political housing advocacy groups to increase the amount of housing for the low-income in the black community.

Local employers should institute affirmative measures to remove barriers to employment that limit the ability of blacks to rent or purchase housing. The university and major local employers could expand the number of blacks working in middle income positions through aggressive recruitment and training, use of specific target goals,[14] and faithful enforcement of antidiscrimination laws.

These recommendations reflect the findings of a review of publicly assisted housing programs in Charlottesville and are limited to that scope; they are not offered as a complete solution to the historical problems of racial discrimination in housing in the city.

NOTES

1. "Text of City's Petition," *Charlottesville Daily Progress* (April 18, 1960), p. 2.
2. Karl Runser, "Housing Site Dropped," *Charlottesville Daily Progress* (September 9, 1966), p. 1.
3. "NAACP Again Says No to Housing," *Charlottesville Daily Progress* (April 21, 1967), p. 25.
4. "Foundation Plans 82 Housing Units," *Charlottesville Daily Progress* (October 22, 1969), p. B-1.
5. Bill Akers, "Council Agrees on Housing Needs in Formal Statement," *Charlottesville Daily Progress* (March 4, 1969), p. 11.
6. Kathleen Brunet, "City to Fight HUD on Housing Policy," *Charlottesville Daily Progress* (August 8, 1986), p. A-1.
7. Jim Ketcham-Colwill, "Some Are Too Poor For Public Housing," *Charlottesville Daily Progress* (July 24, 1983), p. A-1.
8. Ibid, p. A-12.
9. Jessie Bond, "City Unlikely to Add Public Housing," *Charlottesville Daily Progress* (October 7, 1985), p. A10.
10. G.A. Tobin ed., *Divided Neighborhoods: Changing Patterns of Racial Segregation* (Beverly Hills, CA: Sage Publications, 1987), p. 230.
11. Timothy M. Kaine, "Housing Discrimination Law in Virginia," *The Virginia Bar Association Journal* (Spring 1990), p. 16.
12. In an unpublished working paper completed in September 1990, the author and Ted Shekell found support that redlining practices appear to be present in two majority black neighborhoods in the city of Charlottesville.
13. Mittie Olion Chandler, *Urban Homesteading: Programs and Policies* (New York: Greenwood Press, 1988), p. 31.

14. Gerald D. Jaynes and Robin M. Williams, Jr. eds., *A Common Destiny: Blacks and American Society* (Washington, DC: National Academy Press, 1989), pp.. 315–323.

9

HOUSING PROBLEMS AND PROSPECTS
FOR BLACKS IN HOUSTON

Robert D. Bullard

Houston was considered the premier Sunbelt city in the 1970s. Much of the growth during this boom period was fueled by the oil industry. The city led the nation in new jobs created and housing starts. The economic growth, however, was not uniformly distributed to all segments of the population—specifically, a large segment of the black community was passed over during the city's housing boom.

Many of the housing problems facing black Houstonians can be traced to the city's anti-public housing sentiment, policies that create and perpetuate racial segregation, and the dismantling of the fair housing enforcement mechanism. Housing discrimination, residential segregation, and other institutional barriers all limit the mobility options for a sizable segment of the black Houston community.

Decent and affordable housing continues to be an integral part of the American Dream. Despite improvements over the past several decades, a sizable segment of the black community continues to be ill-housed and unable to realize this dream. This article examines housing problems and prospects for blacks in Houston, the nation's fourth largest city. Houston was Boomtown USA in the 1970s, growing through tremendous inmigration of people and frequent annexation of outlying areas, and with City Hall and the Chamber of Commerce always boasting of its low-cost, no-zoning, probusiness method of operation. But in the shadow of the Houston high-rise "petropolis" (a city built on the petrochemical industry) was another city, ignored by and invisible to city boosters and the media. Black Houston, the largest black community in the South, remained largely untouched by the economic and housing boom of the 1970s but was severely hurt by the bust of the 1980s.

This analysis is divided into five major sections. First, housing trends

and residential patterns of black Houstonians are discussed. Second, the
city's federally subsidized housing initiatives are assessed. Third, the
politics associated with low-rent public housing in Houston are considered. Fourth, growing ghettoization of Houston's black poor is chroni-
cled. Barriers to free choice in the housing market are then covered. The
final section presents conclusions.

BLACK HOUSTON: POPULATION, HOUSING AND NEIGHBORHOODS

The Houston metropolitan area was comprised of 2.9 million persons
in 1980 of which over 521,512 (18.2 percent) were black. The city of
Houston included some 1.6 million persons with over 440,257 blacks
(about 28 percent of the city population). The city's minority community
(mainly blacks and Hispanics) comprised over 45 percent of the city's
population in 1980.[1] Houston's black community also was the fastest
growing black community in the South, growing by 39 percent between
1970–1980.

The Houston metropolitan area led the nation in housing starts in the
decade of the seventies. Over 487,000 new housing units were built in the
area between 1970 and 1980 (a 72.4 percent increase). The bulk of the
new housing construction was concentrated in the suburbs with only
modest amounts of construction taking place in inner-city minority areas.

Lower-income and minority neighborhoods were largely passed over
during the peak period of Houston's housing boom, however. A case in
point is Houston's Fourth Ward or Freedmen's Town, the oldest black
neighborhood in the city. Following the Civil War, thousands of newly
freed slaves moved into the Fourth Ward to found the Freedmen's Town
neighborhood. The neighborhood became the center of black social, cultural, political, and economic life for black Houstonians. Black settlers
had acquired much of the land in Freedmen's Town by the 1880s. However, the years of the Great Depression and subsequent decades saw a
steady decline in owner-occupancy rates in the neighborhood. By 1980,
less than 5 percent of the housing in the neighborhood was owner-
occupied. For the most part, the Fourth Ward has become an area of
elderly black renters, and lower-income persons, factors that heighten the
prospects of wholesale displacement of incumbent residents from this
neartown area. The neighborhood has been under "siege" for some
time.[2]

In addition to the Fourth Ward, two other wards experienced economic and infrastructure decline in the 1970s and 1980s. The Third and Fifth Wards, for example, each have a rich history. These two neighborhoods emerged as mostly black neighborhoods as a result of increased housing demands and pressures in the post–World War II era. Blacks in the 1960s began to move southward from the Third Ward and northward from the Fifth Ward. The city's black community can still be found along this north-south corridor (See Figure 1). Houston's black community is located in a broad belt that extends from the south central and southeast portions of the city into the north central and northeast sections of the city. The black population is largely located on the eastern half of the city with smaller enclaves in northwest and southwest Houston.

Although the boundaries of the city's black community have been extended beyond the traditional black areas away from the central business district, blacks remain residentially segregated from whites. One measure of segregation is the index of dissimilarity. This index ''ranges from 100 when every block is either 100 percent black or zero percent black, to zero when every city block has the same ratio of blacks to the total as the entire city.''[3] The 1980 segregation index revealed that over 81 percent of Houston's blacks would have to move in order to achieve on each block the same racial mix as in the city as a whole. In 1970, the city's segregation index was 93. The distribution of the city's black population in 1970 and 1980 is presented in Figures 2 and 3. Overall, black Houstonians became less segregated and more decentralized in the 1970s.

While blacks have been moving into Houston's suburbs in the post–World War II era, their share of the suburban residents actually declined in the past two decades. For example, the black share of Houston's suburban population dropped from 12.9 percent in 1960 to 8.8 percent in 1970; blacks comprised only 6.2 percent of Houston's suburban population in 1980. The 80,000 blacks in Houston's suburbs represent by far a smaller number than might be expected from the size of the central-city black population of more than 400,000.[4]

The black suburbanization trend has often meant successive ''spillover'' from predominately black wards, or an extension of the segregated housing pattern that has typified the central city. Black Houston residents often become resegregated or ''ghettoized'' in suburbia. In other cases, older black suburban enclaves such as Riceville, Bordersville, Carvercrest, and Acres Homes have been encircled by new residential and commercial construction with few of the new amenities benefiting the

FIGURE 1
Predominantly Black Houston Neighborhoods

1. Third Ward	9. Sunnyside	17. Carverdale
2. Fourth Ward	10. South Park	18. Acres Homes
3. Fifth Ward	11. Almeda Plaza	19. Shepherd Park
4. Foster Place/	12. Hiram Clarke	20. Studewood Heights
MacGregor	13. Chasewood	21. Settegast
5. West End	14. Briargate	22. Trinity Gardens
6. Kashmere Gardens	15. Riceville	23. Scenic Woods
7. Pleasantville	16. Carvercrest-	24. Northwood Manor
8. Clinton Park	Pineypoint	25. Bordersville

Source: From *Invisible Houston: The Black Experience in Boom and Bust*, by Robert Bullard. Published by Texas A & M University Press, 1987. Base map by Key Maps, Inc.

nearby black residents. For example, the Houston city council annexed the all-black Riceville community in 1965. However, as late as 1982, this small black community in the rapidly growing southwest sector of Houston did not have running water, sewer or gas connections, sidewalks, paved streets, or regular garbage service.

Many of the inner-city black neighborhoods continue to lose residents

FIGURE 2
Black Population in Houston-Harris County, 1970

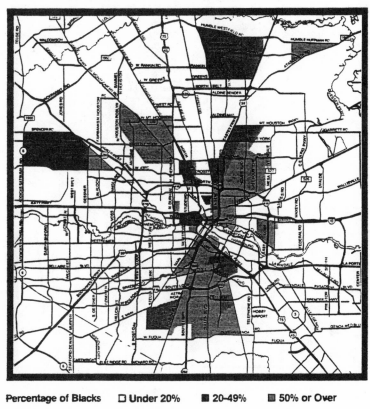

Percentage of Blacks □ Under 20% ■ 20-49% ▤ 50% or Over

Source: From *Invisible Houston: The Black Experience in Boom and Bust*, by Robert Bullard. Published by Texas A & M University Press, 1987. Base map by Key Maps, Inc.

and a substantial share of their low- and moderate-income housing stock. Most noticeable, neighborhood decline is manifested through an increasing number of boarded up and abandoned buildings and empty lots that dot many inner-city neighborhoods. Limited income is a major factor that prevents many residents in these areas from competing for housing in other neighborhoods. Thus, families with limited incomes are caught between rising housing costs and a dwindling supply of decent and affordable housing in Houston's inner-city areas.

A disproportionately large share of black Houstonians continue to be ill-housed despite the efforts made by government. Inadequate housing is often clustered in inner-city minority areas where a large share of the

FIGURE 3
Black Population in Houston-Harris County, 1980

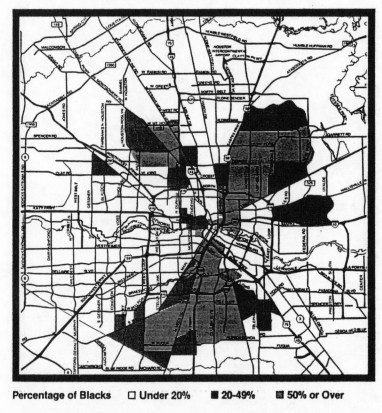

Percentage of Blacks ☐ Under 20%   ■ 20-49%   ▦ 50% or Over

Source: From *Invisible Houston: The Black Experience in Boom and Bust*, by Robert Bullard. Published by Texas A & M University Press, 1987. Base map by Key Maps, Inc.

city's poor also reside. The housing options and opportunities (e.g., owning vs. renting) that are available to blacks and other ethnic minorities have been shaped largely by (1) government housing policies, (2) institutional discrimination in the housing market, (3) housing construction priorities of builders, and (4) demographic changes and uneven development that have taken place in the city. The end result of these factors is reduced housing choices and limited residential amenities for black and lower-income residents.[5]

Federal housing policies were the chief sponsor of suburban development in the past four decades. Much of the current residential housing patterns and problems can be traced directly to the government's role during the fifties and sixties.[6] Moreover, the failures of the government's first "attack" on the nation's urban housing problem through urban renewal have been well documented. To a great extent, the "rehousing of displaced residents was subordinated to the primary goal of clearance and redevelopment."[7]

FEDERALLY SUBSIDIZED HOUSING FOR THE POOR

The U.S. Housing Act of 1937 and subsequent Texas enabling legislation led to the establishment of the Housing Authority of the City of Houston (HACH). The city's housing authority is responsible for construction of housing under the low-rent housing program. A two-pronged approach was used in carrying out the early mission of the local housing authority: (1) to clear slums and "blighted areas," and (2) to provide decent, safe, and sanitary housing. The early housing authority boards emphasized the slum clearance provision. Land acquisition for public housing projects was often mired in controversy. The passage of the local public housing referendum is a major contributing factor in determining the current size of the city's public housing stock. Conventional public housing construction in Houston received a major setback in 1950 when a referendum passed that limited the number of public housing units. Few public housing developments were built in the city between 1952 and 1975.

In an attempt to allow low- and moderate-income households to compete for decent, uncrowded, and safe housing in the private market, the federal government initiated the Section 8 rental assistance program. The subsidy program was created under the Housing and Community Development Act of 1974 and allowed low-income families to secure housing in privately owned buildings, which ordinarily would have rents that were prohibitively high for such families. The owners of housing in the program receive funds from the federal government to supplement rents from low-income tenants. The federal government pays a subsidy equal to the difference between the rents that low-income families can afford and federally certified fair-market rents for housing units. Thirty percent of the household income is the standard for what a low-income household could afford to pay toward rent.

The strategy for providing housing under Section 8 met with some difficulty that was not anticipated by its framers: (1) the program ignored

the shortage of decent housing that existed in many areas despite increased demand, (2) it did not take into consideration possible discrimination
based on race, sex, number of children, and welfare status, and (3) some
landlords were unwilling to rent to Section 8 program participants because they objected to the "fair market rent" ceilings that were determined by the U.S. Department of Housing and Urban Development. The
rent ceiling issue became especially critical in Houston during the seventies when demand for private market apartments was high and vacancy
rates were low.[8]

Houston's housing authority is the largest of the forty public housing
authorities in the Houston-Galveston area. Its annual operating budget is
over $50 million, and in 1983, it had a total of 9,893 units of subsidized
housing serving over 25,000 persons.[9] A breakdown of the Housing
Authority's subsidized units indicates that it owned and managed 4,077
units of public housing in fifteen developments scattered across the city.
By 1990, the number of subsidized units had increased to 12,808 of
which 4,443 were located in public housing developments.

Still, Houston—Texas's largest city—provided far fewer units of public housing than the 7,110 units in Dallas and the 8,300 units in San
Antonio. Although Houston and Philadelphia are similar in size, Philadelphia has more than 23,020 units of public housing. More than 13,000
persons were on the Houston Housing Authority waiting list for assisted
housing in 1987.[10]

In 1990, the Houston Housing Authority provided a total of 7,999 units
of Section 8 assisted housing. Historical patterns of racial and economic
segregation are often perpetuated by Houston's Section 8 housing program. Black program participants, for example, generally secure housing
in mostly black neighborhoods, while white program participants secure
housing in mostly white neighborhoods. A large share of the black Section 8 tenants secure housing in high-density "poverty pockets," where
housing is often deteriorating, deficient, and abandoned. Overall, Houston's Section 8 housing program has had a minimal effect in reversing
residential housing segregation among lower-income black households.

The need for additional units of low-rent and assisted housing in Houston far exceeds the current supply.[11] At least one-fifth of the city's more
than 600,000 households are inadequately housed and could qualify for
some type of housing assistance. Black Houstonians, in particular, are
more likely to be ill-housed than the larger community.

THE POLITICS OF HOUSTON'S PUBLIC HOUSING

The city's aging and rapidly deteriorating public housing stock represents an additional problem to the local housing authority in its effort to provide decent, safe, and sanitary housing for low- and moderate-income families. These problems are exacerbated by dwindling financial resources, weakened political commitment, and growing citizen opposition to public housing. Public housing has become a volatile political issue that has the potential of creating protests from both suburban whites as well as inner-city blacks.

White suburbanites fear their neighborhoods will be targets for low-rent public housing developments as a result of federal site selection policies that aim to preclude construction of new subsidized units from "impacted" areas (i.e., neighborhoods with large concentration of minorities and low-income residents). Suburban residents also fear that lower-income housing projects would adversely affect their property values and the overall quality of life in their respective neighborhoods. The fear is shallow since most new low-rent public housing still goes into impacted areas because HUD modified its procedures to allow construction in impacted areas if there is an overriding need for housing and suburbs block construction in their jurisdictions. Black inner-city residents, on the other hand, fear that public housing developments are being programmed for failure through a policy of neglect.

There is a discernible pattern to the location of "family" developments and "elderly" developments as part of the low-rent public housing program (see Table 1). Houston's public housing developments that are designed for families tend to be located on the eastern half of the city, where the black population is concentrated. Seven of the twelve housing developments designed for families are located in mostly black census tracts and eight family developments are located on Houston's eastside. On the other hand, two of the three housing authority's high rise developments designed for elderly tenants are located on Houston's westside. Only one of the developments designed for elderly tenants is located in a mostly black census tract.

It is becoming increasingly difficult to build family developments in Houston. A case in point involved the 1982 decision by the Houston Housing Authority to approve the construction of two family developments in predominately white neighborhoods. The housing authority approved the construction of a $5 million, 105-unit low-income housing

TABLE 1
Houston Housing Authority Developments–1990

Development	Houston Location	Number of Units	Percent Black in Census Tract[a]
Family			
Allen Parkway Village	Southwest	1,000	63.4
Clayton Homes	Southeast	348	17.3
Cuney Homes	Southeast	564	99.4
Ewing	Southeast	42	47.2
Forest Green	Northeast	100	78.8
Irvington Village	Northwest	318	6.2
Kelly Village	Northeast	333	94.3
Kennedy Place	Northeast	60	94.3
Lincoln Park	Northwest	264	60.6
Long Drive	Southeast	100	1.3
Oxford Place	Northwest	230	4.3
Wilmington House	Southeast	108	99.5
Elderly			
Bellerive	Southwest	210	4.7
Lyerly	Northwest	200	56.5
Telephone Road	Southeast	200	35.4

[a]Percentages are based on 1980 Census figures.
Source: Housing Authority of the City of Houston (January 1990).

development in the Westbury area. The census tract in which the proposed project was to be built had an ethnic composition of 89 percent white, 4 percent black, and 7 percent Hispanic. The selection of the mostly white neighborhood in southwest Houston triggered protests, demonstrations, and legal action. The proposed project was ultimately killed after the developer had problems securing the $5 million loan to begin construction.

Citizen opposition to the proposed development influenced the housing authority later to revise its application to the U.S. Department of Housing and Urban Development from a family development to one that would house elderly persons. An elderly development on the proposed site in the mostly white Westbury area would likely have generated less controversy than the original proposal for a family development. Historically, the city's assisted family developments are comprised of minority tenants (i.e., blacks, Hispanics, and Indochinese), while the low-rent elderly housing developments are occupied primarily by whites.

Another case involved a proposed public housing development slated to be built in northwest Houston. A $3.5 million, 80-unit public housing development was approved in 1982 by the Houston Housing Authority for the predominately white Spring Branch area. The census tract in which the low-income housing development was to have been built is 87 percent white, 4 percent black, and 9 percent Hispanic. Residents of the Spring Branch area were also able to generate enough support at the various levels of government to convince the developer not to purchase the land for the proposed project. The housing authority subsequently dropped the controversial low-income family development planned for this middle-income neighborhood. The Houston Housing Authority also met intense public opposition from its proposal to build a family development near mostly-white Pasadena—a city in Harris County (bordering Houston) known for its ultraconservative politics.

RACE AND THE GHETTOIZATION OF THE POOR IN HOUSTON

The ethnic composition of the city's assisted housing developments in 1976 and 1990 is presented in Tables 2 and 3. Minority households for both time periods (1976 and 1990) were more likely to be housed in family developments. Whites, on the other hand, were more likely to be found in assisted developments designed for the elderly. As late as 1984, for example, whites comprised the vast majority of tenants in the housing authority's high-rise developments designed for the elderly. In that year whites made up 64.1 percent of the tenants in the Lyerly development, 72.9 percent in the Bellerive development, and 70.9 percent in the Telephone Road development. By 1990, over half of the tenants in the Lyerly and Bellerive elderly developments were minority households. Whites still made up the majority of tenants in the Telephone Road development in 1990.

TABLE 2
Ethnic Composition of Houston Housing Authority Developments–1976

Ethnic Composition of Developments[a]

Housing Development	No. of Units	Percent Black	Percent Hispanic	Percent White	Percent Asian/ Other	Percent Black in Census Tract[b]
Family						
Allen Parkway Village	1,000	66.0	3.0	26.0	5.0	84.3
Clayton Homes	348	58.0	32.0	3.0	7.0	18.4
Cuney Homes	564	99.0	1.0	-	-	99.0
Irvington Village	318	25.0	55.0	20.0	-	7.1
Kelley Village	333	100.0	-	-	-	99.1
Elderly						
75 Lyerly	200	7.0	4.0	89.0	-	43.3
Bellerive	210	1.0	4.0	95.0	-	0.1

[a]Ethnic composition of housing developments as of September 1976 was calculated by the Houston Housing Authority.
[b]Census tract data are based on the 1970 census figures.

Although gains were made in expanding the supply of low-cost housing available to Houstonians, the city experienced some slippage in family developments. A case in point is the loss of apartments in the 1,000-unit Allen Parkway Village development. The future of Houston's mostly black Fourth Ward is often linked to the fate of Allen Parkway Village, one of the city's oldest public housing projects. This linkage is highlighted by the commonly held belief that "as goes Allen Parkway Village, so goes the Fourth Ward." Allen Parkway Village has been the subject of much speculation as a result of the housing development's close proximity to the downtown area. The public housing project has experienced a dramatic change in its tenant population beginning in the mid-seventies. Blacks comprised 66 percent of the project tenant population in 1976, while Asians made up only 5 percent of the project tenants. The black tenant population in Allen Parkway Village dropped to 34 percent in 1984 while the Indochinese tenant population, mostly ref-

TABLE 3
Ethnic Composition of Houston Housing Authority Developments–1990

Housing Development	No. of Units	Percent Black	Percent Hispanic	Percent White	Percent Asian/ Other	Percent Black in Census Tract[b]
Family						
Allen Parkway Village	1,000	62.2	4.5	11.1	22.2	63.4
Clayton Homes	348	60.0	19.5	0.5	20.0	17.3
Cuney Homes	564	98.1	1.3	0.4	0.2	99.4
Irvington Village	318	53.9	38.8	4.7	2.6	6.2
Kelly Village	333	95.7	0.8	1.5	2.0	94.3
Lincoln Park	264	98.5	1.0	0.5	0.0	0.6
Oxford Place	230	93.9	1.5	3.8	0.8	4.3
Forest Green	100	97.8	1.1	1.1	0.0	13.7
Ewing	42	88.9	2.8	8.3	0.0	47.2
Kennedy Place	60	88.3	5.0	0.0	6.7	94.3
Wilmington House	108	89.1	0.0	0.0	10.9	99.5
Long Drive	100	87.3	8.0	3.4	1.3	1.3
Elderly						
75 Lyerly	200	35.6	20.1	43.8	0.5	4.7
Bellerive	210	12.6	24.8	46.6	16.0	56.5
Telephone Road	200	29.9	10.8	57.8	1.5	35.4

[a]Ethnic composition of housing developments as of January 1990 was calculated by the Houston Housing Authority.
[b]Census tract data are based on the 1980 Census figures.

ugees, increased to over 58 percent of the project in 1984. The 1976 and 1980 period was the crucial era that established Allen Parkway Village as a project for "refugees" (see Table 4), although occupancy of the project has changed somewhat since then.

The political implication of the housing authority replacing blacks with Asian refugees is fairly obvious: the demolition of a public housing project that housed primarily Indochinese refugees would cause less political "fallout" than demolition of the same project housing a predominately black tenant population. The city's black population constitutes a

TABLE 4
Ethnic Composition of Allen Parkway Village
for Selected Years

Year	Percent Black	Percent Hispanic	Percent White	Percent Asian/Other	Percent Total
1976	66.0	3.0	26.0	5.0	100.0
1980	45.8	2.3	10.9	41.0	100.0
1983	33.1	2.0	6.9	58.0	100.0
1984	34.1	2.8	5.0	58.1	100.0
1990[a]	62.2	4.5	11.1	22.2	100.0

[a]The 1000-unit Allen Parkway Village development in January, 1990 had only 45 units that were occupied.
Source: Houston Housing Authority, Housing Management Division, *Allen Parkway Village Summary Reports* (1990).

potent political bloc. The ethnic composition of the project remained stable in 1983 and 1984. The physical conditions of the forty-six year old Allen Parkway Village project has been rapidly deteriorating over the years to the point that most of the apartments in the development, including many of the occupied units are neither decent, safe, nor sanitary. Only 45 apartments in the 1,000-unit development were occupied in January of 1990—28 by blacks, 10 by Asians, 5 by whites, and 2 by Hispanics.

A 1983 study analyzed the housing conditions in the Allen Parkway Village development and housing options for the surrounding Fourth Ward Neighborhood.[12] The housing authority's board voted to demolish the project. Its proposal called for replacement units, elderly mid-rise housing in the Fourth Ward, and incentives to leverage additional low- and moderate-income housing units that might result from the new construction of housing on the 37-acre site as well as future housing development within the larger Fourth Ward neighborhood. The federal government subsequently refused to approve the housing authority's replacement plan, thereby blocking demolition of the project.

BARRIERS TO FREE CHOICE

While many barriers to decent and affordable housing for Houstonians have been overcome, a sizable portion of the city's black population still does not enjoy complete freedom in the housing market. It has been two decades since the Federal Fair Housing Act of 1968 banned racial discrimination in housing. Persistent barriers and obstacles to free choice provided the main impetus for the 1988 Fair Housing Amendments Act.

Discriminatory practices complicate the housing search for thousands of black Houstonians. The various forms of discrimination also contribute to the decline of many inner-city neighborhoods and deny a substantial segment of the community a basic form of wealth accumulation and investment through home ownership.[12] The practices of refusing to sell or lease housing to blacks, coding records and applications to indicate racial preferences of landlords, selective marketing and advertising, racial steering, redlining, and threats or acts of intimidation continue to be problems that limit the housing alternatives available to black households.

Houston's black homeseekers generally must expend more time, effort, and resources than whites for the same end. Realtors and lending institutions often serve as "gatekeepers" in distributing housing and residential packages. The number of black homeowners would probably be higher in the absence of housing discrimination by realtors and lending institutions. Some 47.2 percent of blacks in the Houston metropolitan area owned their homes in 1980 compared with 58.8 percent of area whites.

The federal government has played an important role in promoting fair housing. However, federal "financial and manpower support to rigorously pursue fair housing efforts have been inadequate."[13] Civil rights violations in the area of fair housing often go uncorrected. Part of this problem is linked to the low priority accorded enforcement of the fair housing laws. The federal government working alone can not eliminate housing discrimination.

The Houston city government, in an effort to promote open housing, passed its Fair Housing Ordinance on July 9, 1975, some seven years after enactment of the Federal Fair Housing Act of 1968. The city ordinance created the Fair Housing Division and charged it with monitoring housing discrimination complaints that originated within the Houston city limits. Houston's Fair Housing Ordinance was patterned after its federal counterpart. The local ordinance prohibited discrimination in the sale, rental, or financing of housing, and discrimination in broker services due to race, color, sex, religion, or national origin.

The city's 1975 fair housing ordinance suffered from some of the same defects that limited its federal counterpart: namely, weak enforcement provisions. Moreover, financial support for the local agency diminished over the years. In 1977, the city agency was staffed by nine full-time employees, four of whom were compliance officers. By 1984, the agency's staff had dwindled to only three persons—an "acting" director, one compliance officer, and a secretary. In 1985, the severely crippled Houston's Fair Housing Division was merged with the city's Affirmative Action Division.

Despite the problems that the local fair housing agency experienced, Houstonians continued to file housing discrimination complaints. A total of 1,617 housing discrimination complaints were received by the city between 1975 and 1982 (see Table 5). Complaint activity fluctuated from year to year, with the greatest number of complaints coming in 1976, the second action year of the fair housing agency. The "newness" of the city's fair housing agency no doubt contributed to the large volume of housing discrimination complaints registered during the program's early years.

The number of housing discrimination complaints registered with the city appears to correlate with the local economic climate and staffing pattern of the local fair housing agency. For example, new housing starts (e.g., building permits), number of fair housing employees, and complaint activity were highest from the mid-seventies through the late seventies. Conversely, a decrease in complaint activity occurred during the economic recessions of the early eighties, and these recessions dramatically affected the fair housing enforcement capability of the city agency.

Housing discrimination complaint activity also differed significantly with the ethnic composition of the neighborhoods where the complaints originated. In general, complaints were more likely to originate from Houston neighborhoods with few minorities. Nearly 57 percent of the city's housing discrimination complaints filed on the basis of race or color in 1979 and 1980 originated from individuals who lived in census tracts where minorities comprised less than 25 percent of the tract population (See Table 6). More than 84.2 percent of the complaints based upon race/color and 92.6 percent of the complaints based upon national origin came from individuals who lived in census tracts where whites were the overwhelming majority.

On the other hand, complaints based on sex did not conform to this pattern. Sex discrimination complaints were concentrated in both minority and nonminority areas. More than 44 percent of the complaints based upon sex were found in census tracts where blacks and Hispanics comprised the numerical majority. Conversely, nearly 41 percent of the cases

TABLE 5
Housing Discrimination Complaint Activity in Houston
1975–1982

Year of Complaint	Number
1975[a]	73
1976	478
1977	233
1978	316
1979	175
1980	120
1981	117
1982	105
Total	1,617

[a]Includes only the period July 9, 1975 through December 31, 1975.
Source: Houston Fair Housing Division (1983).

that alleged sex discrimination in the housing search originated from individuals who lived in census tracts where minorities comprised less than 25 percent of the population.

These data show that sex discrimination in the housing industry complicates the housing search for women, and especially minority women, in both minority and white neighborhoods. Black and Hispanic women are often the victims of the triple "whammy" of racial, sex, and family status (e.g., single parent status) discrimination.[14]

CONCLUSION

Federally assisted housing for the poor has been pushed down the

TABLE 6
Type of Alleged Housing Discrimination by Percent Minority
in Complaint Census Tracts, Houston 1979–1980[a]

| | Type of Alleged Discrimination | | | |
Percent Minority in Complaint Census Tract	Race/ Color	National Origin	Sex	Total
Less than 25	118 (56.4%)	18 (66.7%)	11 (40.7%)	147 (55.9%)
25–49	58 (27.8%)	7 (25.9%)	4 (14.8%)	69 (26.2%)
50 or over	33 (15.8%)	2 (7.4%)	12 (44.5%)	47 (17.9%)
Total	209 (100.0%)	27 (100.0%)	27 (100.0%)	263 (100.0%)

[a]There were 295 housing discrimination complaints filed with Houston's Fair Housing Division in the years 1979 and 1980. The above analysis, however, is based upon 263 files in which type of discrimination was recorded. Thirty-two case files did not list this item.
Source: City of Houston Fair Housing Division (1982).

national agenda. It is also a low priority at the local level. Few cities, including Houston, can afford to have their public housing taken out of the market. However, the nation's public housing developments are in such a state of disrepair that they are literally falling down. This housing problem is a national disgrace.

The weakened federal commitment to providing decent, safe, and affordable housing for low- and moderate-income households has left Houston and many other housing authorities with extreme fiscal problems that are not likely to disappear in the near future. Additionally, the "politicization" of public housing site selection (especially family developments) and citizen opposition further complicate the job of local housing authorities. Few neighborhoods welcome public housing developments, especially family developments, in their backyards. The "NIMBY" (not in my backyard) phenomenon (used mostly by residents of white neighborhoods) has stalled the local housing authority's efforts to expand the mix of federally assisted housing for low- and moderate-income individuals.

Although Houston, the nation's fourth largest city and largest city in the South, has made modest gains in improving the quantity of low-rent housing stock—mainly through the Section 8 program—it still lags behind other cities of comparable size when it comes to subsidized housing for families and the elderly. The 1990s will offer some crucial challenges for big-city housing authorities faced with dwindling resources. The solution to this problem does not lie in demolishing low-income housing developments.

Houstonians still must contend with institutional housing barriers. Housing discrimination complaints increase as blacks and other persons of color venture into mostly white areas seeking housing. Black Houstonians bear the brunt of housing discrimination. Housing discrimination denies a significant portion of the black population decent and affordable housing. Moreover, discrimination denies them a basic form of investment (through home ownership) and contributes to the decline of many inner-city neighborhoods.

After getting a late start in fair housing—the city council passed a local ordinance creating the Fair Housing Division some seven years after the federal fair housing legislation—Houston's commitment to nondiscriminatory housing was weakened by the dismantling of the local fair housing agency. The phasing out of the Fair Housing Division sent a clear signal that nondiscriminatory housing is *not* a priority of the Houston city government.

Finally, the goal of decent and affordable housing for all Houstonians has yet to be realized. Racial discrimination blocks housing opportunities for many black Houstonians. The Houston city government needs to take a more aggressive stance in dismantling the remaining institutional barriers in the housing market. The time has come for the city to enforce antidiscrimination laws in housing—a federal mandate—with the same vigor it enforces other laws.

NOTES

1. U.S. Bureau of the Census, *State and Metropolitan Area Data Book 1982* (Washington, D.C.: Government Printing Office, 1982), p. 386.

2. For a detailed discussion of Houston's wards and the city's other mostly black neighborhoods see Robert D. Bullard, *Invisible Houston: The Black Experience in Boom and Bust* (College Station, Texas: Texas A & M University Press, 1987); Beth A. Shelton, Nestor Rodriguez, Joe R. Feagin, Robert D. Bullard, and Robert D. Thomas, *Houston: Growth and Decline in a Sunbelt Boomtown* (Philadelphia: Temple University Press, 1989); Robert D. Bullard, *In Search of the New South: The Black Urban Experience in the 1970s and 1980s* (Tuscaloosa: University of Alabama Press, 1989), chapter 2.

3. Karl E. Taeuber, "Racial Residential Segregation, 28 Cities 1970–1980," CDE Working Paper, University of Wisconsin, Madison (March 1983), p. 1.

4. See Larry Long and Diane De Are, "The Suburbanization of Blacks," *American Demographics* 3 (September 1981), p. 20; Robert D. Bullard, "Black Housing in the

Golden Buckle of the Sunbelt," *Free Inquiry* 8 (November 1980), 169–172; Robert D. Bullard and Odessa L. Pierce, "Black Housing in a Southern Metropolis: Competition for Housing in a Shrinking Market," *The Black Scholar* 11 (November/December 1979), 60–67.

5. For a thorough discussion on minority housing see Jamshid A. Momeni (ed.), *Race, Ethnicity and Minority Housing in the United States* (Westport, CT: Greenwood Press, 1986); also Robert D. Bullard, "Persistent Barriers in Housing Black Americans," *Journal of Applied Social Sciences* 7 (Fall/Winter 1983), 19–31.

6. G.L. Houseman, "Access of Minorities to Suburbs," *The Urban Social Change Review* 14 (1981), 11–20.

7. W.R. Morris, "The Black Struggle for Fair Housing: 1900–1980," *The Urban League Review* 5 (Summer 1981), 6–7; Robert D. Bullard, "The Black Family: Housing Alternatives in the 80s," *The Journal of Black Studies* 14 (March 1984), 341–351.

8. Robert D. Bullard, "Does Section 8 Promote An Ethnic and Economic Mix?" *Journal of Housing* 7 (July 1978), 364–365.

9. Housing Authority of the City of Houston, *Annual Report* (Houston: Housing Authority of the City of Houston, 1984), 3.

10. See Robert D. Bullard, *Invisible Houston*, pp. 40–49; John Gilderbloom, Mark Rosentraub, and Robert D. Bullard, *Designing, Locating and Financing Housing and Transportation Services for Low Income, Elderly and Disabled Persons* (Houston: University of Houston Center for Policy Research, 1987), pp. 21–28; Joe R. Feagin, *Free Enterprise City: Houston in Political and Economic Perspective* (New Brunswick: Rutgers University Press, 1987), pp. 261–264.

11. Robert Aprea, Robert D. Bullard, Jeff Baloutine, and Jacqueline Alford, *Allen Parkway Village/Fourth Ward Technical Report* (Houston: Housing Authority of the City of Houston, 1983).

12. See Robert D. Bullard and Donald L. Tryman, "Competition for Decent Housing: A Focus on Housing Discrimination in a Sunbelt City," *The Journal of Ethnic Studies* 7 (Winter 1980), 51–63; Franklin James, Betty L. McCummings and Eileen A. Tynan, *Minorities in the Sunbelt* (New Brunswick, NJ: Rutgers University Center for Urban Policy Research, 1984); and Robert D. Bullard, *Invisible Houston: The Black Experience in Boom and Bust* (College Station, TX: Texas A & M University Press, 1987); Robert D. Bullard, ed., "Blacks in Heavenly Houston." Pp. 16–44 in *In Search of the New South: The Black Urban Experience in the 1970s and 1980s* (Tuscaloosa, AL: University of Alabama Press, 1989).

13. U.S. Commission on Civil Rights, *The Federal Fair Housing Enforcement Efforts* (Washington, D.C.: Government Printing Office, 1979), p. 230.

14. See J.G. Greene and G.P. Blake, *How Restrictive Rental Practices Affect Families with Children* (Washington, D.C.: National Neighbors, Inc., for U.S. Department of Housing and Urban Development, 1980); Wilhelmina A. Leigh, "Barriers to Fair Housing for Black Women," *Sex Roles* 21 (1989), 69–84.

10

HOUSING FOR BLACKS:
A CHALLENGE FOR KANSAS CITY

William E. (Gene) Robertson

City planners, neighborhood groups and financial institutions, and
other business partners need to develop a comprehensive plan to increase affordable housing for minorities and to integrate neighborhoods. Kansas City, Missouri is a city with a high potential for good
housing for all of its citizens, but adequate housing continues to elude
many of its black residents. Compared to other U.S. cities of similar
size, Kansas City has good housing stock, but a large number of black
people are suffering from a shortage of low rent housing. In addition,
among Kansas Citians, blacks have the lowest quality housing stock.
Two reasons for the deficit in housing for black Americans in Kansas
City are demolitions among the low-rent housing stock and discrimination in housing rentals.

Kansas City, Missouri has always been a "City of Vision." It has
often been called the easternmost western city, reflecting a willingness to
try new ideas and accept new people, and yet it is a "casual city." The
people of Kansas City are generally easy to get along with and friendly.

Development has been one of the ideas and concepts most appealing to
Kansas Citians, although business development has outpaced residential
development in the city. When housing is considered—as with the upscale residential developments such as Soho West, Quality Hill, the River
Quay, and the Historic Government Center—there is little interest in
low-income housing. Low-income housing is perceived mainly as a bar-
rier to development and a threat to developers. Lip service may be given
to mixed-income housing, but rarely has this become a reality. Yet if this
city would confront the need for development in the housing sector, then
comprehensive development would be addressed forthrightly and posi-
tively.

This article examines the challenges that confront black Americans

TABLE 1
Households, Population, and Tenure by Race
in Kansas City, MO, 1980

	No. of Households	Population Distribution	% of Households that Rent
White	130,342	74.38%	40%
Black	41,158	23.49%	48%
American Indian	723	.41%	61%
Asian	1,154	.66%	67%
Hispanic	1,819	1.04%	46%
Other	31	.02%	N/A
TOTAL	175,227	100.00%	42%

Source: U.S. Population Census
Supplied by the Office of Social Economic Data Analysis
University of Missouri-Columbia

seeking housing in Kansas City. The first section provides background information on the city population and housing stock. The second section discusses the housing market features that have major impacts on black Americans. The third and final section provides an overall assessment of housing for blacks in Kansas City.

POPULATION AND HOUSING

According to the Census, Kansas City contained 448,028 people in 175,227 households in 1980. By 1986, the city's population had decreased to 441,170. In Table 1, the number of households according to race is shown, as well as the percentage of those households that rent and the population distribution by race.

The three counties adjoining Kansas City, MO that constitute its closest suburbs are Jackson, Clay, and Platte. Of these three counties, Jackson is the only one with any tracts hosting minority populations of 50 percent or greater. Minorities residing in tracts with 50 percent or more minority population in Jackson County represent 48 percent of the total minority population in the metropolitan Kansas City area.

According to the Kansas City Board of Realtors, in 1980, the average price of a house was $47,737. By 1989 the average price of a house sold had risen to $64,223 and the number of houses sold was 582.

The physical housing stock in Kansas City is strong compared to homes in eastern cities. These homes were built later, generally of brick, stone and other sturdy materials, because population growth occurred later in the Midwest and West than in the East. Consequently, many of the homes can be easily rehabilitated because the house shell is very strong.

However, housing conditions in central city areas are less desirable than in other parts of the metropolitan area. (See Exhibits 1, 2, and 3). The average housing condition scores in the central portion of Kansas City, illustrated in Exhibits 1, 2, and 3, indicate that the best housing (1.0) exists in areas 25, 28, 72, and 73. These areas border the largest concentration of black residents (except area 44). The housing in the worst condition, area 70, is located in the heart of the central city. In the north portion of Kansas City, where there are fewer black residents, housing condition is considerably better, with the lowest areas having only a 2.6–2.9 scores (see Exhibit 2).

For example, as of mid-March 1989, within the central city, there were 993 boarded, fire damaged, vacant and vandalized buildings containing 2,269 living units. An additional 899 buildings within the central city were presumably unavailable for occupancy because they had no water service during all of 1988.

There is without question a correlation among poverty, race, and housing conditions, when one observes poor housing conditions in Kansas City. In the South and East sections of Kansas City, the black population is very small. There are a few pockets of low-income whites with poor housing conditions (see Section 59 of Exhibit 3). In general, housing lived in by blacks is in poorer condition in the inner city than white housing in the urban core and on the outskirts of Kansas City.

Vacant lots and boarded or vandalized houses are frequently cited in conjunction with criminal activity, from personal assaults to drug sales. Their presence can speed the exodus from a neighborhood of those persons who are able to leave and can directly cause the deterioration of adjacent property.

HOUSING MARKET FEATURES AND BLACK AMERICANS

In recent years, the sector of the housing market that serves low-income and minority residents in Kansas City has experienced several changes. First, an increasing number of units have been demolished and not replaced. Second, rents have increased in the areas that serve minority households, partly due to the shortage induced by the demolitions. Third,

EXHIBIT 1
1987–88 Housing Conditions Average Unit Score

Central Portion of Kansas City, Missouri 1980 Census Tracts

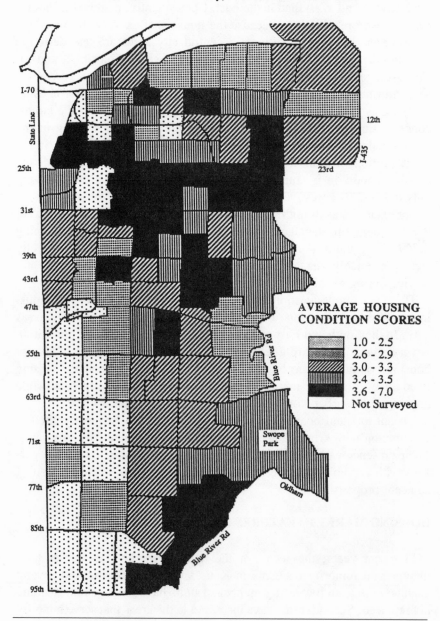

EXHIBIT 2
1987–88 Housing Conditions Average Unit Score

North Portion of Kansas City, Missouri 1980 Census Tracts

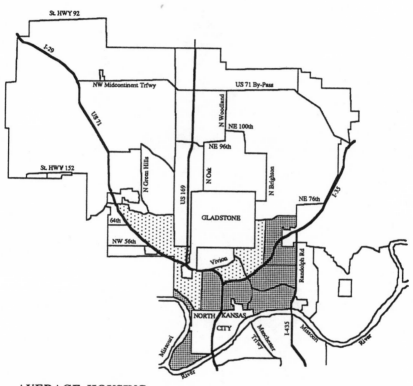

AVERAGE HOUSING
CONDITION SCORES

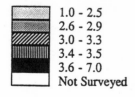

1.0 - 2.5
2.6 - 2.9
3.0 - 3.3
3.4 - 3.5
3.6 - 7.0
Not Surveyed

EXHIBIT 3
1987–88 Housing Conditions Average Unit Score

South and East Portions of Kansas City, Missouri 1980 Census Tracts

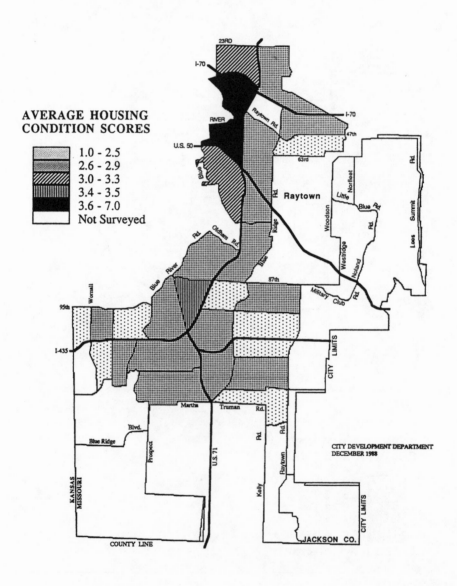

federal housing assistance has been reduced, further limiting the options for low-income households. Finally, perceived and actual housing market discrimination have made it difficult for black Americans to move from areas of minority concentration.

Housing Demolition

Over the past nine years, more than 6,200 units have been demolished and lost to low-income households due to the acquisition of land for construction of new upscale developments and the renovation of older areas. Only 27 percent of these units have been replaced through new construction. In particular, from 1980 through 1988, 4,010 housing units were demolished in the central city area.[1] Eighty-eight percent of all residential demolition in Kansas City took place within that area. The boundaries the city has used to determine where much of the demolition has taken and will take place are contiguous with the boundaries the city residents perceive as the "black area of Kansas City" (See Exhibit 4).

During the same period, 1,695 housing units were constructed in the study area. Forty-three percent of those units were built in Quality Hill, Union Hill, Westport, and the Plaza area. Of the 19,403 housing units built in the entire city during the same period, less than 9 percent were located within the study area.

To some degree, the removal of older central city housing stock is part of the natural evolution of a city. It is the result of new development in older areas, the migration of city residents to the suburbs, the wearing out of buildings over long periods of service without substantial maintenance, changes in local and federal tax codes affecting rental property, and changes in ownership and income patterns within a neighborhood. Yet as noted earlier, much of the Kansas City housing stock could be preserved rather than replaced because of the sturdiness of building materials.

Rents

At a time when the overall local rental housing market is as soft as it has been in years, the situation at the low end of the rental market is exactly the opposite. Social service agencies are finding it increasingly difficult to locate housing for their clients, even in traditionally affordable central city neighborhoods. If a building has been demolished, no one can live in it. If it has been boarded or left vacant and vandalized, no one

EXHIBIT 4
Building the Wall Along Troost Avenue

Over several decades the black population of Kansas City has moved southward but remained segregated within its own neighborhoods. The shaded portions below are census tracts where the black population was 50 percent or more of all residents.

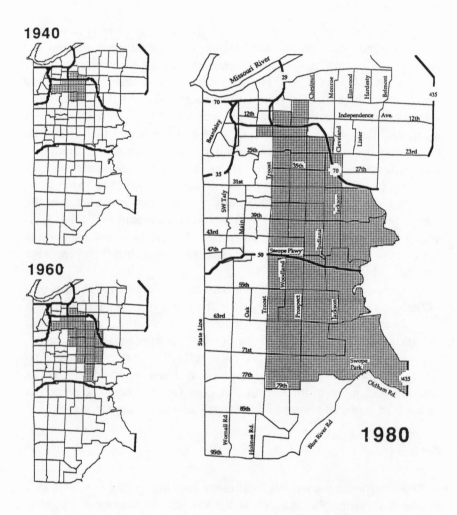

should be living in it. Since the bulk of lower-priced rental housing can be found in the central city, removal of units in those neighborhoods dramatically reduces the options for lower-income renters.

What is apparent is that too many low-income families are competing for too few affordable housing units. As in a game of musical chairs, some families are left standing when the music stops. Evidence of those left standing is provided by Kansas City's centralized Homeless Hotline. In 1988, the Hotline logged 6,210 unduplicated requests for emergency shelter space on behalf of families representing 12,654 people.

Federally Subsidized Housing

From Urban Renewal through Model Cities to Community Development Block Grants,[2] the federal government has been the primary funder of housing and neighborhood development activity. The past eight years have witnessed a steady withdrawal of a federal presence in these areas which has not been replaced at the local level.

Since 1981, federal funding for new activity in low-income housing has been cut by 76 percent, from more than $33 billion to under $8 billion. During this same period, the annual number of new federally assisted housing units has dropped from more than 200,000 to approximately 25,000.[3]

The primary federal initiative to involve the private sector in the production of affordable housing is a low-income housing tax credit enacted in 1986. That legislation has been extended to the end of 1991. The only other significant contributors to the stock of affordable housing are nonprofit community development corporations which also have had their federal funding reduced considerably in the past decade.

As testament to this in Kansas City, the housing authority's Section 8 rent subsidy program has been closed for two years due to a long waiting list. The housing authority has 3,524 apartments in the Section 8 subsidy program but only 256 are vacant. Up to 3,000 persons have applied for these 256 units.[4]

Yet when plans to build or purchase subsidized housing are aired, there is a big outcry from the neighborhood involved. For example, on January 21, 1990, city and state officials met with more than five hundred South Kansas City residents—both black and white—who thought a plan by the Kansas City housing authority was bringing too many subsidized units into some blue collar communities. The residents felt that many of the targeted areas were already integrated and that increasing the number of low-income housing units would only start another slum in their area. The black mayor pro tem and the Kansas City human relations director agreed with the residents.[5] Jackson County issued an order to stop the housing authority's plan to appropriate any properties in the specified areas. The housing authority plan appeared to lack the balance needed to prevent the target areas from losing their stability.

HOUSING MARKET DISCRIMINATION

The remaining problem facing black Kansas City residents is the perceived discriminatory practices that prevent former residents of substandard or demolished housing from seeking alternative housing outside the black areas of the central city.

In 1988, Kansas City was ranked as the twentieth most-segregated city in a study of housing in fifty-nine metropolitan areas in the United States. A nationwide study of racial residential segregation shows that Kansas City's segregation index of ninety on a scale of one-hundred in 1970 had dropped only four points to eighty-six in 1980.[7] This means that in 1970, 90 percent of the households of either racial group would have needed to move to enable all blocks in the city to have the same percentage of blacks and whites as for the city overall. By 1980, 86 percent of the households of either racial group would have needed to move to enable all blocks in the city to have the same percentage of blacks and whites as for the city overall.

This fact was also brought to light when the federal court ordered the Kansas City School District to dismantle its traditional dual system of education, which was the direct result of persistent housing segregation and "white flight." One question that remains unanswered is whether these patterns were primarily the result of the real estate practice of steering racial minorities into certain neighborhoods or merely the result of housing consumers exercising their freedom of choice.

A summary report of a survey of housing discrimination in Kansas City by the Kansas City human relations department states that Kansas City remains a segregated city in spite of local, state, and federal fair housing laws.[6] The Department of Human Relations undertook an eighteen-month study of real estate practices in the Kansas City housing market from June 1, 1987 to November 30, 1988, as they relate to race. The department studied forty-seven apartment complexes and forty real estate agencies dispersed across the city. This study audited the complexes and agencies by sending blacks, and then whites—matched for socioeconomic characteristics and housing requirements—to inquire about housing to see if discriminatory practices were in fact occurring.

The results of the rental audits demonstrated negative differential treatment of blacks in the areas of apartment availability, application fees, waiting lists, and reference requirements. Discrimination against blacks was observed 8.4 percent of the time because rental agents falsified information on the availability of rental units and 11.7 percent of the time because rental agents falsified information on the terms and conditions of rental housing. The falsification of availability and different rental terms and conditions translated into 30 instances of discrimination out of 158 rental audits.

Examples of methods used to discriminate against black renters include:

- denials by owners or managers that vacancies exist when they do;
- quoting higher rental rates;
- not mentioning rent specials, such as one month's free rent or no deposit required;
- offering later, and often more inconvenient, move-in dates; and
- saying that their names must be placed on a waiting list even though units are available.

A similar audit of the sales market focused on housing availability, courtesy shown by the agent, services provided, amount of information solicited by the agent of the prospective buyer, and steering activities. A detailed examination of the evidence produced by this study reveals pockets of steering. Out of the 11,300 sales transactions in Kansas City between September 1988 and September 1989, if steering occurred with actual sales transactions to the same degree as in the sales market audits, (i.e., 20 percent), there would have been 2,260 incidents of steering. There were clear attempts to steer white and black auditors into and away from certain areas, as evidenced by the concentrations of black and white auditor results.

An additional study has been undertaken by the greater Kansas City Community Housing Resource Board to determine the percentage of new rental housing development in areas of different minority concentrations. Three adjoining counties were the focus of the study: Jackson, Clay, and Platte counties. Because Jackson County is the only county in the target area that hosts census tracts with minority populations of 50 percent or greater, it is the focus of this analysis.

The shading on the Jackson County census tract map signifies minority populations of 90 percent or greater, 85 percent to 89 percent, and 50 percent to 84 percent (Exhibit 5). The area of over 50 percent minority concentration represents 19.6 percent of the total Jackson County population and receives 5.34 percent of the new rental housing development activity. In comparison, the south and east tracts (Exhibit 3), chosen for their demographic similarity yet containing less than 50 percent minority concentrations, represents 12.27 percent of the total Jackson County population and receives 9.26 percent of the new rental housing development activity. Ten census tracts host new rental housing development activity of five-hundred units or greater. These tracts have an average minority population of 8.6 percent and account for over 40 percent of all new rental housing development in a three-county area.

This isolated comparison study suggests that there is a negative correlation between the percentage of minorities in the three-county area and the development of new rental housing. The ratios of the percentage of the representative population to the percentage of new rental housing activity in the minority areas and midtown areas, respectively, are 1:.27 and 1:.73.

ASSESSMENT OF HOUSING FOR BLACKS IN KANSAS CITY, MO

Kansas City has problems of housing shortage for black Americans. The shortage arises from several factors: demolition of many of the units in areas that blacks have inhabited traditionally, rent increases on the remaining units in traditionally black areas, reduced federal housing assistance, and discriminatory housing market practices that limit the areas in which blacks can seek and acquire units.

Local groups have played an active role in trying to address some of these problems. For instance, the Neighborhood Housing Services of Kansas City, Inc., a nonprofit development corporation, has tried to forestall demolitions of units through renovations. In addition, the 4,963 Neighborhood Organization has been active since the early 1970s, to foster racial integration in Kansas City. The 4,963 Neighborhood Organization has established its own housing office to ensure that black and white people were shown the same houses throughout the entire neighborhood and to prevent builders from putting up more duplexes and

A Challenge for Kansas City   207

EXHIBIT 5
Minorities as a Percentage of Total Population

Jackson County, Missouri 1980 Census Tracts

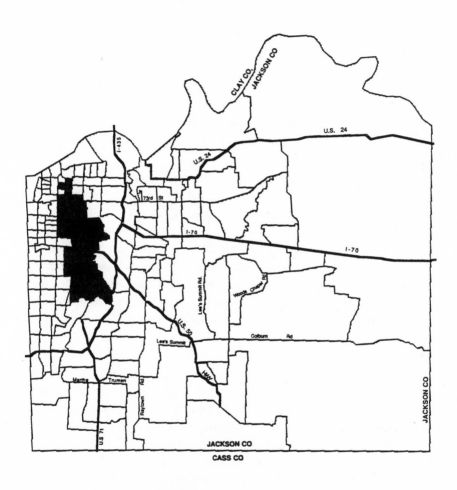

LEGEND

■ > 86% MINORITY POPULATION

☐ < 85% MINORITY POPULATION

converting old homes into multifamily dwellings, actions that could degrade the value of houses in predominantly single-family neighborhoods. Of its 3,300 houses, the 4,963 Neighborhood Organization has black occupants in 228 of them (7 percent) and Hispanics in 99 (3 percent).

Concerted, systematic policy plans and actions by the city, however, have been minimal. A comprehensive plan—including neighborhood residents participating in projects run by the city and developers to provide capital improvements, rent subsidies, and rehabilitation loans as well as a code enforcement strategy directed toward supporting citizens in their quest for affordable housing—would be a stabilizing force. All of Kansas City's neighborhoods are worth preserving, and a comprehensive plan should advocate infill housing where there are presently vacant spaces in existing neighborhoods.

Mixed uses in the neighborhoods should be strongly emphasized, not to the detriment of the residential area but rather as a complement to it. Under certain circumstances, mixed commercial, industrial and residential uses may enhance the stability of a particular Kansas City neighborhood. Other cities in the United States are forming urban development programs and related housing initiatives. One likely type of program is tax increment financing and linkage funding wherein some developers are charged a fee per square foot for gross floor space in both commercial and residential developments in excess of a certain amount. Property tax revenue, as well as the income from urban renewal land, also could be used in innovative ways to support housing development.

Neighborhoods must look beyond their borders at the larger context and form coalitions to complement and strengthen their redevelopment process. Community development corporations (CDCs) that have built and rehabilitated housing nationwide have been hamstrung by the meager amounts of public and private funding available to them, but they are an essential element in any comprehensive neighborhood redevelopment process. CDCs have knowledge and skill which should not be wasted and, thus, should be encouraged and supported to take a leading role. The city and county could issue bonds to finance housing and to promote racial and economic integration. Businesses could invest technical knowledge and resources.

Everyone has a stake in developing viable affordable housing for all Kansas Citians. A joint community partnership to address this effort should involve, and would benefit, everyone.

NOTES

1. *Where Has All the Housing Gone?* A Report on the Shrinking Inventory of Central City Housing (The Greater Kansas City Community Foundation and Affiliated Trusts, 1988).

2. Ibid., p. 17.

3. Frederic G. Reamer, "Affordable Housing Crisis in Social Work," *Social Work* 34, 1 (January 1989), p. 6.

4. Barbara Shelly, "City Predicts 3,000 May Apply for Section 8 Aid," *The Kansas City Star* (May 19, 1989).

5. William Hollan and Glenn E. Rice, "Public Housing Meeting Draws 500," *The Kansas City Times* (January 22, 1990).

6. *A Survey of Housing Discrimination in Kansas City, Missouri*, prepared by the Kansas City human relations department (1988).

7. *Report on Community Housing Resource Board: Racial Discrimination in the Rental Housing Market*, prepared by Marlene Muller, Mid-America Regional Council intern, (July 18, 1988).

11

RECENT CHANGES IN THE HOUSING STATUS OF BLACKS IN LOS ANGELES

J. Eugene Grigsby III and Mary L. Hruby

In the aftermath of reductions in federal housing assistance programs during the 1980s, many cities are experiencing severe shortages of affordable housing. It is particularly difficult for low income and minority households to find and maintain adequate, low-cost housing.

This article describes how Los Angeles has responded to this need through implementation of a particular housing policy and financing strategy. It specifically examines what impacts this program has had in producing affordable housing in the city's low-income, minority neighborhoods. Recommendations for further public action on housing needs in Los Angeles are also offered.

The 1982 draft report by the Presidential Commission on Housing Task Force provided early signs that dramatic changes in federal housing policy were about to be launched. A key premise of the report was that by and large the national goal of providing a decent home and suitable living environment for Americans had been achieved.[1] Paradoxically, the report indicated that affordability might continue to be a problem for certain sectors of the population (e.g., first-time home buyers and low-income households). The proposed solution for this affordability problem was to expand the economy. The assumption was that individuals would be able to earn enough to purchase affordable housing in the market place and that an adequate supply of housing would be produced, allowing individuals to "trade up," thus making more affordable housing available. As a consequence, federal resources directed toward assisting low-income households would no longer be needed.

Conspicuous by its absence was any indication of what impacts withdrawal of federal involvement might have on different locales, particularly in light of the fact that economic vitality and housing markets differ so greatly in various parts of the country. Furthermore, the report did not analyze the potential locational dimensions of housing affordability or provide any indication of whether or not particular minority groups, because of their low income status and/or housing discrimination, might bear the brunt of this persistent housing crisis.[2]

A 1988 National Task Force on Housing reaffirmed that housing affordability, particularly for low-income households and blacks, remains a national problem. Furthermore, the report points out that the federal government's withdrawal from housing assistance has exacerbated this affordability crisis.[3] Solutions to this crisis have fallen squarely on the shoulders of local governments. Mechanisms to stimulate housing at the local level, such as density bonus programs, inclusionary zoning, redevelopment, and linkage fees—which require commercial developers to fund or build affordable housing—have been woefully inadequate to significantly impact the magnitude of the housing affordability problem, particularly for blacks.

Most local governments seek to address this affordability crisis devoid of any understanding of both the spatial components of poverty and the close overlaps between poverty and minority residential neighborhoods. For example, in 1980, 70 percent of Los Angeles' black population lived in three of the city's thirty five planning districts. The median household income for whites in Los Angeles was $17,931 but for blacks it was $10,756. In 1988, the average selling price of a home in Los Angeles was $263,000 and the median monthly rent for one-and-two bedroom multifamily units was over $800 per month. Thus, if required to leave their existing residential units, a significant number of these blacks would have extreme difficulty securing affordable housing.[4]

In Los Angeles, the preferred local housing strategy is to encourage the production of new units through the conversion of land uses, generally single family to higher density multifamily units. This process is often referred to as land recycling. Through the redevelopment process, land recycling in Los Angeles is generating revenues that are being used to finance affordable housing. The primary funding mechanism is tax increment financing, a method of funding public investment in areas slated for redevelopment by recapturing, for a time, all or a portion of the increased tax revenue that may result if redevelopment stimulates private investment.

The robust nature of Los Angeles' economy produced 106 million square feet of commercial construction from 1980 to 1988. Within redevelopment areas this growth has given Los Angeles the opportunity to generate nearly a half billion dollars in revenues, 20 percent of which must, by state law, be spent on affordable housing. This capability is particularly important given the diminished federal role in affordable housing production.

As such, Los Angeles epitomizes the federal philosophy that expanding the economy will, in and of itself, solve the housing crisis for low-income households. However, the assumption that an expanding economy would produce a sufficient number of new units to allow affordable "trickle down" housing to become available has apparently not worked, at least not for low-income blacks in Los Angeles.

The purpose of this article is to examine what impact the city housing strategy, as implemented by the Community Redevelopment Agency, has had in producing affordable housing for blacks. Data from the Los Angeles Building and Safety file, which indicates the type and location of all residential construction and demolition taking place between 1980 and 1988, were used to describe the housing picture for the city and its black residential areas.[5] Income and minority status data came from the 1980 census and from a 1987 special census conducted in Los Angeles. Information on housing programs and policies was obtained from published reports and interviews with various city officials.

THE BLACK COMMUNITY IN LOS ANGELES

Since its inception as a city in 1781, blacks have been counted among Los Angeles' residents. Twenty-six of the original forty-four settlers had some African ancestry, thus, making blacks the majority group among the city's first inhabitants.[6] This majority status quickly disappeared, however, with continued immigration of new settlers.

The beginning of the modern black community resulted from the land boom of 1887–88, as the city's black population increased to 1,258 persons in 1890, up from 102 just ten years earlier.[7] Unlike the residential patterns of today, the first black citizens were not residentially segregated. Blacks could and did live throughout the city.[8]

Between 1910 and 1920, California's black population is estimated to have increased by 16,000 persons, with the majority concentrating in the Los Angeles area. As was the case with the earlier black immigrants, the new wave of blacks was not relegated to segregated residential neighborhoods. They tended to locate in a number of different areas. One black neighborhood developed on the southeastern edge of the downtown business district, and others formed in several different directions from downtown.[9]

Los Angeles' Black Neighborhoods Grow

It was only during the 1920s and 1930s that the formation of distinct black districts, as well as increased residential segregation became evident. White flight coupled with restrictive covenants and discriminatory housing practices resulted in the concentration of new immigrants in the Central Avenue area south of downtown. By 1925, most blacks were living in one area stretching nearly thirty blocks down Central Avenue and several blocks east to the railroad tracks. A few detached residential islands were also evident. For the next fifteen years these areas of black residence were surrounded by established white areas closed to black occupancy by restrictive covenants, even though the black population of the city expanded to about 65,000 by 1940.[10]

The demand for workers during World War II served as a major attraction for the next wave of black residents. While Los Angeles' white population increased by 41 percent in the 1940s, the black population increased 112 percent.

Similarly, in the 1950s and 1960s, the proportion of blacks increased significantly. Blacks comprised 7.6 percent of the area's population in 1960 and 10.8 percent in 1970. In terms of residential location, the 1940s saw blacks locating south of what had been a white border street (Slauson Avenue). The vast majority of blacks, however, continued to reside north of Slauson and there was a large increase in the number of blacks residing in Watts.

During the 1960s, the three largest black neighborhoods, Central Avenue–Furlong Tract, Watts, and West Jefferson became intertwined. For the next two decades expansion of blacks into the adjacent communities of West Adams, Crenshaw, Leimert Park and Mid-Wilshire steadily progressed.

Blacks Become The New Minority

By 1970, however, the region began to experience a totally different set of immigration patterns. Hispanics comprised 14 percent of the region's population in 1970. By 1980, their numbers had increased to 24 percent and today Hispanics constitute 28 percent of the population. Forecasts to the year 2010 indicate that the Hispanic population is expected to reach 40 percent of the area's residents (see Figures 1,2 and 3).[11]

The size of the Asian and "other" population, which includes Japanese, Chinese, Koreans, Vietnamese, Filipinos, Iranians, Russian Jews, Armenians, etc., doubled between 1970 and 1980. It is projected to grow at a slow but steady rate over the next ten to fifteen years.

The black population declined during the same time period. Blacks represented 17.3 percent of the city's population in 1970 and 12.6 percent in 1980. Today blacks comprise approximately 10 percent of the city's population and are not expected to exceed this proportion in the foreseeable future.

Blacks Are Not Enjoying The Benefits Of A Growing Economy

Accompanying these shifts in population trends over the past decade has been a strong resurgence in the area's economy. For example, the volume of United States trade moving across the Pacific exceeded flows across the Atlantic. Paralleling this trend, imports and exports through Los Angeles' customs districts have grown more than 20 percent since 1970. International trade-related jobs, now 10 percent of the total, are projected to increase to one job in six by the year 2000. The region's financial services industry has surpassed New York in terms of domestic deposits, and the region's banks and savings and loans hold 10 percent of the nation's deposits and 60 percent of the state's. In addition, the Los Angeles area will continue to attract foreign capital; already over 140 banks from 35 nations have located in the region.[12]

Furthermore, Los Angeles' strong diversified industrial base is also projected to expand. The manufacturing sector is the only one among postindustrial cities in North America that has continued to grow. Three hundred and fifty thousand businesses are located in the Los Angeles area. Seventy-five percent of these businesses employ fewer than ten people and yet the gross regional product is so great that the Southern California economy ranks eleventh among nations in the world.[13]

During the past decade this tremendous prosperity has resulted in over 51 million square feet of new office construction, nearly 8 million square feet of additional hotel space and over 18 million square feet of retail space. Net industrial space has increased by over 4 million square feet and over 106,000 new residential units have been built.[14]

FIGURE 1
City of Los Angeles: White Population

As Percentage of Total Population

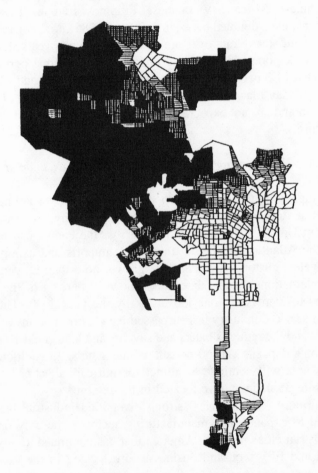

By Census Tracts 1980

Percent White

75% - 100%
50% - 75%
25% - 50%
0% - 25%

FIGURE 2
City of Los Angeles: Black Population

As Percentage of Total Population

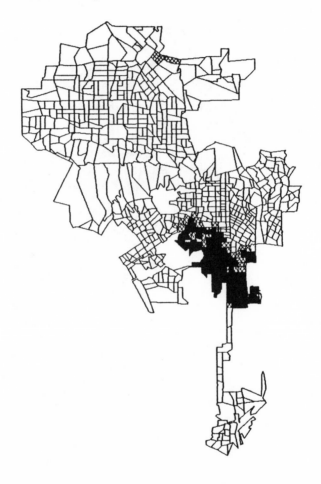

By Census Tracts 1980

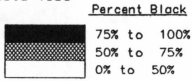

Percent Black

75% to 100%
50% to 75%
0% to 50%

FIGURE 3
City of Los Angeles: Hispanic Population

As Percentage of Total Population

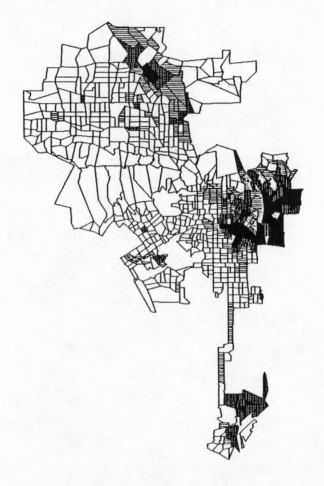

By Census Tracts 1980

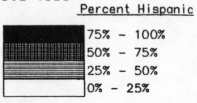

Percent Hispanic

75% – 100%
50% – 75%
25% – 50%
0% – 25%

Little of this development activity has occurred within black communities. Figure 4 presents an index of residential, commercial, and industrial development that has occurred in all of Los Angeles' black neighborhoods between 1980 and 1987. A 1.0 on the index means that development within the black community is at parity with the development occurring within the rest of the city. Greater than one would mean that more development was occurring in black neighborhoods and a score of less than one indicates that less development is occurring within black neighborhoods.

As shown in Figure 4, black neighborhoods have been "underdeveloped" compared to development that has occurred throughout the city. If development activity is used as a surrogate measure for capital investment, data presented in Figure 4 demonstrate rather dramatically just how little investment has been directed toward the black community. Black communities are not benefiting from the tremendous economic prosperity shared by the region as a whole.

As Ong and his colleagues have pointed out, despite employment growth, Los Angeles has not escaped the problem of increasing income inequality.[15] Their research suggests that economic and population restructuring have reinforced old forms of inequality and pushed up the poverty level.[16] Perhaps of greater concern is the fact that this increased level of poverty is not randomly distributed but instead is increasingly concentrated among minorities and women and bounded geographically. A growing poverty level has contributed significantly to the housing crisis of blacks in Los Angeles.

The Growing Housing Crisis in the Land of Plenty

As described in the report of a Blue Ribbon Committee on Housing, appointed by Mayor Tom Bradley, Los Angeles has approximately 1.2 million housing units, 40 percent owner-occupied, and 60 percent renter-occupied. During the last decade the net growth in the supply has been 14,000 units per year, over 90 percent as rental housing. At the same time the net growth in the population has been 25,000 households, resulting in a gap between supply and demand of approximately 11,000 units per year.[17]

The report points out that the effect on lower income groups of this imbalance between supply and demand is exacerbated by a rapid loss of affordable units. Of the 4,000 units demolished annually, 60 percent are rentals, and 80 percent of the rentals are affordable to very low income

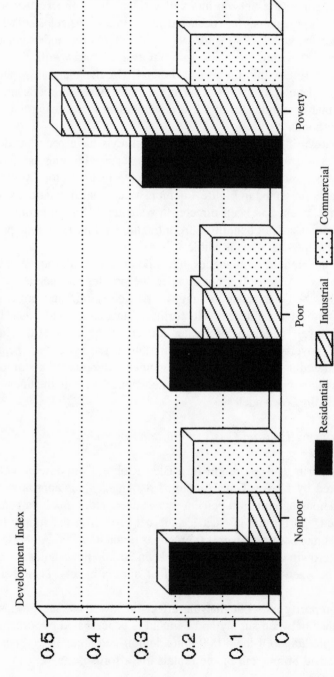

FIGURE 4
Development in Black Neighborhoods
1980 to 1987

Development Index

Residential   Industrial   Commercial

Source: Los Angeles Building & Safety File
Compiled by: Paul Ong & Eugene Grigsby

households.[18] Compounding this problem is the fact that Los Angeles has over 19,000 rental units whose federally subsidized status will soon expire with the expectation that the majority of these low-income units will revert to market rate rents.

It is within this context of a growing economy and continued population growth that we next examine what these changes have meant for the housing status of black neighborhoods. Data for Hispanic communities are also presented to compare the housing status of the city's other large minority group with that of black communities. We then examine how city policies and redevelopment activities have contributed to the production of affordable housing in these two communities.

HOUSING IN LOS ANGELES: 1980 TO 1988

In this section we examine the outcomes of Los Angeles' policy of fostering the production of new housing as a means of addressing the housing crisis. To conduct this analysis, data from the Los Angeles Building and Safety File have been aggregated by selected city planning areas. In order to be selected for detailed analysis at least 60 percent of the planning area's population had to be either black or Hispanic. As a result, three planning areas were identified as black neighborhoods and three as Hispanic neighborhoods.

Data presented in Table 1 show the relative concentration of the two minority groups within the planning areas we have selected for more detailed analysis. Blacks are the more highly concentrated of the two groups. Seventy-nine percent of all blacks residing in Los Angeles live in the area designated as black and within this area 70 percent of the residential population is black.

The city's Hispanic population is not nearly as concentrated. Less than one-third of the city's Hispanic population lives in the Hispanic designated area. However, within Hispanic areas there is a high degree of residential concentration. Seventy percent of the Hispanic area is comprised of Hispanics. The different levels of minority concentration suggest that the changes in the amount and type of housing stock are likely to have different impacts on each of these communities.

The Citywide Supply

From 1980 to 1988, the number of housing units in Los Angeles increased by 8.95 percent. A total of 2,332 new single family housing

FIGURE 5
1980 Black Population Distribution
City of Los Angeles

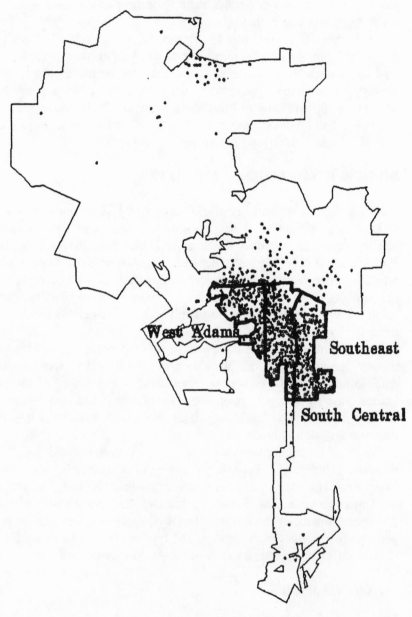

FIGURE 6
1980 Hispanic Population Distribution
City of Los Angeles

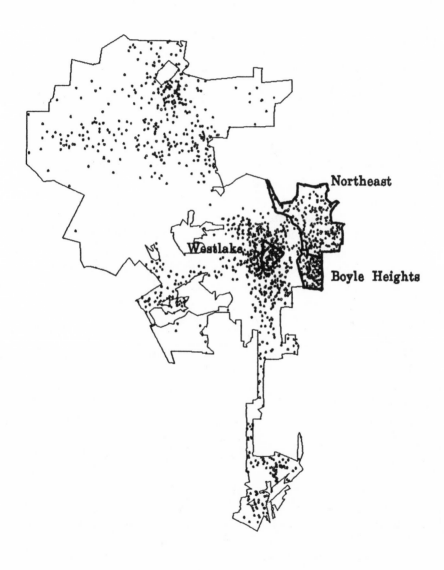

TABLE 1
Planning Area Minority Populations

	Total	Area	% of City	% of Area
Black	495,292	389,464	79	70
Hispanic	816,415	259,094	32	70

Source: Compiled from data in the 1986 City of Los Angeles Housing Element.

units were constructed within the city, representing a .44 percent increase in this type of housing. Nearly 19,000 condominiums were also built during this period. The total number of two-unit buildings (duplexes), however, declined by 399.

Higher density multiunit housing was, by far, the most prevalent type of construction. A total of 85,738 of these units were built, representing a 12.95 percent increase. Stated another way, from a total of 106,461 housing units constructed during this period, multiunits represented 81 percent of the new housing stock (see Table 2).

Housing In Minority Communities

In terms of the geographic distribution of net new housing, Table 3 shows that the smallest net increase in such housing occurred in the black community. Only 3,266 new housing units were added during this eight-year period, representing a 1.61 percent increase in the area's total housing stock. This contrasts with 14,046 net new units within the Hispanic community, an 11.15 percent increase. Thus, of the 17,312 additions of new housing within the black and Hispanic communities, the black community received 19 percent and the Hispanic community 81 percent.

The type of new housing added also differed between the two communities (see Table 4). The black community experienced a net gain in single family units, a total of 94. The Hispanic community had a net loss of 194 single family units. The Hispanic community, however, experienced a net gain of 8,492 condominium units, 99 percent of all construction of this type in minority communities, and nearly half (45%) of new units built citywide. The black community experienced a smaller net increase in multiunits, 2,795, or 33 percent of these units within minority communities.

TABLE 2
Change in the Distribution of Housing Stock by Type
For the City of Los Angeles
1980 to 1988

Housing Type	1980	1988	Net Change	% Change
Single Family	526,792	529,124	2,332	.44
Condominium	NA	NA	18,790	
Duplex	NA	NA	-399	
Multiunit	662,130	747,868	85,738	12.95
Total	1,188,922	1,295,383	106,461	8.95

Source: Compiled from the Los Angeles City Planning Department Building and Safety File.

Are New Units Sufficient To Meet The Needs Of A Growing Population?

Citywide, the production of housing is not keeping pace with population growth. While the population increased by nearly 12 percent, the number of housing units increased by just under 9 percent, resulting in a continued lag between housing production and population growth.

As shown in Table 5, population growth within the minority communities is consistent with that of the city as a whole, with the rate of population growth in the black community being slightly lower; however, the rate of housing production is slower. In the black community the number of households increased by 1.6 percent while the population grew by 8.8 percent. In the Hispanic community housing production nearly matched population growth; the number of households increased by 11.2 percent, while the population increase was only 12.61 percent. These data suggest that the pressure for housing within minority communities is

TABLE 3
Change in the Number of Housing Units
by Selected Geographic Areas
1980 to 1988

Geographic Area	1980	1988	Net Change	% Change
Citywide	1,188,922	1,295,383	106,461	8.95
Minority Areas				
Black	202,810	206,076	3,266	1.61
Hispanic	125,999	140,045	14,046	11.15
	----------	---------	--------	-----
Total	328,809	346,121	17,312	5.26

Source: Compiled from the Los Angeles Planning Department Building and Safety File.

likely to be greater than it is citywide, particularly since a disproportionate number of the city's low income population live in these neighborhoods and minority households tend to be larger.[19]

Are New Units Affordable?

While it is important to know that the number of units being produced annually is not keeping pace with population growth, an equally important question is, How affordable are the units being produced? Data in Tables 6 and 7 show that the gap between income and the cost of housing is growing, particularly within the minority communities. While the housing shortage and the affordability issue are serious problems for the city as a whole, they are acute within minority communities.

For example, the average selling price of a home in the black community is $88,000. A potential black buyer would have to pay $17,600 as a 20 percent down payment, closing costs of approximately $3,500 and then be in a position to qualify for a $70,400 mortgage. At 9 percent

TABLE 4
Net Change in Housing Units by Type
1980 to 1988

Geographic Area	Single	Condo	Duplex	Multiunit
Citywide	2,332	18,790	-399	85,738
Minority Areas				
Black	94	101	276	2,795
Hispanic	-194	8,492	87	5,661
	-----	------	------	------
Total	-100	8,593	141	8,456

Source: Compiled from the Los Angeles Planning Department Building and Safety File.

annual interest this would mean that a thirty-year fixed mortgage would require payments of $566 per month, excluding taxes and insurance. Given current lending practices in Los Angeles, an annual income of $37,800 would be needed to qualify for this mortgage. Based upon income data presented in Table 7, this potential buyer would not be able to qualify for a home loan. He or she would, however, be able to rent an existing unit (average price of $450 within the black area), but not a new market rate unit with average prices ranging between $800 and $900. Even a less expensive new unit would rent for $600 to $700, putting it outside the affordable price range for many black residents.

It is equally important to examine the number and type of units that have been removed from minority communities. As shown in Table 8, 17.7 percent of all of the residential units removed from the city between 1980 and 1988 were in the black and Hispanic communities (9.2% and 8.5% respectively). Within the black community, of the 3,799 units removed, 1,037 (27.3%) were single family units. In the Hispanic community, 30.4 percent of the residential units removed were single family. However, the majority of units removed from both these minority communities were multiunits (66.8% in the black community and 64.0% in the Hispanic community).

TABLE 5
Changes in Population
1980 to 1989

Geographic Area	1980	1989	Increase	% Change
Citywide	2,966,850	3,310,057	343,207	11.56
Minority Areas				
Black	558,020	607,188	49,168	8.8
Hispanic	368,732	415,852	47,120	12.6

Source: City of Los Angeles, Planning Department Population Estimate and Housing Inventory as of October 1, 1989.

The units removed represent some of the most affordable dwellings in these communities (average rents of $300 per month). Even though new units are labeled as affordable (average rents of $700 per month) this notion of "affordability" is not achievable given community income levels. The new units may be affordable to the general housing market in the Los Angeles metropolitan area, but certainly are not affordable to a sizable segment of the minority population. Thus, the removal of any units that are not replaced by ones with rents or mortgage rates comparable to those removed will force lower-income households to pay a larger proportion of their income for housing, increase the chances of "doubling up," force some people out of the community and/or into the ranks of the homeless population, or push them into the shadow market of illegal dwellings (e.g. garages).[20]

LOS ANGELES HOUSING POLICIES AND PROGRAMS

Housing Policies

The Housing Element of the city's general plan provides the policy framework guiding programmatic activities undertaken by the city. For the past decade, however, there has been no central department within

TABLE 6
Changes in Housing Costs
1980 to 1988

	Average Selling Price		Average Rent (Monthly)	
	1980	1988	1980	1988
Geographic Area				
Citywide	115,358	263,300	277	833
Minority Areas				
Black	N.A.	88,000	210	450
Hispanic	N.A.	169,000	203	717

Source: 1980 average rental data come from the *Housing Plan: An Element of the General Plan*, City of Los Angeles, December 1986. 1988 data come from the Sewer Permit Allocation Draft Environmental Impact Report, Volume II Technical Analyses, September 1989.

Los Angeles city government responsible for implementing housing policies or programs.[21] The 1986-adopted Housing Element which is currently undergoing a state-required periodic revision, indicates the city's orientation toward housing:

- provision of adequate housing, emphasizing rental units, and housing for low- and moderate-income and special needs households (e.g. homeless, disabled)
- housing design that is environmentally sound, safe and energy-conserving
- promotion of equal opportunity for all persons to rent, buy, rehabilitate or build housing throughout the city
- encouraging housing assistance and services for people displaced as a result of city actions

TABLE 7
Changes in Average Annual Earnings
1980 to 1988
(All male workers 16 to 64, Constant 1987 Dollars)

			Effective
	1980	1988	Change
Geographic Area			
Citywide	$30,364	$32,702	$2,338
Minority Areas			
Black	$19,824	$23,105	$3,281
Hispanic	$20,758	$20,063	$-695

Source: Holly Van Houten, "The Cost of Not Being Anglo," in Ong, et. al., *The Widening Divide: Income Inequality and Poverty in Los Angeles* (Graduate School of Architecture and Urban Planning, University of California, Los Angeles, June 1990).

- improvement and conservation of existing residential neighborhoods
- development of new housing units to meet the city's housing needs
- provision for the availability of access to all public facilities and services for all neighborhoods throughout the city
- maximum feasible involvement of residents and organizations in housing programs of direct interest to them
- continuation of the city's rent control and rental market ordinances to insure residents are being served while rights and interests of renters and landlords are protected

Specific strategies for accomplishing each objective can be categorized as follows:

Private market incentives: land write-downs and construction subsidies; density bonuses; lower depreciation schedules for rental construction; factory, site-built and mobile housing; tax benefits to preserve and rehabilitate housing; historic preservation; reduce regulatory and administrative barriers to housing production.

Public sector support: bond financing; expedite permit and plan check processing; inventory vacant/reusable public lands and properties for possible housing uses; maintain public housing; commercial and neighborhood revitalization to support a stable residential base; encourage a variety of housing types; minimize and mitigate displacement as a result of public development/redevelopment activities; encourage relevant city agencies to give priority consideration to low-cost housing within their planning and development processes; determine neighborhood housing needs.

Regulatory processes: code enforcement; housing inspection and rehabilitation; seismic safety reinforcement of older buildings; enforcement of antidiscrimination and fair housing laws; assure code flexibility to reduce unnecessary constraints on housing production; rent, condominium conversion and demolition control.

Community participation: maintain local neighborhood planning advisory councils; disseminate information on city's housing programs; maintain ethnic, age, income and cultural diversity where it exists.

Legislative advocacy: lobby for federal and state housing assistance funds and legislation to stimulate development of affordable housing in the market place.

City Agencies Responsible For Housing

Four agencies, the City Housing Authority, the Planning Department, Community Development Department and the Community Redevelopment Agency have responsibility for housing and housing-related activities in Los Angeles. Only the last two have direct responsibility for housing rehabilitation and/or production. Their participation in the production of housing for low-income households is discussed in the following section.

Housing Authority of the City of Los Angeles. The Housing Authority of the City of Los Angeles (HACLA) is responsible for providing safe, sound rental housing affordable for low-income households. Currently, there are 21 public housing projects owned and operated by the Housing Authority. These projects account for 8,800 units of assisted housing with a population of approximately 34,000 low-income residents, senior citizens, disabled and handicapped persons. All the public housing projects were constructed in the late 1940s and through the 1950s. There have been no additions to the public housing stock since that time.[22]

The Housing Authority also administers the Section 8 Housing Assistance Payments Program and the Housing Voucher Program. Currently,

TABLE 8
Housing Types Removed Citywide and From Minority Communities
1980 to 1988

	Citywide	Black	%	Hispanic	%
Single	9,239	1,037	27.3	1,066	30.4
Duplex	2,084	226	6.0	198	5.6
Multiunits	30,129	2,536	66.8	2,243	64.0
	-----	-----	-----	-----	-----
Total	41,452	3,799	100.1*	3,507	100.0

*Total does not add to 100 due to rounding

Source: Compiled from the Los Angeles Planning Department Building and Safety File.

there are more than 22,000 certificates assigned to households within the City of Los Angeles. The housing subsidy represented by these two programs is assigned to the individual as opposed to the location. The head of the household is qualified for the program through the HACLA. Once a determination is made that the family or individual qualifies for the program, the certificate is issued. The family or individual is then provided with a list of property owners who are willing to participate in the program at rent levels approved by the federal Department of Housing and Urban Development.

Planning Department. The Planning Department has no direct role in housing production but is responsible for preparing the state-mandated Housing Element as a part of the city's General Plan. This element affects the number, location and regulatory procedures impacting new housing. The department analyzes and projects needs for physical facilities and services, providing input to officials in the Community Development Department and the Community Redevelopment Agency. It administers the citizens' advisory groups who participate in reviewing plans for the city's thirty-five designated neighborhood planning areas. The department also evaluates the effectiveness of new programs designed to meet projected needs, potentially giving it a significant position to assess how city policies and programs have addressed various aspects of the housing crisis.

Community Development Department. The Community Development Department (CDD) administers the city's Housing and Community Development Block Grant (CDBG), Job Training Partnership Act (JTPA), Community Services Block Grant and Rent Control Program. With the exception of rent control, these are federally funded grant entitlement programs.

CDD's primary responsibilities are to coordinate and analyze information from various city departments and agencies as these relate to the Housing and Community Development Program. Other related activities include maintaining resident advisory groups in project areas, to propose and monitor housing programs as well as related social, economic and environmental activities, and to prepare the city's Housing Assistance Plan.[23]

Rehabilitation of existing units is the major focus of CDD's housing efforts. Since the city adopted an inclusionary zoning ordinance in 1983 to provide density bonuses for developments designating a percentage of their units for low-income households, CDD has participated in 164 projects which produced 6,884 units. Of these units 1,778 (26%) were deemed affordable for low-income households.

The Community Redevelopment Agency. The Community Redevelopment Agency of the City of Los Angeles (CRA) was established in 1948 under the Community Redevelopment Law of California.[24] The CRA is charged with improving the economic and social conditions within given locations through redevelopment. Before a redevelopment area can be declared, state law requires that the CRA prove that blight exists, demonstrate that redevelopment can rid the area of blighting conditions and prescribe specific remedies. Citizen participation is achieved through advisory committees. These committees, comprised of residents, property owners and businessmen in the project area review all major aspects of redevelopment. The agency also operates a single-family and multi-family housing rehabilitation loan program, and assists developers in building rental and owner housing.

Because CRA has had the major responsibility for implementing the city's housing production policies, the remainder of this section will

TABLE 9
Housing Produced by the Community Redevelopment Agency[28]

	Rehabs	New	L/M	Senior
Citywide	4,727	10,418	3,054	3,401
Minority Areas	1,655	3,423	399	180
Black	967	1,788	113	180
Hispanic	688	1,635	286	0

L/M = Low- and moderate-income housing

Source: Compiled from annual reports produced by the City of Los Angeles Community Redevelopment Agency.

focus on what CRA-sponsored activities have done to increase the supply of housing in Los Angeles, with a particular focus on how this agency has increased affordable housing within minority communities.

Housing And The Redevelopment Process

The Community Redevelopment Agency has been responsible for the production of 10,418 new units.[25] Twenty-nine percent of these units were developed for low- and moderate-income households.[26] Thirty-four hundred new senior units were built. Given available data, it is not possible to determine if any of these senior units were also counted as part of the low- and moderate-income units (see Table 9).

Using data in Table 10, we can examine the distribution of CRA-sponsored units between the two minority communities. The black community received 17.2 percent of the CRA-sponsored units and the Hispanic community 15.7 percent. However, the majority of all CRA -sponsored units (67.1% or 6,995) were developed outside of these predominately minority residential areas.

TABLE 10
CRA-Produced Housing Citywide and Within Minority Communities
1980 to 1988

Geographic Area	Total Net New Units	CRA Units	% of Total
Citywide	106,461	10,418	9.7
Minority Areas	17,312	3,423	19.8
Black	3,266	1,788	54.7
Hispanic	14,046	1,635	11.6

Source: Compiled from annual Community Develoment Department reports and telephone interviews with CRA officials.

As shown in Table 11, 87 percent of the low- and moderate-income units built were outside of the minority communities, and over 95 percent of the senior units were constructed in nonminority areas. The distribution of low- and moderate-income units between black and Hispanic neighborhoods is not even. The black community received 3.7 percent of these units and 9.4 percent were built in the Hispanic community. The number of CRA-sponsored senior units was also quite unevenly distributed between the two communities. The number of senior units constructed within the black community equaled 180 or 5.3 percent of the total number of these types of units produced by CRA.

CONCLUSIONS

Withdrawal of federal funding has forced local governments to seek alternative strategies for meeting the rising demand for affordable housing. In Los Angeles, a number of different approaches have been initiated, with the preferred strategy that of using the redevelopment process as a catalyst for stimulating the production of new housing.

TABLE 11
CRA-Produced Low/Mod and Senior Units
1980 to 1988

Geographic Area	LOW/MOD	% OF TOTAL	SENIOR	% of Total
Citywide	3,054	100.0	3,401	100.0
Minority Areas	399	13.0	180	5.3
Black	113	3.7	180	5.3
Hispanic	286	9.4	0	0.0

Source: Compiled from annual Community Redevelopment Department reports and telephone interviews with CRA officials.

Findings in this article show that between 1980 and 1988, the Los Angeles Community Redevelopment Agency was responsible for the production of 10,418 new units, nearly 10 percent of the total of 106,461 net new housing units produced during this period. Twenty percent of all of the units produced by CRA were in black and Hispanic communities. Within the black community, CRA produced over 50 percent of the total net new units. While the total increase in the number of households was only 1.6 percent, the population in the black community increased by 8.8 percent, providing further evidence that overcrowding is likely occurring. Furthermore, 3,799 affordable units were removed from the black community and were replaced by nearly 7,000 units.[27] CRA takes credit for 1,788 of these units but indicates that only 113 were affordable. Clearly, CRA has played a significant role in the production of housing in the black community.

However, two serious flaws can be identified in spite of the apparent success of the agency in producing new units within minority communities. First, to our knowledge, there are no records to verify that the new units produced in minority areas were actually occupied by minorities. A random visit to many of these newly constructed units strongly suggests that minorities are not really occupying the new housing being constructed in their communities. Within the black community, for example, much of the housing has been constructed in conjunction with the University of Southern California. Consequently, it is more likely that students and persons associated with the university are the beneficiaries of this housing, and not local residents seeking a place to live. Similarly, in the Hispanic neighborhoods, much of the new housing is now being occupied by whites, not new Hispanic immigrants, who comprise the largest proportion of the growth in population in this community.

The second concern is that the new units produced, in spite of the goal of maintaining affordability, simply have not achieved this objective. Given the low income levels of large numbers of Los Angeles residents, many newly built "affordable" units within a cluster of market rate units, will never actually be affordable for a significant number of households. Even if we overlook the fact that minorities may not be occupying the new units constructed within areas (assuming that they may have the "opportunity" to occupy these units at some future point in time), it is very difficult to overlook the fact that new units produced are simply outside of the price range of a significant number of minority households in need of housing. One might argue that this "affordability gap" is being made up in part through the use of housing vouchers and Section 8 certificates. No doubt this is partially true, but the availability of this form of housing assistance is limited. Furthermore, for minorities to rely solely on this mechanism as a way of achieving affordable housing will, in combination with housing discrimination, tend to relegate them to specific geographic areas, requiring them to live in the oldest units, and preclude them from securing new housing.

To address these concerns, the city needs to do several things. First, the annual rate of housing production must be increased. The recent creation of a Housing Trust Fund, in addition to the ongoing efforts of the Community Redevelopment Agency, should help. The key to producing truly affordable units is to control the cost of land and/or the cost of money, the two elements of new construction which impact cost the most. If the city purchased vacant lots and/or abandoned properties and made this land available at a nominal fee to any developer willing to construct affordable housing (using the HUD criteria of low- and very-low-income), then land cost would be contained. Similarly, the city could use funds from the Housing Trust and monies from tax increment financing generated through the redevelopment process to finance construction at nominal rates. The city could also consider providing second mortgage loans of $10,000 to $15,000 at no interest and payable upon sale of the property. Precedent for this approach can be found in the Nehemiah East Project in New York. This organization is able to offer new 2- and 3-bedroom units for $55,000 to $60,000. The key to its success is the fact that the city provides the land free of charge, does the preliminary site preparation and offers second mortgages payable upon sales of the property. The city of New York has also created a guaranteed mortgage pool similar to the Community Reinvestment Act Loan fund recently created in the State of California.

But increasing the production of new units, in and of itself, is no guarantee that either low-income individuals or minority group members will actually occupy this new housing. The city also needs to develop a monitoring mechanism to determine in which areas of the city newly produced units are being located and to identify if targeted groups are actually occupying these units. Periodic reports on the results of this monitoring should be made to elected officials and the public. In talking with CRA staff members we learned that many of them did not know whether or not their senior units were for the low- and moderate-income. Nor did they know how many of all newly produced units were for the low- and moderate-income. Currently, the agency has no way to produce a complete picture of its housing activities for the city as a whole. The agency does not have a citywide reporting mechanism in place and none of the agencies responsible for housing policy have required it.

While it is certainly desirable to produce more affordable housing in Los Angeles, especially for minority households, it is not realistic to assume that this goal can be achieved without, at the same time, increasing household incomes. Linking housing production to economic development for low income minority communities should also become a priority objective for the city. It is quite likely that reducing the amount of income paid for housing from 40 percent of total income to 30 percent, may be a much more cost-effective strategy than either building the required number of affordable units and/or subsidizing households to achieve the same objective.

As a major participant in the Pacific Rim economy, Los Angeles will continue to generate and attract economic wealth. It will also attract those who are seeking to share in this prosperity. New immigration in combination with continued population growth through natural increase has already put a serious strain on the existing housing market. Those who face income or other barriers to housing access do and will continue to experience these strains most severely. The challenge to decision-makers in Los Angeles is how to use the benefits of this prosperity to meet the basic needs of a diverse and growing population.

NOTES

1. White House Presidential Housing Task Force Report, (1982).

2. Analysis of data from the Annual Housing Survey suggests that the issue of housing affordability for blacks has a definite spatial component. Nationally between 1970 and 1980 more rental housing units occupied by black Americans were removed from their residential areas than were added. In addition, new rental units constructed were disproportionately occupied by whites, and had rent rates significantly above those of the units which had been removed, i.e. new construction did not increase the supply of affordable rental housing in black neighborhoods, J. Eugene Grigsby and Mary L. Hruby, "A Review of the Status of Black Renters, 1970–1980, *The Review of Black Political Economy*, Vol. 13, No. 4 (Spring 1985).

3. *A Decent Place to Live: the Report of the National Housing Task Force*, Advance Copy (March 1988).

4. For this paper affordable housing is defined as housing that can be secured by households whose incomes are less than or equal to 120% of Los Angeles County's median income, adjusted for family size.

5. For planning purposes the City of Los Angeles Planning Department subdivides the city into 35 different community planning districts. Specific community plans designating land use policies are prepared for each of these plan areas.

6. Lawrence deGraaf, "City of Black Angeles: Emergence of the Los Angeles Ghetto, 1890–1930," *The Pacific Historical Review*, Vol. 39, No. 3 (August 1970), p. 327.

7. *Ibid.*

8. *Ibid.*, p. 329.

9. Howard J. Nelson, William A.V. Clark , *Los Angeles: The Metropolitan Experience*, (Ballinger Publishing Company, Cambridge, Massachusetts, 1976), p. 36.

10. *Ibid.*

11. Southern California Association of Governments, *Baseline Population Trends and Projections* (1986).

12. *L A 2000: A City for the Future*, Final Report Los Angeles 2000 Committee, (1988).

13. *Ibid.*, p. 58.

14. See *Economic Development in Los Angeles*, A report prepared by The Planning Group for the 2000 Partnership (December 1989).

15. Paul M. Ong, Project Director, *The Widening Divide: Income Inequality and Poverty in Los Angeles*, The Graduate School of Architecture and Urban Planning, University of California, Los Angeles, June 1990, p. 14.

16. *Ibid.*, p. 17.

17. *Housing Los Angeles Affordable Housing for the Future*, Report of the City of Los Angeles Blue Ribbon Committee for Affordable Housing (December 1988).

18. *Ibid.*, p. 9.

19. The average household size within the Hispanic neighborhoods is 3.30 compared to 2.70 within the black community. City-wide the figure is 2.31.

20. A 1987 Los Angeles Times survey estimated that at least 42,000 garages were being rented illegally as residential units.

21. Following a recommendation of the Mayor's Blue Ribbon Committee for Affordable Housing, the city recently hired a housing coordinator.

22. The Housing Authority is currently negotiating with a private developer to sell one of its public housing projects. As a condition of the sale the developer will replace the existing 400 units at no cost to the city. In addition, another 100 units of affordable senior housing is being proposed.

23. The Southern California Association of Governments requires that all local jurisdictions that apply for federal HCD Block Grant money prepare Housing Assistance Plans. The purpose of the plan is to indicate how the housing needs of limited income households will be met.

24. Now codified as Division 24, Part 1, of the California Health Code.

25. Since the inception of the agency, they report that over 20,000 new units have been constructed. Unfortunately, the agency has no records available that will allow us to verify this claim.

26. Data for this report were compiled from annual reports produced by CRA. Not all of these reports indicated how many of the newly produced units were for low- and moderate-income households.

27. Data from the Building and Safety File indicate that between 1980 and 1988, 7,000 new housing units were constructed in the black community.

28. Reports reviewed to obtain citywide data included; Beacon Street, Bunker Hill, Central Business District (CBD), Hollywood, North Hollywood, Pico Union, Pico Union #2, China Town, Little Tokyo and the black and Hispanic areas.

Reports reviewed to compile data for the black area included; Adams, Hoover and Watts. The Hispanic area reports included; Boyle Heights, Monterey Hills, Lincoln Heights.

Data reported in the CRA annual reports are cumulative since the particular project area's inception, with the exception of Boyle Heights and the CBD. The Boyle Heights report covers only 1986 through 1987. Data for the CBD reflect only 1986 through 1989 information.

Lincoln Heights and Boyle Heights are not formal redevelopment project areas. They are, however, project revitalization areas where CRA has been actively involved in housing rehabilitation efforts.

IV

Postscript

POSTSCRIPT

The circumstances described in the housing markets of the cities and metropolitan areas featured in Sections II and III of this volume have probably changed since these chapters were written. Housing markets in general are dynamic, and there is no reason to think that these were not.

Because of this presumed dynamism, preliminary data from the 1990 Census were examined and are compared with the market characteristics reported in Sections II and III. In Section II, in the chapter entitled "Trends in the Housing Status of Black Americans Across Selected Metropolitan Areas," trends between 1970 and 1980, and 1980 and 1984 were discussed for the following metropolitan areas: Birmingham, AL; Buffalo, NY; Cleveland, OH; Indianapolis, IN; Memphis, TN; Milwaukee, WI; Newport News, VA; Oklahoma City, OK; Providence, RI; Salt Lake City, UT; and San Jose, CA. In Section III, housing market characteristics in the 1970s and 1980s, and federal assistance programs that have had particular impacts on black Americans are discussed for Atlanta, GA; Baltimore, MD; Buffalo, NY; Charlottesville, VA; Houston, TX; Kansas City, MO; and Los Angeles, CA. Preliminary 1990 data (population, percent minority, number of households, number of units, tenure, crowding, value of units, and gross contract rent) for all of these housing markets are discussed below.

METROPOLITAN AREAS: 1990 ANALYSES (SECTION II)

Data from the 1990 Census for the eleven metropolitan areas analyzed in Section II—Birmingham, Buffalo, Cleveland, Indianapolis, Memphis, Milwaukee, Newport News, Oklahoma City, Providence, Salt Lake City, and San Jose—reflect the workings of the housing markets in those places over the decade of the 1980s. The predictable relationship between the growth rates of the population, of households, of housing units, and of crowding within units seems to have existed. Crowding, median value or rent, and ownership rates also interact as one might predict. The following paragraphs detail some of these relationships.

Population, number of households, and number of units all increased during the 1980s for nine of the eleven metropolitan areas. In all the metropolitan areas, except Buffalo and Cleveland, the population, the number of households, and the number of housing units all increased between 1980 and 1990 (see Tables 1 and 2). In Buffalo and Cleveland, however, while the number of households and the number of units increased, the population decreased—by around 4 percent in both places.

The opposing trends of growth in the number of households and the number of housing units and decline in population should translate into a reduction in crowding, as measured by the percent of units with more than one person per room (see Table 2). In the case of Buffalo and Cleveland, it does. Between 1980 and 1990, the percent of units with more than one person per room declined from 1.9 percent to 1.3 percent in Buffalo and from 2 percent to 1.5 percent in Cleveland. In addition, though, crowding declined in seven of the other metropolitan areas, where population, number of households, and number of units all grew. Only in San Jose did crowding worsen during the 1980s—10.5 percent of the units there had more than one person per room in 1990, while only 5.3 percent of the units did in 1980.

Although the population in most of these eleven metropolitan areas increased between 1980 and 1990, its mix changed very little (see Table 1). In all places, the percentage of blacks increased or remained nearly constant, while the percentage of persons of Spanish origin did likewise in most places. The largest relative increases for blacks were in Milwaukee (3 percentage points) and Providence (1 percentage point). The share of Spanish-origin households increased noticeably in five places—Milwaukee, WI (from 2.5 percent in 1980 to 3.6 percent in 1990); Newport News, VA (from 1.6 percent in 1980 to 2.3 percent in 1990); Oklahoma City, OK (from 2.2 percent in 1980 to 3.6 percent in 1990); Providence, RI (from 2.1 percent in 1980 to 4.6 percent in 1990); and San Jose, CA (from 17.5 percent in 1980 to 21.0 percent in 1990).

Between 1980 and 1990, although the home ownership rate both rose and fell, depending on the metropolitan area, the rate fell in seven of the eleven places (see Table 2). In Buffalo, Indianapolis, Milwaukee, Oklahoma City, Providence, Salt Lake City, and San Jose, the home ownership rates fell. In most places the rate fell only slightly, while in Buffalo and Oklahoma City, it fell by more than 3 percentage points, and in

TABLE 1
Demographic Characteristics of Selected Metropolitan Areas, 1990

	Population					Households		
	1980	1990	Percent Change 1980–90	Percent Black	Percent Spanish Origin	1980	1990	Percent Change 1980–90
Birmingham, AL MSA	884,014	907,810	2.7	27.1	0.4	316,381	345,328	9.1
Buffalo, NY CMSA[a]	1,242,800	1,189,288	-4.3	10.3	2.0	445,475	461,803	3.7
Cleveland, OH PMSA	1,898,800	1,831,122	-3.6	19.4	1.9	694,401	712,362	2.6
Indianapolis, IN MSA	1,166,600	1,249,822	7.1	13.8	0.9	418,485	480,010	14.7
Memphis, TN MSA[b]	913,472	981,747	7.5	40.6	0.8	311,996	356,997	14.4
Milwaukee, WI PMSA	1,397,000	1,432,149	2.5	13.8	3.6	500,684	537,722	7.4
Newport News, VA MSA[c]	1,160,300	1,396,107	20.3	28.5	2.3	385,929	493,536	27.9
Oklahoma City, OK MSA	860,969	958,839	11.4	10.5	3.6	321,546	367,775	14.4
Providence, RI (2 PMSAs)[d]	925,917	984,238	6.3	3.7	4.6	330,632	369,262	11.7
Salt Lake City, UT MSA[e]	910,222	1,072,227	17.8	1.0	5.8	289,379	347,531	20.1
San Jose, CA PMSA	1,295,071	1,497,577	15.6	3.8	21.0	458,519	520,180	13.4

Source: State and Metropolitan Area Data Book 1986; Selected Population and Housing Characteristics, 1990 Census

Notes: MSA is metropolitan statistical area; PMSA is primary metropolitan statistical area; and CMSA is consolidated metropolitan statistical area.

[a]Full name is Buffalo-Niagara Falls, NY CMSA.
[b]Full name is Memphis, TN-Arkansas-Mississippi MSA.
[c]Full name is Norfolk-Virginia Beach-Newport News, VA MSA.
[d]Represents two PMSAs: Providence, RI PMSA and the Pawtucket-Woonsocket-Attleboro, RI-MA PMSA.
[e]Full name is Salt Lake City-Ogden, UT MSA.

TABLE 2
Characteristics of Housing Units in Selected Metropolitan Areas, 1990

	Number in 1980	Number in 1990	Percent Change 1980–90	Percent Owner-Occupied	Percent with 1.01+ Persons per Room	Median Value of Owned Units	Median Contract Rent of Rented Units
Birmingham, AL MSA	341,006	376,897	10.5	69.0	2.4	$59,200	$260
Buffalo, NY CMSA[a]	474,247	492,516	3.9	60.5	1.3	$71,800	$290
Cleveland, OH PMSA	734,110	758,984	3.4	65.4	1.5	$34,100	$332
Indianapolis, IN MSA	451,319	517,893	14.8	63.8	1.9	$66,800	$342
Memphis, TN MSA[b]	332,079	385,214	16.0	61.4	4.3	$64,800	$297
Milwaukee, WI PMSA	521,505	562,031	7.8	59.4	2.5	$76,900	$376
Newport News, VA MSA[c]	413,364	537,101	29.9	58.9	3.0	$87,000	$398
Oklahoma City, OK MSA	352,321	425,043	20.6	64.3	3.1	$54,500	$286
Providence, RI (2 PMSAs)[d]	357,977	398,581	11.3	55.7	N/A	N/A	N/A
Salt Lake City, UT MSA[e]	306,639	370,967	21.0	67.4	4.3	$71,000	$313
San Jose, CA PMSA	473,817	540,240	14.0	59.1	10.5	$289,400	$715

Source: State and Metropolitan Area Data Book 1986; Selected Population and Housing Characteristics, 1990 Census

Notes: MSA is metropolitan statistical area; PMSA is primary metropolitan statistical area; and CMSA is consolidated metropolitan statistical area. N/A means not available.

[a]Full name is Buffalo-Niagara Falls, NY CMSA.
[b]Full name is Memphis, TN-Arkansas-Mississippi MSA.
[c]Full name is Norfolk-Virginia Beach-Newport News, VA MSA.
[d]Represents two PMSAs: Providence, RI PMSA and the Pawtucket-Woonsocket-Attleboro, RI-MA PMSA.
[e]Full name is Salt Lake City-Ogden, UT MSA.

Providence, it fell nearly 4 percentage points. In San Jose, the ownership rate declined only slightly—from 59.7 percent to 59.1 percent—despite the fact that the median value of owned units more than doubled during the 1980s (from $109,400 to $289,400). In fact, because the percent of units with more than one person per room nearly doubled over the decade in San Jose, it appears that the high rate of ownership has been maintained there in part because of the increase in the household size. In Indianapolis, Milwaukee, Oklahoma City, and Providence, the declines in the ownership rate might be due to the regional economic downturns that occurred during the 1980s.

CASE STUDY CITIES: 1990 ANALYSIS (SECTION III)

The discussions about the housing conditions of blacks in the case studies in Section III, center around the central city or innermost areas of the metropolitan areas (of Atlanta, Baltimore, Buffalo, Charlottesville, Houston, Kansas City, and Los Angeles). Unfortunately, the 1990 data with which to make comparisons for these places are specific to the metropolitan areas. Thus, the comparisons will not be as targeted as would be ideal.

Between 1980 and 1990, the percentage of blacks declined in three of the seven study cities (Charlottesville, Houston, and Los Angeles) (see Table 3). In the other four metropolitan areas, the percentage of blacks in the entire population increased slightly. Over the same time period, the population share of persons of Spanish origin increased in every city, in some by considerable proportions. In the Houston, TX PMSA, the share of persons of Spanish origin in the population grew from nearly 15 percent in 1980 to over 21 percent in 1990. In Los Angeles, persons of Spanish origin increased from about 28 percent to nearly 38 percent (almost two-fifths) of the population between 1980 and 1990. In two of the three places in which the share of the black population decreased, the share of the Spanish-origin population increased.

The relationship among population, number of households, and number of housing units, described above for the Section II metropolitan areas, also holds for the seven case study areas (see Tables 3 and 4). That is, between 1980 and 1990, in all cities except Buffalo, the population, the number of households, and the number of housing units all increased. In Buffalo, the city common to Section II and Section III, although the number of households and the number of housing units increased, the population declined. This combination of trends is an easy explanation

TABLE 3
Demographic Characteristics of Selected Metropolitan Areas, 1990

	Population					Households		
	1980	1990	Percent Change 1980–90	Percent Black	Percent Spanish Origin	1980	1990	Percent Change 1980–90
Atlanta, GA MSA	2,138,143	2,833,511	32.5	26.0	2.0	756,597	1,056,427	39.6
Baltimore, MD MSA	2,199,497	2,382,172	8.3	25.9	1.3	765,830	880,145	14.9
Buffalo, NY CMSA[a]	1,242,800	1,189,288	−4.3	10.3	2.0	445,475	461,803	3.7
Charlottesville, VA MSA	113,568	131,107	15.4	14.4	1.1	40,241	48,709	21.0
Houston, TX PMSA	2,734,617	3,301,937	20.7	18.5	21.4	973,162	1,186,375	21.9
Kansas City, MO-KS MSA	1,433,464	1,566,280	9.3	12.8	2.9	529,012	602,347	13.9
Los Angeles, CA PMSA[b]	7,477,422	8,863,164	18.5	11.2	37.8	2,730,469	2,989,552	9.5

Source: State and Metropolitan Area Data Book 1986; Selected Population and Housing Characteristics, 1990 Census

Notes: MSA is metropolitan statistical area; PMSA is primary metropolitan statistical area; and CMSA is consolidated metropolitan statistical area.

[a]Full name is Buffalo-Niagara Falls, NY CMSA.
[b]Full name is Los Angeles-Long Beach, CA PMSA.

TABLE 4
Characteristics of Housing Units in Selected Metropolitan Areas, 1990

	Number in 1980	Number in 1990	Percent Change 1980–90	Percent Owner-Occupied	Percent with 1.01+ Persons per Room	Median Value of Owned Units	Median Contract Rent of Rented Units
Atlanta, GA MSA	809,008	1,174,007	45.1	62.3	3.0	$89,800	$441
Baltimore, MD MSA	809,784	938,979	16.0	63.7	2.4	$101,200	$399
Buffalo, NY CMSA[a]	474,247	492,516	3.9	60.5	1.3	$71,800	$290
Charlottesville, VA MSA	43,248	51,932	20.1	59.4	2.3	$93,800	$415
Houston, TX PMSA	1,104,164	1,355,821	22.8	54.9	8.1	$64,300	$339
Kansas City, MO-KS MSA	570,093	657,351	15.3	65.4	2.1	$66,500	$346
Los Angeles, CA PMSA[b]	2,855,578	3,163,343	10.7	48.2	18.2	$226,400	$570

Source: State and Metropolitan Area Data Book 1986; Selected Population and Housing Characteristics, 1990 Census

Notes: MSA is metropolitan statistical area; PMSA is primary metropolitan statistical area; and CMSA is consolidated metropolitan statistical area.

[a]Full name is Buffalo-Niagara Falls, NY CMSA.
[b]Full name is Los Angeles-Long Beach, CA PMSA.

for the reduction in crowding over the previous decade in Buffalo, although it does not explain the reduction in crowding in Atlanta, Baltimore, Charlottesville, and Kansas City over the same period.

While crowding decreased during the 1980s in most of the case study cities, in two of them (Houston and Los Angeles), crowding increased substantially (see Table 4). In Houston, where house prices and rents increased only modestly, the increased crowding may be associated with the increased percentage of persons of Spanish origin and the tendency for Spanish-origin households to be bigger than black or white households (see Table 3). In Los Angeles, the increased crowding is probably associated with both the increase in the cost of housing and the increase in the share of the population of Spanish origin there. Between 1980 and 1990, the median value of owned units rose from $88,000 to $226,400. Median contract rents also more than doubled, from $277 to $570, over the period (see Table 4).

Ownership rates increased in only three of the seven places (Atlanta, Baltimore, and Charlottesville) (see Table 4). In the other four places, ownership rates declined—by nearly 4 percentage points in Houston and over 3 percentage points in Buffalo. Houston seems to be the area that experienced the greatest number of changes in its housing market over the 1980s—the share of crowded units increased; the percent of black households decreased; the percent of Spanish-origin households increased; and the home ownership rate declined.

CONCLUSIONS

Although minor changes have taken place between 1980 and 1990 in the character and circumstances of the housing markets described in the chapters in Sections II and III, the basic patterns noted seem to have maintained. For example, of the three metropolitan areas that lost population between 1970 and 1980 (Buffalo, Cleveland, and Milwaukee), two (Buffalo and Cleveland) also lost population between 1980 and 1990. On the other hand, areas such as Atlanta, Houston, and Los Angeles were big gainers in population over both decades. The mix of the racial groups in the populations of these areas remained fairly stable, although the share of persons of Spanish origin increased in many places. Home ownership rates fell in a majority of the metropolitan areas studied, as did the rate for the nation as a whole over the 1980–90 decade.

Preliminary 1990 Census data sketch the outlines of changes that have transpired in metropolitan housing markets over the decade of the 1980s.

Further analysis of these and other metropolitan areas—as well as analysis of their associated central cities—using 1990 Census data is clearly warranted.

GLOSSARY
Federal Housing Subsidy Programs

The federal housing subsidy programs described below are in chronological order by date of program authorization. The first to be discussed is the Low-Rent Public Housing program authorized in 1937, followed by the Urban Renewal program established in 1949. The third topic is a set of mortgage insurance programs of the Federal Housing Administration (FHA)—the Section 221 (d) (3) Below Market Interest Rate (BMIR), Section 236, and Section 235 programs. Fourth is the Community Development Block Grant (CDBG) program, established in 1974, followed by all the Section 8 subprograms, most of which also were authorized by the same 1974 legislation as CDBG. The final program to be discussed is the Nehemiah Housing Opportunity Grants program authorized in 1988.

LOW-RENT PUBLIC HOUSING PROGRAM

The low-rent public housing (LRPH) program, established by the U.S. Housing Act of 1937, provides reduced-rent publicly owned dwellings for lower-income families and for elderly, handicapped, or displaced individuals.[1] The federal government finances both the construction and operation of these projects, which are administered by local housing agencies (LHAs).[2] The LRPH program currently shelters about 1.4 million households and provides about one-third of all federal housing assistance.

Since 1937, the calculation of tenant rents for LRPH has changed in ways that have affected the populations served. Between 1937 and 1949, the eligible tenant population was defined as those of the lowest income group able to pay the rents LRPH required to be financially self-sufficient. In 1949, eligibility was redefined to target those whose net incomes at the time of admission to the projects did not exceed five times the rents of their units.[3] Because the process of setting the rent levels was thus detached from the assessment of funds needed to operate the units, the LHAs faced shortfalls in operating expenses, which they tried to meet by raising rents. Later, to limit rent increases, the Brooke-Cranston Amendment of 1969 established 25 percent of adjusted tenant income as the maximum tenant rent. The 1981 Omnibus Budget Reconciliation Act increased the maximum tenant rent to 30 percent of adjusted tenant income—effective immediately for new tenants and to be effective by 1986 for current tenants, using 1 percent annual increments.[4]

The adjusted tenant income used as a base for rent calculations results after subtracting several items from gross tenant income.[5] These items are: $550 per dependent; $400 for an elderly family; medical expenses in excess of 3 percent of annual income per family; child care expenses essential to the ability of an adult to work; 10 percent of earned family income; and any payment by a family member for child support or alimony for someone in another household (up to a certain limit).[6]

The LHAs select tenants and compile waiting lists of households for LRPH and for the other programs they administer. The LHAs also are responsible for maintenance and management of projects.

URBAN RENEWAL PROGRAM

The 1949 Housing Act established the Urban Renewal program with the objective of reducing construction costs by lowering the cost of land for newly constructed rented and owned projects. Under the program, localities could use the power of eminent domain to acquire land. Any buildings would be razed and the lots sold at auction to private developers who would build anew on the land. Households dislocated by urban renewal were entitled both to payments for their housing and land and to relocation assistance. The program is no longer active, although redevelopment activities now take place under the Community Development Block Grant (CDBG) program.

The Urban Renewal program has been criticized for razing standard units and for eliminating housing for the poor without replacing it in like quantity. In some places, though, LRPH and Section 236 projects that house the poor and the near-poor have been built on land cleared because of the Urban Renewal program.

FEDERAL HOUSING ADMINISTRATION MORTGAGE INSURANCE PROGRAMS

Mortgage insurance provided by the Federal Housing Administration (FHA) under the Section 221 (d) (3) Below Market Interest Rate (BMIR), Section 235, and Section 236 programs is covered here. The programs for multifamily projects—the BMIR and the Section 236 programs—are discussed first, followed by the discussion of the Section 235 program that insures single-family mortgages made by private lenders.

Section 221 (d) (3) BMIR Program

Under the BMIR program, authorized in 1961, the FHA insured forty-year mortgage loans made by private lenders to developers of multifamily projects. In return for this insurance, the developers agreed to rent their units to tenants with incomes (at the time they moved in) no greater than 95 percent of the median for families in the area, adjusted for family size. In addition, the FHA provided the developer an up-front subsidy that effectively reduced the mortgage interest rate to 3 percent.[7] Public entities, nonprofit organizations, and limited-dividend entities—that is, profit-motivated organizations whose ongoing pre-tax return on investment is limited to 6 percent per year on the original investment—all could sponsor projects under the BMIR program. As of November 1986, about 1,170 BMIR project mortgages (with an associated 148,000 dwelling units) were outstanding.[8] The BMIR program was active until 1968 when it was replaced by the Section 236 program.

Rents for tenants in BMIR projects reflect the reduced mortgage interest rates paid by project owners. BMIR tenants pay the following sum for rent: a fixed component sufficient to amortize a 3-percent mortgage; plus an allowance set by HUD to cover operating costs: plus (in the case of limited-dividend sponsors) an allowance for return on investment. Tenants whose incomes rise above 110 percent of the income limit for new occupants (that is, 110 percent of 95 percent of the area's median income) have their rents raised by 10 percent.

To enable very-low-income families to afford rents in BMIR projects, beginning in 1965, rent supplements were made available.[9] Under the Rent Supplement program, HUD agreed to subsidize certain project tenants for up to forty years to reduce their rents. Very-low-income tenants receiving rent supplements pay rents equal to the greater of 30 percent of

their adjusted incomes or 30 percent of the fixed rent component (from
the rent calculation). Gradually, all rent supplement assistance contracts
are being replaced with Section 8 assistance contracts.

Under certain conditions, after twenty years of their forty-year mortgage terms, limited-dividend owners of BMIR projects are eligible to
prepay their mortgages without HUD's permission.[10] Prepaying their
mortgages ends the requirement to rent their units to tenants with incomes, when moving in, no greater than 95 percent of the median family
incomes in their areas. Prepaying also would allow the owner, at his
discretion, to convert his project to a use other than renting to lower-
income tenants. Owners of about 540 BMIR projects, representing 76,000
units, were estimated to be eligible to prepay their project mortgages
between 1986 to 2001.[11] To preclude the potential loss of these units
through mortgage prepayment by BMIR project owners, the Congress
established a procedure to provide incentives for owners to retain their
BMIR projects for use by lower-income tenants.[12]

Section 236 Program

The 1968 Housing and Urban Development Act established the Section
236 program to replace the BMIR program. Although the Section 236
program provided FHA insurance for mortgages on multifamily projects
developed privately by the same types of sponsors as did the BMIR
program, the mortgage interest on Section 236 loans was subsidized
through a different mechanism. In the Section 236 program, the mortgage
was made at the market rate, and HUD provides subsidy payments directly to the project owner. These payments cover the difference between
the monthly payments that would amortize the mortgage at the market
rate and the amount needed to amortize the mortgage at a rate as low as
1 percent, the rate at which tenant rents are calculated. Projects are rented
to families whose incomes upon admission are 80 percent or less of the
area's median income, adjusted for family size. Although the program
was permanently suspended as part of the January 5, 1973 moratorium on
federal housing assistance, as of November 1986, about 3,870 federally
insured Section 236 project mortgages (with an associated 433,000 units)
were outstanding.[13]

Most tenants in Section 236 projects pay what is called ''basic rent,''
the sum of: the amount needed to amortize a 1-percent mortgage; plus an
allowance for operating costs; plus (in the case of a limited-dividend
sponsor) an allowance for return on investment. When 30 percent of a

tenant's adjusted income exceeds the basic rent, the tenant pays for rent 30 percent of income up to a maximum, known as the "market rent." The "market rent" is identical to the "basic rent" except that it includes an allowance to cover the mortgage insurance payment, and its component to amortize the mortgage is calculated at a level sufficient to pay off the loan at the full unsubsidized interest rate at which it was written.

Very low income tenants in Section 236 projects received supplementary assistance first through the Rent Supplement program and then through the Rental Assistance Payments (RAP) program. Under the Rent Supplement program, rents for assisted tenants equal the greater of the following: 30 percent of adjusted income; or 30 percent of the basic rent. Rent supplements were available for the full forty-year mortgage term. Beginning in 1974, the RAP program subsidized some low-income tenants in Section 236 projects by reducing their rents to 30 percent of adjusted income. The RAP program made up the difference between the unit's basic rent and 30 percent of adjusted tenant income.

Limited-dividend sponsors of Section 236 projects are able to prepay under the same conditions as limited-dividend BMIR program sponsors. Owners of about 2,370 Section 236 projects (with an associated 258,000 units) are estimated to be able to prepay between 1986 and 2001.[14] The procedure established in the 1990 Cranston-Gonzalez National Affordable Housing Act that requires HUD to offer incentives to induce owners not to prepay their mortgages also applies to the Section 236 programs.

Section 235 Program

Although the Section 235 Homeownership Assistance program has operated in three different forms—original, revised, and restructured—the 1987 Housing and Community Development Act terminated the program on October 1,1989. Although it did not extend the program beyond the end of fiscal year 1989, the HUD Reform Act of 1989 (enacted December 15, 1989) authorized the refinancing of Section 235 mortgages under certain conditions.[15]

The original program, established in 1968, provided a homeownership interest reduction subsidy for lower-income families. Eligible families paid at least 20 percent of their adjusted monthly incomes toward their monthly mortgage payments. The balance was made up by federal assistance payments, which could not exceed the difference between the required mortgage payment at a market rate and the amount that would be required on a mortgage of the same amount bearing an interest rate of 1 percent. The original program was discontinued by the housing moratorium of January 5, 1973.

The revised program, activated in 1976, required eligible homeowners to make a downpayment of 3 percent of the cost of acquisition of a newly constructed or substantially rehabilitated unit, as well as to pay 20 percent of their adjusted monthly incomes toward mortgage payments. The monthly assistance payment was calculated as the difference between mortgage costs at the then-current subsidized interest rate and the mortgage costs at the FHA maximum interest rate in force at the time of insurance endorsement. The Housing and Urban-Renewal Recovery Act of 1983 (P.L. 98–181) authorized the restructured Section 235 program, with ten years of interest-subsidy payments and with homeowners required to contribute a minimum of 28 percent of adjusted income toward monthly mortgage payments. Assistance payments are the lesser of: (1) the difference between the total monthly payment for principal, interest, taxes, insurance, and the mortgage insurance premium (MIP) on the mortgage at the market rate and 28 percent of the borrower's adjusted monthly income; or (2) the difference between the monthly payment for principal, interest, and MIP on the mortgage at the market rate and the monthly payment for principal and interest alone at the then-current subsidized interest rate. At the end of fiscal year 1989, 2,780 units were under payment in the restructured program.

Under the restructured Section 235 program, the Homeownership Assistance Fund was established (by the Housing and Urban-Rural Recovery Act of 1983) to receive recaptured budget authority, cash, and interest earnings. These funds may be used, to the extent approved by appropriation acts, to provide additional Section 235 assistance payments for mortgagors, who are unable to assume the full mortgage payments after the guaranteed ten years of assistance payments.

COMMUNITY DEVELOPMENT BLOCK GRANT PROGRAM

The 1974 Housing and Community Development Act established the Community Development Block Grant (CDBG) program to consolidate a wide range of community development activities directed toward neighborhood revitalization, economic development, and improved community facilities and services. Neighborhood revitalization can include either the rehabilitation or substantial reconstruction of housing.[16] Federal aid is provided both to entitlement communities (metropolitan cities and urban counties) and on a nonentitlement basis to states and small cities. No less than 70 percent of CDBG funds must be used for activities that benefit low- and moderate-income persons.[17] The program is still active.

The legislation establishing the CDBG program conditions receipt of CDBG funds on the willingness of a community to provide low- and moderate-income housing within its boundaries.[18] A locality may be awarded a CDBG only if it has filed either a Comprehensive Housing Affordability Strategy (CHAS) or a Housing Assistance Plan (HAP) identifying the general locations of proposed housing for lower-income persons.[19] These locations must be selected to "promote greater choice of opportunity and to avoid undue concentrations of assisted persons in areas containing a high proportion of low-income persons."[20] This requirement is to foster the spatial deconcentration of assisted housing throughout the metropolitan areas that receive CDBG funds. Additional subsidized housing would be built in areas of minority concentration only when "necessary to meet overriding housing needs."

The CDBG program also has a little-used feature, the Areawide Housing Opportunity Plan (AHOP), with the objective of fostering spatial deconcentration of assisted housing. Under the AHOP, areas would get bonuses of additional funds for housing and community development if the central cities and their suburban jurisdictions could agree on a plan to apportion housing for low-income and minority families more evenly among themselves.

SECTION 8 PROGRAM

The Section 8 program, also established by the 1974 Housing and Community Development Act, ushered in a new wave in federal rental assistance programs. Like the CDBG program, the Section 8 Rental Assistance program was part of the thrust towards spatial deconcentration and expanded housing opportunities for lower-income households. It has subsidized very-low-income and low-income households living in privately owned, newly constructed, rehabilitated, and existing units. The authority to fund units under the new construction and substantial rehabilitation subprograms has been repealed, however, except in conjunction with housing for the elderly and handicapped.[21] During fiscal year 1990, HUD Secretary Kemp terminated the Moderate Rehabilitation subprogram under Section 8, except for the funding of single-room occupancy units for the homeless.[22] During fiscal year 1990, all Section 8 subprograms had outstanding commitments to assist over 2.5 million households.

In all the Section 8 subprograms—the major subprograms are new construction, substantial rehabilitation, moderate rehabilitation, existing-housing, and vouchers—HUD makes payments to cover the gap between a rent level that the agency estimates and the rental payments made by assisted tenants. Rental assistance payments on behalf of lower-income tenants go either directly to owners of newly developed or rebuilt housing or through LHAs to owners of existing dwellings. Assistance payments are made for from five to forty years in the Section 8 subprograms.[23] To continue receiving assistance payments for their tenants, owners must maintain their units to meet the quality standards set by HUD.

The minimum tenant rental payment in Section 8 is 30 percent of adjusted income, and the income adjustments are the same as in the Low-Rent Public Housing (LRPH) program. Tenants receiving vouchers can pay more than 30 percent of their incomes toward rent, however. Eligible tenants must have incomes, adjusted for family size, of less than or equal to 80 percent of the area median in all subprograms except vouchers, where incomes must be less than or equal to 50 percent of the area median. Family income and composition are re-examined annually.

Existing Housing (Moderate Rehabilitation and Finders-Keepers)

The Section 8 existing-housing program subsidizes lower-income households through both its moderate rehabilitation and finders-keepers subprograms. Owners of existing dwellings in need of a modest amount of rehabilitation may upgrade their units and lease them to lower-income tenants at subsidized rents under the moderate rehabilitation component of the Section 8 existing-housing program. The finders-keepers program aids lower-income families who lease standard quality privately owned apartments, houses, or congregate units of their choosing.[24]

Property owners who wish to rehabilitate moderately substandard housing to rent to lower-income families can receive rental assistance payments covering the difference between the maximum rent for the unit and the tenant rental payment. Moderate rehabilitation involves a minimum expenditure of $3,000 per unit and can include work on common areas or systems to upgrade them to decent, safe, and sanitary condition. It also could include the replacement or repair of major building systems or components in danger of failure to comply with HUD's housing quality standards. Program abuses uncovered in this program in 1989 resulted in the recall of all unobligated program funds. Funds from 1989 have been carried over to 1990 for use in a revised program to rehabilitate only SRO units for the homeless.

The finders-keepers program subsidizes lower-income renters living in standard quality, privately owned, existing units of their choosing, which lease at rents not exceeding HUD-established rent maximums for their market areas and family sizes. Potential program participants receive an eligibility certificate, which they have 60 days to use by locating a suitable unit and a landlord willing to rent to them. Successful certificate recipients then qualify for monthly rental assistance payments on their behalf from HUD. These monthly payments cover the difference between the rent stated on the lease (with the HUD-established maximum as the ceiling) and the tenants' rental payments.[25]

Vouchers

The Section 8 voucher program was designed to maximize the ability of tenants to find standard housing within the existing inventory, as well as to enable very low income families to afford to rent rehabilitated and newly constructed units. It was authorized as a demonstration by the Housing and Urban-Rural Recovery Act of 1983 and established as a permanent Section 8 program option by the Housing and Community Development Act of 1987. The LHAs operating the Section 8 existing-housing program also administer the voucher program.

Vouchers are available to previously unassisted families with incomes no greater than 50 percent of the area median income, adjusted for family size. Families assisted by other federal programs also are eligible, even if their incomes are above 50 percent of the area median.[26] Seventy percent or more of the vouchers made available in a given year must give preference for occupancy to families who, at the time they are seeking assistance, occupy substandard housing, are involuntarily displaced, or are paying more than 50 percent of their incomes for rent. Other units are to be made available for occupancy according to the preference system established by the LHA.[27]

The HUD-established market rent does *not* serve as a ceiling on unit rents in the voucher program, although voucher assistance payments are determined relative to a payment standard that generally equals this HUD-established rent. The voucher subsidy payment equals the difference between the payment standard and the tenant rental payment of 30 percent of adjusted household income. An assisted family may lease a unit whose rent exceeds the payment standard but must pay the excess without additional subsidy; in this case, the tenant rent payment would exceed 30 percent of adjusted income. Families leasing units that rent for less than the payment standard pay that much less than 30 percent of their adjusted incomes for housing. Voucher assistance payments can be adjusted as frequently as annually.[28]

NEHEMIAH HOUSING OPPORTUNITY GRANTS PROGRAM

The Nehemiah Housing Opportunity Grants program was authorized by the 1987 Housing and Community Development Act (signed into law in February 1988); it establishes a revolving loan fund that provides money to nonprofit organizations to make loans to moderate-income families who are purchasing homes developed by these nonprofits under this program.[29] Housing developed through the Nehemiah program is to be concentrated in given neighborhoods in a conscious effort to rebuild depressed areas of cities. All homes must be located in a single neighborhood in which the median family income does not exceed 80 percent of the median family income for the area. The federal program is similar to a state-fostered Nehemiah program developed and operated by church groups in Brooklyn, NY.

Each loan made through this program must be for no more than $15,000, be interest-free, be secured by a second mortgage held by the Secretary of HUD for the property involved, and be repayable to the Secretary upon sale, lease, or other transfer of the property. Families eligible to participate in the program must have incomes below either the local or the national median family income, whichever is higher. In general, the downpayment must equal 10 percent of the sales price of the home.

The first funding for the Nehemiah program in 1989 of $20 million was not formally obligated during 1989. Thus, in 1990, the $20 million from 1989 was available in addition to $25 million newly appropriated for 1990, for a total of $45 million.[30] The 1991 Appropriations Act for the Departments of VA and HUD, and Independent Agencies (P.L. 101–507) provided $35 million for Nehemiah Housing Opportunity Grants. The 1990 Cranston-Gonzalez National Affordable Housing Act (P.L. 101–625), however, repeals the legislation that establishes this program, as of October 1, 1991. Thus, program funds not obligated before that date can not be used thereafter.

NOTES

1. Lower-income households have incomes less than or equal to 80 percent of the median incomes in their metropolitan areas.

2. Public housing authorities (PHAs) are a type of LHAs. The generic label for local agencies that operate federal housing programs is LHA, although the PHA is the most commonly encountered such agency.

3. This change affected the financial viability of LRPH and led to the federal government providing not only construction financing but also operating subsidies. Operating subsidies were first provided in 1961.

4. Although 30 percent of adjusted household income is the usual tenant contribution, income-eligible tenants actually pay for rent the greater of: 30 percent of adjusted family income, 10 percent of monthly gross (unadjusted) income, or the shelter allowance from welfare assistance payments. Ten percent of a household's unadjusted monthly income generally is the minimum payment required of all participants.

5. The same deductions from income are used to define adjusted income for both the LRPH program and the Section 8 program.

6. The limit (as a deductible from gross income) for child support or alimony payments for someone outside of the household is the lesser of (a) the legal limit or (b) $550 for each individual for whom the payment is made.

7. The government provided this subsidy by purchasing market-rate mortgages from private lenders, then either reselling the loans at reduced prices as 3-percent-interest-rate mortgages, or holding them in the federal portfolio while charging project owners only 3 percent interest.

8. Wilhelmina A. Leigh and Carla Pedone, *The Potential Loss of Assisted Housing Units as Certain Mortgage-Interest Subsidy Programs Mature*, Staff Working Paper (Washington, DC: Congressional Budget Office, March 1987), p. 12.

9. The terms "very low income" and "low-income" are used to describe the target populations of federal housing assistance programs. "Very low income" families have incomes no greater than 50 percent of the area's median income, adjusted for family size. "Low-income" families have incomes no greater than 80 percent of the area's median.

10. If none of the units in projects with limited-dividend owners have received rent supplements or any other form of supplemental assistance, these owners are able to repay without HUD's permission, at this point in the mortgage term. Limited-dividend owners who purchased their projects from nonprofit owners are not eligible to prepay without HUD's permission; nor are nonprofit or public sponsors or owners.

11. See Leigh and Pedone, pp. 12–13.

12. Title II of the 1987 Housing and Community Development Act—also known as the Emergency Low Income Housing Preservation Act of 1987—established a procedure requiring advance notification and HUD approval of any proposed prepayment of a mortgage insured by either the BMIR or the Section 236 programs. In Section 221 (General Prepayment Limitation) of Subtitle B (Prepayment of Mortgages Insured Under the National Housing Act) of Title II, a two-year moratorium was established on prepayments. The moratorium resulted because the following conditions were met: If any U.S. or state court invalidates the requirements established by this section, an owner of eligible low-income housing located in the geographic area subject to the jurisdiction of that court may not prepay, and a mortgagee may not accept prepayment of a mortgage on such housing during the two-year period following the date of invalidation.

Although Subtitle B was to have been repealed (and the moratorium lifted) on February 5, 1990, two years after the effective date of the 1987 Act, the HUD Reform Act of 1989 extended the date of repeal until September 30, 1990, to afford Congress time to develop a more permanent solution to the problem. That more permanent solution was provided in Subtitles A and B of Title VI (Preservation of Affordable Rental Housing) in the Cranston-Gonzalez National Affordable Housing Act (P.L. 101–625). This title is known as The Low-Income Housing Preservation and Resident Homeownership Act of 1990

(LIHPRHA).

The LIHPRHA applies to Section 221 (d)(3) BMIR projects; Section 221 (d)(3) projects with rent supplement or Section 8; Section 236 projects; and HUD-held projects formerly insured under those programs that, under pre-February 5, 1988 contracts or regulations, are eligible for prepayment without HUD approval within 24 months. The Act establishes fair market value incentives for owners to retain their projects as low-income housing and a fair market price for owners to sell their projects as low-income housing. If no willing or able purchaser is found for a given project, owners would be allowed to prepay. Incentives for owners to retain projects as low-income housing include: providing greater access to residual receipts; providing increased rents; and financing capital improvements through the flexible subsidy program.

13. See Leigh and Pedone, p. 12.

14. See Leigh and Pedone, p. 12–13.

15. Section 125 in Subtitle B (Management Reform) of Title I (Reforms to Department of Housing and Urban Development) of P.L. 101–235 (Department of Housing and Urban Development Reform Act of 1989) authorizes the HUD Secretary to insure refinanced Section 235 mortgages. Because this measure is intended to reduce federal expenditures in this program, by refinancing mortgages initially made at higher rates in a lower-interest-rate environment, the Secretary also is authorized to provide financial incentives to the borrowers to encourage refinancing.

The 1990 Appropriations Act for the Departments of Veterans Affairs (VA) and Housing and Urban Development (HUD), and Independent Agencies (P.L. 101–144) provided similar authority for the HUD Secretary to periodically review each Section 235 assistance payments contract to determine if refinancing the mortgage, loan, or advance of credit would result in sufficient savings to the federal government to warrant the refinancing. Financial assistance to encourage refinancing would include such things as the payment of reasonable mortgage or loan origination fees, discount points, and other refinancing expenses, or the payment of an amount less than or equal to 1 percent of the principal refinanced.

16. Title V (Community Development and Miscellaneous Programs), Subtitle A (Community And Neighborhood Development and Preservation), Section 510 (Limited New Construction of Housing Under the CDBG Program) of the 1987 Housing and Community Development Act added substantial reconstruction as a new category of eligible activity under the CDBG program. Substantial reconstruction can take place with housing owned and occupied by low- and moderate-income persons under the following circumstances: (1) if the need for reconstruction was not determinable until after rehabilitation under this section had begun; or (2) if the reconstruction is part of a neighborhood rehabilitation effort and the grantee (a) determines that the housing is not suitable for rehabilitation and (b) demonstrates to the satisfaction of the HUD Secretary that the cost of substantial reconstruction is much less than the cost of new construction and less than the fair market value of the property after substantial reconstruction.

17. The 1987 Housing and Community Development Act increased the targeting percentage from 51 to 60 percent, while the 1990 Cranston-Gonzalez National Affordable Housing Act increased this figure to 70 percent.

18. The dispute in Yonkers, NY over building low-income housing in non-minority areas stems from the receipt of CDBG funds by Yonkers in the late 1970s, conditioned on building scattered site housing for low-income households.

19. Whichever is filed—the CHAS or the HAP—must be approved by the HUD Secretary before CDBG funds can be awarded. See Title IX, Subtitle A, Section 905 of the Cranston-Gonzalez National Affordable Housing Act (P.L. 101–625).

20. Congress, House, Committee on Banking, Finance and Urban Affairs, Subcommittee on Housing and Community Development, *Discrimination in Federally Assisted Housing Programs*, report on "Subsidized Housing and Race," prepared by the Office of General Counsel, U.S. Department of Housing and Urban Development, 99th Cong., 1st sess., 1985, Part I, Serial No. 99–83, p. 104.

21. The 1983 Housing and Urban-Rural Recovery Act repealed the authorizations for the Section 8 new construction and substantial rehabilitation programs, except in conjunction with Section 202 housing for the elderly and handicapped.

22. Because of irregularities and scandals recently uncovered with respect to the Moderate Rehabilitation program, several measures were taken that led to termination of program funding except for SRO units for the homeless. In April 1989, HUD canceled a funding round for the Moderate Rehabilitation program and requested that in 1990, all funds be devoted to disaster relief efforts. The Appropriations Committee (1990 Appropriations Act for the Departments of VA and HUD, and Independent Agencies) approved the use of 70 percent of the Moderate Rehabilitation funding for disaster assistance programs but required that the remaining 30 percent be used for SRO units for the homeless. Funding for these SRO units was to be administered according to the reforms of the Moderate Rehabilitation program made in Title I, Subtitle B (Management Reform), Section 127 (Reform of the Moderate Rehabilitation Program) of the HUD Reform Act of 1989 (P.L. 101–235). Changes would require a minimum expenditure of $3,000 per unit; require the HUD Secretary to take into account the existence of tax credits on Moderate Rehabilitation projects and to reduce Moderate Rehabilitation assistance accordingly; and prohibit assistance to any project of more than 100 units.

23. The initial maximum terms under the Section 8 subprograms were: five years for vouchers; fifteen years for existing-housing and moderate rehabilitation; and either twenty, thirty, or forty years for new construction and substantial rehabilitation, depending on the type of project financing. Section 8 existing-housing certificates now are issued for five-year terms, per the HUD-Independent Agencies Appropriations Act (P.L. 100–404).

24. Congregate housing facilities provide some common services for residents and are most frequently occupied by the elderly or handicapped.

25. The maximum allowable rent, or fair market rent (FMR), is defined as the 45th percentile of rents of standard quality units occupied by recent movers but excluding units built in the last two years.

26. For example, tenants of public housing projects that are sold or demolished, and tenants displaced from Section 8 projects when their owners fail to renew their contracts also are eligible to receive vouchers.

27. These preference rules for project occupancy were established by Title V, Section 501 of the Cranston-Gonzalez National Affordable Housing Act (P.L. 101–625).

28. Section 143 of Subtitle A in Title I (Housing Assistance) of the 1987 Housing and Community Development Act. Prior to passage of this Act, voucher assistance payments could be adjusted only twice during their five-year term.

29. See Title VI of the Housing and Community Development Act of 1987 (P.L. 100–242) for the language that authorizes the Nehemiah Housing Opportunity Grants Program.

30. This total was reduced to $44.2 million by the transfer of funds for other purposes and by the sequestration of funds to meet Gramm-Rudman-Hollings targets.

ABOUT THE AUTHORS

Sheila Ards is a research scholar at the Urban Institute in Washington, DC and a lecturer in the School of Public Affairs at the University of Maryland, College Park.

Robert D. Bullard is associate professor of sociology at the University of California-Riverside.

J. Eugene (Gene) Grigsby III is associate professor of urban planning in the Graduate School of Architecture and Urban Planning at the University of California-Los Angeles.

William M. Harris, Sr. is professor of city planning in the Department of Urban and Environmental Planning in the School of Architecture at the University of Virginia, Charlottesville.

Mary L. Hruby is staff consultant to The Planning Group, Inc., in Los Angeles.

Wilhelmina A. Leigh was principal analyst at the U.S. Congressional Budget Office in Washington, DC when this information was compiled. She is now senior research associate at the Joint Center for Political and Economic Studies in Washington, DC.

David A. Macpherson is assistant professor of economics at Miami University, Oxford, OH.

Nancy Olmsted is a recent graduate of the University of Virginia with a Master of Planning degree.

Alfred D. Price is associate professor and director in the Department of Planning and Design in the School of Architecture and Planning at the State University of New York at Buffalo.

Veronica M. Reed is executive director of the Indiana Association of Community Economic Development in Indianapolis.

William E. (Gene) Robertson is professor and chair of the Department of Community Development at the University of Missouri-Columbia.

Carla J. Robinson is assistant professor of economics and director of the Honors Program at Spelman College, Atlanta, GA.

James B. Stewart is vice provost and professor of labor studies and industrial relations at The Pennsylvania State University, University Park. He is also editor of *The Review of Black Political Economy*.